Student Study Guide

FINANCIAL ACCOUNTING

Student Study Guide

FINANCIAL ACCOUNTING

Sixth Edition

Walter T. Harrison Jr.
Charles A. Horngren

Alan Campbell
Michael Flores
Wichita State University

PEARSON
Prentice
Hall

Upper Saddle River, New Jersey 07458

VP/Editorial Director: Jeff Shelstad
Senior Acquisitions Editor: Wendy Craven
Project Manager: Kerri Tomasso
Associate Director Manufacturing: Vincent Scelta
Production Editor & Buyer: Wanda Rockwell
Printer/Binder: Courier, Bookmart Press

10 9 8 7 6 5 4 3 2 1
ISBN 0-13-149953-X

Contents

Chapter 1

THE FINANCIAL STATEMENTS

CHAPTER OBJECTIVES

The learning objectives for this chapter are as follows:

1. Use accounting vocabulary for decision making
2. Apply accounting concepts and principles
3. Use the accounting equation to describe an organization
4. Evaluate operating performance, financial position, and cash flows
5. Explain the relationships among the financial statements

CHAPTER OVERVIEW

The focus of this chapter and of the whole book is the basic financial statements for a corporation. The basic financial statements begin with the income statement, which is also known as the statement of operations. The second basic financial statement for a corporation is the statement of retained earnings. The next basic financial statement is the balance sheet, which is also known as the statement of financial position. The last major financial statement is the statement of cash flows. This chapter explains what each basic financial statement includes.

People need information to make decisions. Accounting supplies much of the information that people need to make business and financial decisions. This chapter discusses some of the concepts and vocabulary that serve as the foundation of accounting. It also includes a discussion of evaluating a company's operating performance, financial position, and cash flows using accounting information. Understanding the role that accounting plays in decision making leads to a better appreciation of the financial statements.

CHAPTER REVIEW

Objective 1—Use accounting vocabulary for decision making

People often confuse accounting with bookkeeping. Accounting differs from bookkeeping in that accounting is an information system that measures business activities, converts date into useful information, and communicates financial information to people. Financial statements are a major part of the process of reporting financial information to decision makers. Accounting is often called the language of business. Exhibit 1-1 illustrates the role of accounting in business.

Understanding the language of accounting helps people make better financial decisions. Decision makers need information, and accounting supplies a part of that information. Decision makers who use accounting information include individuals, businesses, investors, creditors, government agencies, and nonprofit organizations.

Two branches of accounting are financial accounting and management accounting. Financial accounting focuses on providing information to people outside the organization. Management accounting produces information for the managers of an organization.

Ethical considerations are very important in accounting. To obtain money from the public, companies must provide investors and creditors with accounting information that is reliable and relevant. Most managers comply with the law and ethical standards in providing accounting information to external users of the financial statements. Some managers, however, provide misleading or false information. For example, a company might overstate its assets, understate its liabilities, overstate its revenues, or understate its expenses to make its financial position and results of operations appear to be better than the actual amounts. Companies such as Enron, Tyco, and WorldCom have made headlines in the news for their corrupt accounting practices.

To increase the credibility of financial statements, a company can have an independent accounting firm audit the financial statements. The auditor then issues an opinion on the fairness of the company's financial statements. In the United States, companies that sell their stock to the public must issue annual financial statements audited by an independent accounting firm.

The American Institute of Certified Public Accountants (AICPA) is the national professional organization for certified public accountants (CPAs). Members of the AICPA must comply with its Code of Professional Conduct, which requires honorable behavior beyond what the law requires. Failure to comply with legal requirements and high ethical standards can force a CPA firm to cease to exist. A recent example is the firm of Arthur Andersen, which was the auditor of Enron Corporation. Arthur Andersen failed to comply with legal requirements and ethical standards in rendering its opinion on the fairness of Enron Corporation's financial statements. Enron Corporation's financial statements were so unreliable that the damage to Arthur Andersen's reputation led to its downfall.

As shown in Exhibit 1-2, a business can operate in one of three legal forms—a proprietorship, a partnership, or a corporation. A proprietorship has one owner. A partnership has as least two owners called partners. A corporation usually has many owners called stockholders or shareholders.

The stockholders of a corporation elect the board of directors. Each stockholder receives one vote for each share owned. The board of directors establishes corporate policy and appoints the officers of the corporation.

Objective 2—Apply accounting concepts and principles

Accountants must prepare financial statements in accordance with generally accepted accounting principles (GAAP). The Financial Accounting Standards Board (FASB) has the primary responsibility for formulating GAAP in the United States. The FASB formulates GAAP based on a conceptual framework as shown in Exhibit 1-3. Accounting information should be useful for making investment and credit decisions. To be useful, accounting information must be reliable, relevant, comparable, and consistent. Reliability means that the information is verifiable and free of error and bias. To be relevant, the information must be able to influence a decision. Timeliness is a key aspect of relevance. Comparable means that a decision maker can use the accounting information to compare different companies. Consistent means that a decision maker can compare the same company from one period to the next.

The most basic accounting concept is the entity concept. An entity is an organization or segment of an organization that for accounting purposes stands apart from other organizations and individuals as a separate economic unit. The entity concept requires that the personal affairs of the owners of a business be kept separate from the business affairs.

The reliability principle states that companies should base accounting information on the most reliable data available. The reliability principle is also known as the objectivity principle. As much as possible, objective information should serve as the basis for accounting information. The information should be free of personal bias and opinions to the maximum extent possible.

> **Study Tip:** While accounting information should be reliable and free from bias, estimates are inherent in accounting.

Another major accounting principle is the cost principle. The cost principle states that a company should record assets and services on the books at their actual cost, which is also known as their historical cost. The company should maintain assets at their historical costs for as long as the company owns the assets. Cost is a more reliable measure than estimated values.

The going-concern concept is the assumption that the entity will remain in operation for the foreseeable future. The going-concern concept provides the foundation for reporting assets at their historical cost. The reason is that the going-concern concept assumes that the business will remain in operation long enough to use the assets for their intended purpose. Market value is not the only value of an asset. An asset also has value for its ability to generate revenues for a business.

The alternative to the going-concern concept is going out of business, often called liquidation. In the event of liquidation, a business values its assets at their current market value rather than at their historical cost.

The stable-monetary concept is the basis for ignoring the effects of inflation. Inflation is a general rise in the general price level. Although inflation erodes the purchasing power of the dollar, accountants ignore the effects of inflation in the accounting records.

Objective 3—Use the accounting equation to describe an organization

The financial statements are the output of the financial accounting process. The accounting equation provides the basis for the financial statements. The accounting equation is the most basic tool of accounting. Exhibit 1-4 illustrates the accounting equation. The accounting equation is as follows: Assets = Liabilities + Owners' Equity.

Assets are the economic resources of a business from which the business expects to receive a future benefit. Examples of assets include cash, accounts receivable, notes receivable, merchandise inventory, office supplies, land, buildings, furniture, equipment, and patents.

Liabilities are the debts of an organization owed to outsiders called creditors. Liabilities represent the creditors' claims against the assets of the organization. Examples of liabilities include accounts payable and notes payable.

> **Study Tip:** Any account that includes the word payable is a liability, but not all liabilities include the word payable.

Owners' equity represents the owners' claims against the assets of the organization. Owners' equity is also called capital for a proprietorship or partnership and stockholders' equity or shareholders' equity for a corporation. The stockholders' equity of a corporation includes two main elements: paid-in capital (also known as contributed capital) and retained earnings.

Owners' equity is a residual amount because it is what is left after subtracting liabilities from assets. The creditors' claims on the assets come first. The equation for calculating owners' equity is as follows: Assets – Liabilities = Owners' Equity

Two subparts of stockholders' equity are paid-in capital and retained earnings. Paid-in capital represents money that the stockholders have invested in the corporation in exchange for its common stock. Retained earnings are the sum of the corporation's net income minus the sum of all of its net losses and dividends since the corporation began. The owners' equity of a proprietorship or partnership does not show separate amounts for paid-in capital and retained earnings. The owner' equity of a proprietorship or partnership is also known as capital.

Revenues are increases in retained earnings from the sale of a company's products or services. Expenses are decreases in retained earnings from costs that have expired in the operation of the business. If a company's revenues exceed its expense, the difference is called net income. If a company's expenses exceed its revenues, the difference is called net loss. Dividends are distributions of assets generated by net income to stockholders.

Dividends are not an expense, but they decrease retained earnings. Exhibit 1-5 illustrates how to calculate the ending balance in retained earnings.

Objective 4—Evaluate operating performance, financial position, and cash flows

The financial statements provide information on a company's operating performance, financial position, and cash flows. The income statement shows how well a company performed over a specific period in terms of revenues, expenses, and the resulting net income or net loss. The statement of retained earnings shows what caused the change in a company's retained earnings over a specific period. The balance sheet shows a company's financial position in terms of assets, liabilities, and owners' equity on a specific date, which is usually the end of the accounting period. The statement of cash flows shows how much cash a company generated or spent during a specific period. It is divided into cash flows from three different activities—operating activities, investing activities, and financing activities. Exhibit 1-6 shows four questions that decision makers might ask and how the different financial statements answer those questions.

The income statement is also known as the statement of operations. Each financial statement must have a proper heading. The first line of the heading of a financial statement is the name of the company, and the second line is the name of the financial statement. The third line of the heading shows the specific period covered for the income statement, statement of retained earnings, and statement of cash flows. The third line of the heading of the balance sheet shows the specific date of the balance sheet. Many companies use the calendar year as their accounting year. Companies may use an accounting year that ends on a month other than December. Such an accounting year is called a fiscal year.

Companies often present financial statements for two years so that the decision maker can compare the financial statements for the two years. Exhibit 1-7 illustrates an income statement that shows the results of operations for each of two consecutive years. Depending on the size of the company, the financial statements may show amounts rounded to the nearest million dollars or to the nearest thousand dollars. The income statement shows two main categories: (1) revenues and gains and (2) expenses and losses. Net income is equal to revenues and gains minus expenses and losses.

Revenues do not always contain the word revenue. For example, net sales revenue is often shown as simply net sales. Expenses do not always contain the word expense. For example, one of the largest expenses for a merchandising company is called cost of goods sold or cost of sales.

The statement of retained earnings provides a summary of the changes in a corporation's retained earnings during the accounting period. It begins with the beginning balance of retained earnings. Net income from the income statement increases retained earnings. A net loss decreases retained earnings. Dividends decrease retained earnings. The ending balance in retained earnings also goes on the balance sheet. If the balance in retained earnings is negative, it is called a deficit. Exhibit 1-8 illustrates a statement of retained earnings.

The balance sheet is the only major financial statement prepared for a specific date rather than for a specific period. The balance sheet is also known as the statement of financial position. It shows a company's assets, liabilities, and owners' equity. Exhibit 1-9 illustrates a balance sheet.

The two main categories of assets on the balance sheet are current assets and long-term assets. Current assets are assets expected to be converted to cash, sold, or consumed in operations within one year or within the normal operating cycle of the business, whichever is longer. Current assets include cash, short-term investments, accounts receivable, notes receivable, merchandise inventory, and prepaid expenses. Long-term assets consist of property, plant, and equipment, intangibles, and investments. Assets included in property, plant, and equipment are also known as plant assets or fixed assets.

The process of allocating the cost of a plant asset to expense is called depreciation. Accumulated depreciation is the total amount of depreciation that a company has taken on its plant assets since it acquired them.

The two categories of liabilities on the balance sheet are current liabilities and long-term liabilities. Another name for long-term liabilities is long-term debt. Current liabilities are debts due within one year or within the normal operating cycle of the business, whichever is longer. Common examples of current liabilities are accounts payable, notes payable within one year, interest payable, and salaries and wages payable. Stockholders' equity is the difference between a company's assets and its liabilities. Stockholders' equity includes common stock and retained earnings. Another name for stockholders' equity is shareholders' equity.

The last major financial statement is the statement of cash flows. It shows cash inflows and cash outflows in the three categories of operating activities, investing activities, and financing activities. Operating activities are activities that generate revenues or cause expenses in the company's major line of business. Investment activities involve the purchase or sale of a company's long-term assets. Financing activities are activities that obtain cash from investors and creditors or return cash to them. The payment of dividends is a financing activity. Exhibit 1-10 illustrates a statement of cash flows.

Study Tip: Cash paid for interest is a cash outflow for an operating activity because interest expense appears on the income statement.

Objective 5—Explain the relationships among the financial statements

The net income or net loss from the income statement also appears on the statement of retained earnings because net income increases retained earnings and a net loss decreases retained earnings. The ending balance of retained earnings from the statement of retained earnings also goes on the balance sheet. The ending balance of cash on the statement of cash flows must be the same balance of cash shown on the balance sheet. Exhibit 1-11 summarizes the relationships among the financial statements.

Investors and creditors make financial decisions by analyzing financial statements. Managers also use financial statements to evaluate the performance of subordinate managers. One example of a financial database is the Electronic Data Gathering, Analysis, and Retrieval (EDGAR) system of the Securities and Exchange Commission (SEC). It includes the financial statements of all public corporations in the United States. The EDGAR database is located online at the SEC's Web site www.sec.gov.

TEST YOURSELF

Matching

Match each numbered term with its lettered definition.

_____ 1. retained earnings

_____ 2. proprietorship

_____ 3. financial accounting

_____ 4. liabilities

_____ 5. corporation

_____ 6. cost principle

_____ 7. management accounting

_____ 8. expenses

_____ 9. assets

_____ 10. going-concern concept

_____ 11. revenues

_____ 12. stable-monetary unit concept

_____ 13. current assets

_____ 14. reliability principle

_____ 15. net income

_____ 16. plant assets

_____ 17. current liabilities

_____ 18. long-term debt

_____ 19. dividends

_____ 20. net loss

A. ensures that accounting records and statements are based on the most reliable data available.

B. decrease in retained earnings that result from operations; the cost of doing business.

C. excess of total expenses over total revenues.

D. acquired assets and services should be recorded at their actual cost.

E. a liability that falls due beyond one year from the date of the financial statements.

F. a business with a single owner.

G. the branch of accounting that provides information to people outside the firm.

H. excess of total revenues over total expenses.

I. assets that are expected to be converted to cash, sold, or consumed within the next 12 months or the normal operating cycle of the business, whichever is longer.

J. distributions of assets generated by net income to stockholders.

K. holds that the entity will remain in operation for the foreseeable future.

L. debts due to be paid within one year or within the operating cycle of the business, whichever is longer.

M. economic obligations or debts payable to individuals or organizations outside the business.

N. increase in retained earnings from delivering goods or services to customers or clients.

O. a business owned by stockholders.

P. long-lived assets such as property, plant, and equipment.

Q. the branch of accounting that generates information for the internal decision-makers of a business.

R. the amount of stockholders' equity that the corporation has earned through profitable operations of the business and has not paid to stockholders.

S. economic resources that are expected to be of benefit in the future.

T. the basis for ignoring the effects of inflation in the accounting records.

Multiple Choice

Circle the best answer.

1. Which financial statement shows cash flows from operating activities, investing activities, and financing activities?
   a. balance sheet
   b. statement of cash flows
   c. income statement
   d. statement of retained earnings

2. The owners of a corporation are called:
   a. stockholders
   b. partners
   c. proprietors
   d. associates

3. GAAP stands for:
   a. generally accepted accounting practices
   b. generally authorized accounting practices
   c. generally accepted auditing principles
   d. generally accepted accounting principles

4. The group elected by the stockholders to set policy for a corporation and to appoint its officers is called the:
   a. executive committee
   b. board of regents
   c. board of directors
   d. policy committee

5. Which of the following is the accounting equation?
   a. Assets = Liabilities + Expenses
   b. Liabilities = Assets + Owners' Equity
   c. Assets = Liabilities + Owners' Equity
   d. Revenues – Expenses = Net Income

6. Which financial statement shows how retained earnings changed during the year?
   a. balance sheet
   b. statement of cash flows
   c. income statement
   d. statement of retained earnings

7. Which financial statement shows a company's financial position at the end of the year?
   a. balance sheet
   b. statement of cash flows
   c. income statement
   d. statement of retained earnings

8. Which financial statement shows the company's revenues, expenses, and net income or net loss?
   a. balance sheet
   b. statement of cash flows
   c. income statement
   d. statement of retained earnings

9. Prepaid expenses are:
   a. expenses
   b. current assets
   c. current liabilities
   d. fixed assets

10. Accounts payable are:
    a. expenses
    b. current assets
    c. current liabilities
    d. long-term debt

11. Activities that increase or decrease a company's long-term assets are:
    a. operating activities
    b. investing activities
    c. financing activities
    d. accounting activities

12. Which financial statement is also known as the statement of operations?
    a. balance sheet
    b. statement of cash flows
    c. income statement
    d. statement of retained earnings

13. Accounting is often called the:
    a. language of business
    b. mathematics of business
    c. rules of business
    d. systems of business

14. Which organization has the primary responsibility for formulating generally accepted accounting principles in the United States?
    a. American Institute of Certified Public Accountants
    b. Financial Accounting Standards Board
    c. American Bar Association
    d. Institute of Management Accountants

15. Which accounting principle is also called the objectivity principle?
    a. going-concern concept
    b. entity concept
    c. cost principle
    d. reliability principle

Completion

Complete each of the following statements.

1. A rise in the general price level is called _____.
2. A(n) _____ _____ is a liability for goods or services purchased on credit and supported only by the credit standing of the purchaser.
3. The basic component of paid-in capital is _____ _____.
4. A _____ year ends on a date other than December 31.
5. A negative balance in retained earnings is called a _____.
6. A(n) _____ is an organization or section of an organization that stands apart for accounting purposes from other organizations and individuals.
7. Accounting lists a going concern's assets at their _____ _____.
8. _____ _____ are business documents that report financial information about a business entity to decision-makers.
9. _____ is an information system that measures business activities, processes the information into reports and financial statements, and communicates the results to decision makers.
10. Without an _____, people would doubt the amounts reported on a company's financial statements.
11. A _____ is an association of two or more persons who co-own a business for profit.
12. The _____ elect the corporation's board of directors.
13. _____ means able to influence a decision.
14. The claim of the owners of a business to the assets of the business is called _____ _____.
15. A _____ _____ is a written promise to pay on a certain date.

True/False

For each of the following statements, circle T *for true or* F *for false.*

1. T F   The word *payable* always indicates a liability.
2. T F   The balance sheet is also called the statement of financial position.
3. T F   Management accounting focuses on providing information to people outside the firm.
4. T F   The accounting firm of Arthur Andersen was the auditor of Enron.
5. T F   Shareholder is another name for stockholder.
6. T F   Reliability means able to influence a decision.
7. T F   Comparable means able to compare a company from one period to the next.
8. T F   Assets should generally be recorded at their appraised values.
9. T F   The cost principle requires that a business maintain an asset at its historical cost for as long as the business owns the asset.
10. T F   The income statement is the most basic tool of accounting.
11. T F   Land is an example of a current asset.
12. T F   Capital is another name for the owners' equity of a business.
13. T F   Dividends are a special type of expense.
14. T F   Cost of goods sold is also called cost of sales.
15. T F   Net income flows from the income statement to the balance sheet.

Exercises

1. Adams Company had a beginning cash balance of $450,000 and ending cash balance of $800,000. The company had net cash inflows from operating activities of $600,000 and net cash outflows for investing activities of $300,000. Calculate the net cash inflows from financing activities or the net cash outflows for financing activities.

2. During the year, Wright Company issued $200,000 of common stock. The company earned $700,000 of sales revenue. The company reported salaries expense of $310,000, rent expense of $60,000, utilities expense of $5,000, supplies expense of $10,000. The company declared and paid $24,000 in dividends. Calculate the net income that Wright Company should report on its income statement for the year.

3. Green Company has current assets of $700,000 and long-term assets of $500,000. Its current liabilities are $300,000, and its long-term debt is $350,000. Calculate the total stockholders' equity.

4. White Company had total revenues were $875,000. Total expenses were $650,000. The beginning balance in retained earnings was $900,000. The company declared and paid $100,000 in dividends. Calculate the ending balance in retained earnings.

5. Given the following information, calculate Rowe Company's current assets.

Merchandise inventory	$400,000
Cash	100,000
Property, plant, and equipment	800,000
Accounts payable	300,000
Accounts receivable	500,000
Retained earnings	1,400,000
Prepaid expenses	200,000
Common stock	600,000

Critical Thinking

Harris Company purchased land for $200,000 at an estate auction. The land has an appraised value of $500,000. Discuss the accounting principles the company would violate if it recorded the land on its books at $500,000.

Demonstration Problems

1. Given the following information, prepare an income statement and a statement of retained earnings for the year ended December 31, 2006, for Brown Corporation.

   Brown Corporation issued $500,000 of common stock in January 2006 and began business. It sold products for $900,000. The products that it had sold cost $500,000. Brown Corporation incurred advertising expense of $30,000, rent expense of $48,000, utilities expense of $7,000, salaries expense of $114,000, and supplies expense of $15,000. Income tax expense was 40% of income before tax. Brown Corporation paid $16,000 in dividends.

2. Given the following account balances as of December 31, 2006, prepare a balance sheet for Weber Corporation.

Accounts payable	170,000
Accounts receivable	240,000
Cash	300,000
Common stock	800,000
Long-term debt	180,000
Merchandise inventory	550,000
Notes receivable (due in 6 months)	100,000
Patents	40,000
Prepaid expenses	20,000
Property, plant, and equipment	390,000
Retained earnings	540,000
Salaries and wages payable	120,000

SOLUTIONS

Matching

1	R	5	O	9	S	13	I	17	L
2	F	6	D	10	K	14	A	18	E
3	G	7	Q	11	N	15	H	19	J
4	M	8	B	12	T	16	P	20	C

Multiple Choice

1	B
2	A
3	D
4	C
5	C
6	D
7	A
8	C
9	B
10	C
11	B
12	C
13	A
14	B
15	D

Completion

1. inflation
2. account payable
3. common stock
4. fiscal
5. deficit
6. entity
7. historical cost
8. Financial statements
9. Accounting
10. audit
11. partnership
12. stockholders
13. Relevant
14. owners' equity
15. note payable

True/False

1. T
2. T
3. F Financial accounting focuses on providing information to people outside the firm. Management accounting focuses on providing information to the firm's managers.
4. T
5. T
6. F Relevance means able to influence a decision. Reliability means verifiable and free of error and bias.
7. F Consistent means able to compare a company from one period to another. Comparable means able to compare different companies.
8. F Assets should be recorded at their historical cost.
9. T
10. F The accounting equation is the most basic tool of accounting.
11. F Land is an example of property, plant, and equipment.
12. T
13. F Dividends are not an expense. Rather, dividends are a distribution of the assets earned from generating net income to the stockholders.
14. T
15. F Net income flows from the income statement to the statement of retained earnings.

Exercises

1.

Ending cash balance	$800,000
Less: Beginning cash balance	(450,000)
Increase in cash	$350,000

Cash inflows from operating activities	$600,000	
Less: Cash outflows for investing activities	(300,000)	
Net cash inflows except for operating activities		300,000
Net cash inflows from financing activities		$ 50,000

2. The issuance of common stock does not generate revenues. A company earns revenue by delivering products or services to customers. The only revenue that Wright Company had was the sales revenue of $700,000. The payment of dividends is not an expense. Dividends are a distribution of cash to the stockholders from the net income earned by the corporation. Wright Company's expenses are $385,000 ($310,000 + $60,000 + $5,000 + $10,000). Wright Company should report $315,000 ($700,000 – $385,000) net income on its income statement for the year.

3. Current assets $700,000
   Long-term assets   500,000
   Total assets $1,200,000

   Current liabilities $300,000
   Long-term debt   350,000
   Total liabilities $650,000

   Total stockholders' equity = total assets – total liabilities
   Total stockholders' equity = $1,200,000 – $650,000
   Total stockholders' equity = $550,000

4. The ending balance in retained earnings is calculated as follows:

Beginning balance in retained earnings		$900,000
Add: Total revenues		875,000
Sub-total		$1,775,000
Less: Total expenses	$650,000	
Dividends	100,000	750,000
Ending balance in retained earnings		$1,025,000

5. The current assets are cash, accounts receivable, merchandise inventory, and prepaid expenses. Therefore, the current assets are calculated as follows:

Cash	$100,000
Accounts receivable	500,000
Merchandise inventory	400,000
Prepaid expenses	200,000
	$1,200,000

Accounts payable is a current liability. The property, plant, and equipment account is a long-term asset. Common stock and retained earnings are stockholders' equity accounts.

Critical Thinking

Harris Company would violate the cost principle and the reliability principle. According to the cost principle, a company should record assets at their historical cost, not at their appraised values. According to the reliability principle, a company should base its accounting information on the most reliable date available. The cost of $200,000 is more reliable than the appraised value of $500,000.

Demonstration Problems

1.

Brown Corporation
Income Statement
For the Year Ended December 31, 2006

Sales revenue		900,000
Operating Expenses		
Cost of goods sold	500,000	
Advertising expense	30,000	
Rent expense	48,000	
Utilities expense	7,000	
Salaries expense	114,000	
Supplies expense	15,000	
Total expenses		714,000
Income before tax		186,000
Income tax expense		74,400
Net income		111,600

Brown Corporation
Statement of Retained Earnings
For the Year Ended December 31, 2006

Retained earnings, January 1, 2006	0
Add: Net income	111,600
	111,600
Less: Dividends	16,000
Retained earnings, December 31, 2006	95,600

2.

Weber Corporation
Balance Sheet
December 31, 2006

Assets		**Liabilities**	
Current Assets:		Current Liabilities:	
Cash	300,000	Accounts payable	170,000
Accounts receivable	240,000	Salaries payable	120,000
Notes receivable	100,000	Total current liabilities	290,000
Merchandise inventory	550,000		
Prepaid expenses	20,000	Long-term debt	180,000
Total current assets	1,210,000	Total liabilities	470,000
Long-term Assets:		**Stockholders' Equity**	
Property, plant, and equipment	390,000	Common stock	800,000
Patents	40,000	Retained earnings	370,000
Total long-term assets	430,000	Total stockholders' equity	1,170,000
		Total liabilities and	
Total assets	1,640,000	stockholders' equity	1,640,000

Chapter 2

TRANSACTION ANALYSIS

CHAPTER OBJECTIVES

The learning objectives for this chapter are as follows:

1. Analyze business transactions
2. Understand how accounting works
3. Record business transactions
4. Use a trial balance
5. Analyze transactions for quick decisions

CHAPTER OVERVIEW

This chapter illustrates how companies record transactions. A transaction is any event that has a financial impact on an organization and which it can measure reliably. A company records its transactions in dollars or other currency. Therefore, a company must assign a dollar value to each transaction. Recording transactions begins the accounting process that enables a company to prepare its financial statements.

A company records its transactions in accounts. An account is the basic summary device of accounting. A company has three basic types of accounts: assets, liabilities, and owners' equity. The owners' equity of a corporation is also known as stockholders' equity or shareholders' equity. The accounting equation is the basic tool of accounting. The accounting equation for a corporation is Assets = Liabilities + Stockholders' Equity. After a company records each transaction, the accounting equation should be in balance.

Assets are the economic resources of a business that provide it with future benefits. When a company incurs a cost, it can be an asset or an expense. The cost is an asset if the cost will provide future benefits to the company. The cost is an expense if the cost will not provide future benefits to the company. Assets common to many businesses include cash, accounts receivable, notes receivable, inventory, prepaid expenses, land, buildings, equipment, furniture, and fixtures.

Liabilities are the debts of a business and represent the creditors' claims to the assets of the business. An account that ends with the word *payable* is always a liability. However, a company can have other liabilities that do not include the word *payable*. An accrued liability is a liability for an expense that a company has incurred, but which it has not yet paid.

Stockholders' equity represents the stockholders' claims to the assets of the corporation. A corporation can have many stockholders' equity accounts, but all corporations will have the accounts Common Stock and Retained Earnings. Common stock represents the stockholders' original investment in the corporation. Retained earnings are the cumulative net income of a corporation minus its cumulative net losses and dividends. Dividends are a distribution of the earnings of the corporation to its stockholders.

Net income occurs when a company's revenues exceed its expenses. A net loss occurs when a company's expenses exceed its revenues. Revenues are a special kind of increase in stockholders' equity, which result from the sale of a company's products and services. Expenses are a special kind of decrease in stockholders' equity, which result from the expiration of costs incurred in generating the revenues. If a cost incurred in the process of generating revenues does not provide the company with any future benefit, the cost is an expense. In addition, costs that were initially assets can become expenses over time as the company uses or consumes the assets.

CHAPTER REVIEW

A checkbook is an example of a single-entry accounting system. It shows where a person received cash, and where a person paid cash, the amounts, and the running balance. However, a business needs more information than a single-entry accounting system provides. To meet these information needs, a business uses double-entry accounting. Each transaction affects at least two accounts.

The end products of a double-entry accounting system are the financial statements. The income statement shows a company's revenues and expenses and the resulting net income or net loss. The users of a company's financial statements find the income statement helpful in evaluating the company's operating performance. The balance sheet reports a company's financial position in terms of its assets, liabilities, and owners' equity. The statement of cash flows shows the sources and uses of a company's cash.

Objective 1—Analyze business transactions

Every transaction affects the financial statements. A business can prepare its financial statements after recording any number of transactions, but most businesses prepare financial statements at the end of the accounting period.

Assume that on December 1, 2005, George Smith formed a corporation called Smith Corporation and contributed $100,000 in cash to the corporation in exchange for its common stock. The transaction would increase the asset Cash $100,000 and increase the stockholders' equity account Common Stock $100,000.

Smith Corporation buys land for $20,000 in cash. The transaction increases the asset Land $20,000 and decreases the asset Cash $20,000. The company now has $80,000 in cash and $20,000 in land for total assets of $100,000. The balance in the stockholders' equity account Common Stock remains at $100,000.

Next, the company paid $10,000 in cash and signed a note for $90,000 for an adjacent parcel of land. This transaction decreases the asset Cash by $10,000, increases the asset Land $100,000, and increases the liability Note Payable $90,000. The company now has $70,000 in cash and $120,000 in land for total assets of $190,000. The company has a note payable of $90,000, which is its only liability. Smith Corporation still has $100,000 in common stock. Therefore, its total liabilities and stockholders' equity are $190,000.

The company obtains a client and provides $25,000 of services on account. A company earns revenue when it performs a service, which may not be the same time that it collects the cash from the client. This transaction increases the asset Accounts Receivable $25,000, and increases Retained Earnings $25,000. The increase in Retained Earnings is due to the service revenue the company earned. Smith Corporation now has $70,000 in cash, $25,000 in accounts receivable, and $120,000 in land for total assets of $215,000. The company has a note payable of $90,000, which is its only liability. Smith Corporation has $100,000 in common stock and $25,000 in retained earnings for total stockholders' equity of $125,000. Therefore, its total liabilities and stockholders' equity are $215,000.

The company purchases $4,000 of supplies on account. This transaction increases the asset Supplies $4,000 and increases the liability Accounts Payable $4,000. Smith Corporation now has $70,000 in cash, $25,000 in accounts receivable, $4,000 in supplies, and $120,000 in land for total assets of $219,000. The company has accounts payable of $4,000 and a note payable of $90,000 for total liabilities of $94,000. Common stock remains at $100,000 and retained earnings remain at $25,000 for total stockholders' equity of $125,000. Therefore, the company's total liabilities and stockholders' equity are $219,000.

The company collected the $25,000 account receivable. This transaction increases Cash $25,000 and decreases Accounts Receivable $25,000. Total assets, liabilities, and stockholders' equity do not change. Smith Corporation now has $95,000 in cash, $4,000 in supplies, and $120,000 in land for total assets of $219,000. The company has accounts payable of $4,000 and a note payable of $90,000 for total liabilities of $94,000. Common Stock remains at $100,000 and Retained Earnings remain at $25,000 for total stockholders' equity of $125,000. Therefore, the company's total liabilities and stockholders' equity are $219,000.

The company paid $4,000 in rent, $1,000 in utilities, and $5,000 in salary to an employee. These transactions decrease Cash $10,000 and decrease Retained Earnings $10,000 because the payments are for expenses, which decrease retained earnings. Smith Corporation now has $85,000 in cash, $4,000 in supplies, and $120,000 in land for total assets of $209,000. The company has accounts payable of $4,000 and a note payable of $90,000 for total liabilities of $94,000. Common Stock remains at $100,000 and Retained Earnings are $15,000 for total stockholders' equity of $115,000. Therefore, the company's total liabilities and stockholders' equity are $209,000.

The company pays $2,000 of its accounts payable. This transaction decreases Cash $2,000 and decreases Accounts Payable $2,000. Smith Corporation now has $83,000 in cash, $4,000 in supplies, and $120,000 in land for total assets of $207,000. The company has accounts payable of $2,000 and a note payable of $90,000 for total liabilities of $92,000. Common Stock remains at $100,000 and Retained Earnings are $15,000 for total stockholders' equity of $115,000. Therefore, the company's total liabilities and stockholders' equity are $207,000.

On December 31, 2005, the company declares and pays a dividend of $3,000. This transaction decreases Cash $3,000 and decreases Retained Earnings $3,000. The payment of the dividend does not affect net income because dividends are not an expense. Smith Corporation now has $80,000 in cash, $4,000 in supplies, and $120,000 in land for total assets of $204,000. The company has accounts payable of $2,000 and a note payable of $90,000 for total liabilities of $92,000. Common Stock remains at $100,000 and Retained Earnings are $12,000 for total stockholders' equity of $112,000. Therefore, the company's total liabilities and stockholders' equity are $204,000.

Exhibit 2-1 summarizes the transactions for a sample company and provides the data for its financial statements. The column for Retained Earnings provides the revenue and expense data for the income statement. Revenues increase retained earnings, and expenses decrease retained earnings. The data for the statement of cash flows are below the Cash account. Cash receipts are sources of cash, and cash payments are uses of cash.

Exhibit 2-2 shows the company's financial statements at the end of its first month of operations. The income statement shows the company's revenues, expenses, and net income. The statement of retained earnings begins with the beginning balance of retained earnings, adds the net income, and then subtracts the dividends to determine the ending balance of retained earnings. The net income comes from the income statement. The balance sheet lists the company's assets, liabilities, and stockholders' equity at the end of the accounting period. Stockholders' equity includes the ending balance of retained earnings from the statement of retained earnings.

Although a company can use a spreadsheet to account for its transactions, it would be very awkward to use because most companies have a large number of transactions. Most companies use a double-entry accounting system to account for their transactions.

Objective 2—Understand how accounting works

The double-entry accounting system shows the dual effects of a transaction on an organization. Each transaction affects at least two accounts. A useful model of an account in the general ledger is the T-account, which uses the capital letter T. The name of the account appears at the top of the T-account. The left side of the T-account is the debit side, and the right side of the T-account is the credit side. Every transaction includes at least one debit entry and one credit entry.

Exhibit 2-3 illustrates the debit and credit rules. A debit increases an asset account, and a credit decreases an asset account. Conversely, a credit increases accounts for liabilities and stockholders' equity, and a debit decreases accounts for liabilities and stockholders' equity. The amount remaining in an account after all of the debit and credit entries is called its balance. Exhibit 2-4 shows the balances of the Cash account and the Common Stock account after the stockholder invested $50,000 in cash in exchange for the company's common stock. The Cash account has a debit balance of $50,000, and the Common Stock account has a credit balance of $50,000. Exhibit 2-5 shows the balances in the T-accounts after the company purchased land for $40,000 in cash. The Cash account has a debit balance of $10,000; the Land account has a debit balance of $40,000; and the Common Stock account has a credit balance of $50,000.

Study Tip: To balance any account, add up all of the debits, including any beginning debit balance. Next, add up all of the credits, including any beginning credit balance. Subtract the lesser total from the greater total. The difference is the balance of the account, and it goes on the side with the greater total.

In addition to Common Stock and Retained Earnings, stockholders' equity also includes revenues and expenses. Revenues and expenses appear on the income statement, but they also affect retained earnings. Revenues are increases in retained earnings that result from rendering services or delivering goods to customers. Expenses are decreases in retained earnings that result from the expiration of costs in the generation of the revenues. Dividends, which are a distribution of the earnings to the stockholders, also decrease retained earnings. Dividends are not an expense.

Exhibit 2-6 shows the expanded accounting equation as Assets = Liabilities + Common Stock + Retained Earnings – Dividends + (Revenues – Expenses). Exhibit 2-7 shows the complete debit and credit rules. Assets are increased by a debit and decreased by a credit. Liabilities, Common Stock, and Retained Earnings are increased by a credit and decreased by a debit. Dividends are increased by a debit and decreased by a credit. Revenues are increased by a credit and decreased by a debit. Expenses are increased by a debit and decreased by a credit.

> **Study Tip:** An increase in dividends or expenses results in a decrease in retained earnings and total stockholders' equity.

Objective 3—Record business transactions

An accountant first records transactions in a journal, which is a chronological record of all the transactions of an organization. This process is called journalizing or making a journal entry. The journalizing process has three steps:

1. Identify the accounts affected by the transaction and classify each account by account type.
2. Determine whether the transaction increases or decreases each of the affected accounts. Apply the debit and credit rules to determine whether to debit or credit each affected account.
3. Record the transaction in the journal. The debit transaction appears first on the left margin. The account or accounts credited appear below the account or accounts debited. The entry to record the account or accounts credited is indented to the right of the account or accounts debited. The entry should include a brief explanation, including any reference to source documents that support the transaction. Source documents include such things as checks, receipts, and invoices.

A ledger is a group of accounts. After a company records its transactions in a journal, the company must copy the information from the journal to the accounts in the general ledger. Exhibit 2-8 shows groupings of the asset, liability, and stockholders' equity accounts in the ledger. The process of copying a transaction from the journal to the accounts in the ledger is called posting. Exhibit 2-9 illustrates how a company posts a transaction from the journal to the accounts in the ledger. Exhibit 2-10 illustrates the flow of accounting information from the transaction through the posting of the transaction to the accounts in the ledger.

The journal entry to record the $100,000 investment of George Smith into Smith Corporation in exchange for its common stock is as follows:

Cash........................	100,000	
Common Stock.......		100,000
Issued common stock.		

The journal entry to record Smith Corporation's purchase of land for $20,000 is as follows:

Land...........................	20,000	
Cash..................		20,000
Paid cash for land.		

The journal entry to record the purchase of an adjacent parcel of land for a $10,000 downpayment and a $90,000 note is as follows:

Land............................	100,000	
Cash....................		10,000
Note Payable.........		90,000

Purchased land for cash and a note payable.

The journal entry to record rendering $25,000 of services on account to a client is as follows:

Accounts Receivable........	25,000	
Service Revenue....		25,000

Rendered services on account.

The journal entry to record the purchase of $4,000 of supplies on account is as follows:

Supplies........................	4,000	
Accounts Payable....		4,000

The journal entry to record the collection of the $25,000 account receivable is as follows:

Cash............................	25,000	
Accounts Receivable		25,000

The journal entry to record the payment of $4,000 in rent, $1,000 in utilities, and $5,000 in salary is as follows:

Rent Expense................	4,000	
Utilities Expense............	1,000	
Salary Expense..............	5,000	
Cash....................		10,000

The journal entry to record the payment of $2,000 of accounts payable is as follows:

Accounts Payable............	2,000	
Cash....................		2,000

The journal entry to record the payment of a dividend of $3,000 is as follows:

Dividends.....................	3,000	
Cash....................		3,000

The income statement, statement of retained earnings, and balance sheet for Smith
Corporation for the month of December 31, 2005, are as follows:

Smith Corporation
Income Statement
For the Month Ended December 31, 2005

Revenue
       Service Revenue………….. $25,000

Expenses
       Salary Expense……………$5,000
       Rent Expense……………. 4,000
       Utilities Expense………… 1,000
       Total Expenses…………..   10,000
Net Income…………………. $15,000

Smith Corporation
Statement of Retained Earnings
For the Month Ended December 31, 2005

Retained Earnings, December 31, 2005………..$ 0
Add: Net Income………………………………. 15,000
Sub-Total………………………………………..$15,000
Less: Dividends……………………………… (3,000)
Retained Earnings, December 31, 2005……….. $12,000

Smith Corporation
Balance Sheet
December 31, 2005

Assets   **Liabilities**

Cash…….. $ 80,000   Accounts Payable………..$ 2,000
Supplies…   4,000   Note Payable……………. 90,000
Land……   120,000   Total Liabilities……… $92,000

                                Stockholders' Equity

                                Common Stock…………$100,000
                                Retained Earnings……… 12,000
                                Total Stockholders' Equity   112,000

                                Total Liabilities and
Total Assets $204,000   Stockholders' Equity $204,000

Exhibit 2-11 shows how the T-accounts for a sample company would appear after all transactions have been posted to the ledger accounts.

Objective 4—Use a trial balance

A trial balance is a list of all the accounts in the ledger with their balances. The trial balance shows assets first, then liabilities, and then the stockholders' equity accounts. The purpose of the trial balance is to prove that total debits equal total credits in the ledger. A company may prepare a trial balance at any time, but usually a company prepares a trial balance at the end of the accounting period. Exhibit 2-12 illustrates a trial balance.

> **Study Tip:** The fact that total debits equal total credits in the ledger does not mean that the accountant has not made an error.

If the trial balance indicates that the total debits do not equal the total credits, the accountant must find and correct the error or errors. A useful place to start this process is to calculate the difference between the total debits and the total credits. The accountant should make sure that each account in the ledger appears with its correct balance on the trial balance. The accountant should also divide the difference by two and determine if that amount appears on the wrong side of an account. For example, if the total debits exceed the total credits by $700, the accountant would look for a $350 entry on the debit side that should be on the credit side. If the difference between the total debits and total credits is divisible by nine, the accountant would look for a transposition error. For example, if the total credits exceeded the total debits by $90, the accountant might find a credit entry for $540 that should be $450.

A chart of accounts lists all of the accounts in the ledger and their account numbers. Exhibit 2-13 illustrates a chart of accounts. The chart of accounts lists accounts by category. Assets appear first, then liabilities, the stockholders' equity accounts, then revenues, and finally expenses.

The normal balance of an account is always on the same side as the increase side. Exhibit 2-14 shows the normal balance of each type of account. Assets, dividends, and expenses have normal debit balances. These accounts are debit-balance accounts. Liabilities, the stockholders' equity accounts Common Stock and Retained Earnings, and revenues have normal credit balances. These accounts are credit-balance accounts.

One format of an account is the T-account format with the debit side on the left of the T and the credit side on the right of the T. A different format has four columns for amounts: (1) debit, (2) credit, (3) debit balance, and (4) credit balance. This format provides a running balance of the account. Exhibit 2-15 shows this account format.

Objective 5—Analyze transactions for quick decisions

Managers often make decisions without the benefit of a complete set of accounting records. A manager can often analyze the effects of a transaction quickly simply by posting the effects of the transaction to T-accounts. The remainder of the book will emphasize the use of accounting information in decision making, which is one of the key functions of management. The better that a manager understands accounting information, the better the manager will be able to make wise decisions.

TEST YOURSELF

Matching

Match each numbered term with its lettered definition.

_____ 1. accounts	_____ 11. credit
_____ 2. revenues	_____ 12. expenses
_____ 3. liability	_____ 13. posting
_____ 4. transaction	_____ 14. trial balance
_____ 5. retained earnings	_____ 15. journal
_____ 6. accrued liability	_____ 16. chart of accounts
_____ 7. double-entry system	_____ 17. assets
_____ 8. debit	_____ 18. ledger
_____ 9. prepaid expenses	_____ 19. dividends
_____ 10. stockholders' equity	_____ 20. accounts payable

A. a chronological record of all company transactions.

B. any event that has a financial impact on the business and can be measured reliably.

C. the basic summary device of accounting.

D. economic resources that provide a future benefit for a business.

E. the book of a company's accounts and their balances.

F. an expense that has not yet been paid.

G. the right side of an account.

H. amounts paid by a corporation to its owners as a return on their investment.

I. the cumulative net income earned by a corporation over its lifetime, minus cumulative net losses and dividends.

J. a debt.

K. the owners' claims to the assets of a corporation.

L. lists all the accounts with their account balances.

M. records the dual effects of each transaction on an entity.

N. increases in stockholders' equity that result from delivering goods or services to customers.

O. a list of all a company's accounts and their account numbers.

P. a debt arising from the credit purchase of inventory.

Q. assets expected to expire or be used up in the near future.

R. copying entries from the journal to the ledger.

S. the left side of an account.

T. the costs of operating a business that decrease stockholders' equity.

Multiple Choice

Circle the best answer.

1. Which of the following reports a company's financial position in terms of assets, liabilities, and owner's equity?
   a. trial balance
   b. balance sheet
   c. income statement
   d. statement of cash flows

2. Which of the following is recorded as a debit?
   a. increases in assets
   b. increases in liabilities
   c. increases in revenues
   d. decreases in assets

3. Which of the following is the accounting equation?
   a. Assets + Liabilities = Owners' Equity
   b. Assets = Liabilities – Owners' Equity
   c. Revenues – Expenses = Net Income
   d. Assets = Liabilities + Owners' Equity

4. Most companies report their financial statements at the end of each:
   a. day
   b. transaction
   c. accounting period
   d. week

5. What is a cost that will provide future benefits to a company?
   a. expense
   b. asset
   c. revenue
   d. liability

6. Credit is the normal balance of:
   a. asset accounts
   b. asset and liability accounts
   c. assets and stockholders' equity accounts
   d. liability and stockholders' equity accounts

7. The process of copying the record of a transaction from the journal to the ledger is called:
   a. posting
   b. journalizing
   c. transferring
   d. moving

8. The process of recording a transaction in the journal is called:
   a. posting
   b. journalizing
   c. initiating
   d. reporting

9. What lists all the accounts in the ledger with their account balances?
   a. journal
   b. trial balance
   c. chart of accounts
   d. checkbook

10. Economic resources that benefit a business are:
    a. assets
    b. liabilities
    c. revenues
    d. expenses

11. The owners' claims to the assets of a corporation are called:
    a. assets
    b. liabilities
    c. stockholders' equity
    d. revenues

12. Which financial statement measures operating performance?
    a. income statement
    b. statement of cash flows
    c. statement of retained earnings
    d. balance sheet

13. What is the effect on total assets when a company collects an account receivable?
    a. increase
    b. decrease
    c. no effect
    d. can increase or decrease depending on the amount collected

14. What is the effect of the payment of dividends?
    a. increases expenses
    b. decreases cash
    c. increases retained earnings
    d. decreases cash and increases expenses

15. The retained earnings shown on the balance sheet comes from the:
    a. income statement
    b. statement of cash flows
    c. statement of retained earnings
    d. checkbook

Completion

Complete each of the following statements.

1. A prepaid expense is an asset because it provides a _____ benefit for the company.
2. A(n) _____ is the record of all the changes in a particular asset, liability, or stockholders' equity.
3. Most business failures result from a shortage of _____ .
4. Accountants often use a(n) _____ to represent an account in the general ledger.
5. The normal balance of an account falls on the side of the account where _____ are recorded.
6. Revenues minus expenses equals _____ .
7. _____ means money and any medium of exchange.
8. Unlike a corporation, a proprietorship has a single _____ account.
9. The statement of cash flows reports the sources and _____ of cash.
10. Although they are not an expense, _____ decrease retained earnings.
11. If the total debits do not equal the total credits on the trial balance, the cause could be a transposition error if the difference is divisible by _____ .
12. The journal is a _____ record of all of a company's transactions.
13. The _____ is a grouping of all the accounts with their account balances.
14. A _____ is any event that has a financial impact on a business and that the business can measure reliably.
15. A(n) _____ liability is a liability for an expense that the company has not yet paid.

True/False

For each of the following statements, circle T *for true or* F *for false.*

1. T F The statement of cash flows reports a company's operating performance in terms of revenues and expenses.
2. T F The Common Stock account shows the owners' investment in the corporation.
3. T F The balance sheet reports the financial position of a company in terms of assets, liabilities, and owners' equity.
4. T F The statement of retained earnings reports the net income or net loss and any dividends declared by a corporation.
5. T F If the total debits do not equal the total credits on a trial balance and the difference is divisible by two, the likely cause of the difference is a transposition error.
6. T F An account receivable is more binding than is a note receivable.
7. T F Most business failures result from a shortage of inventory.
8. T F Cash includes bank account balances.
9. T F Generally accepted accounting principles prohibit a company from using more than one revenue account.
10. T F A company's expenses increase when it purchases office supplies for cash.
11. T F Revenues increase the retained earnings of a corporation.
12. T F The income statement shows a company's revenues and expenses and the resulting net income or net loss.
13. T F Accounts Receivable is a liability.
14. T F Land is an asset.
15. T F Posting is recording a business transaction in a journal.

Exercises

1. State whether each of the following independent transactions increased, decreased, or did not affect total assets.

(1) Provided $10,000 of services to clients on account. _____

(2) Collected $6,000 of accounts receivable. _____

(3) Purchased $1,500 of supplies on account. _____

(4) Paid $800 on accounts payable. _____

(5) Paid $1,000 dividend to stockholders. _____

2. State whether each of the following would be recorded as a debit or as a credit.

(1) Increase in Accounts Receivable   _____

(2) Decrease in Accounts Payable   _____

(3) Increase in Dividends   _____

(4) Increase in Service Revenue   _____

(5) Decrease in Cash   _____

(6) Increase in Notes Payable   _____

(7) Increase in Common Stock   _____

(8) Increase in Rent Expense   _____

3. Prepare journal entries to record each of the following transactions.

(1) Issued common stock for $250,000.

(2) Purchased land for $100,000 in cash.

(3) Purchased $11,000 of supplies on account.

(4) Rendered $10,000 services to clients and received immediate payment.

(5) Paid $900 on accounts payable.

(6) Rendered $25,000 of services to clients on account.

(7) Collected $16,000 of accounts receivable.

(8) Paid rent expense of $4,000.

(9) Paid utilities expense of $850.

(10) Paid $2,000 in dividends.

4. Given the following account balances, prepare a trial balance for Williams Company as of January 31, 2006. All balances are normal balances. Be sure that the trial balance has a proper heading and that the accounts appear in the proper order.

Accounts Payable	$ 19,000
Utilities Expense	$ 1,000
Land	$509,000
Common Stock	$500,000
Cash	$ 26,000
Service Revenue	$ 18,000
Dividends	$ 2,000
Accounts Receivable	$ 14,000
Retained Earnings	$ 29,000
Rent Expense	$ 3,000
Supplies	$ 5,000
Salary Expense	$ 6,000

5. The marketing manager of Boley Business Consulting has proposed an advertising campaign that would cost $10,000. The campaign is expected to increase revenues by $50,000, but it would also require an increase in salaries of $20,000. What is the estimated effect of the advertising campaign on net income?

Critical Thinking

Clampit Company prepared its trial balance and learned that the total debits exceeded the total credits by $9,000. Discuss at least three possible causes of the difference.

Demonstration Problems

1. Prepare journal entries for each of the following transactions that occurred during March 2006 for Nickerson Corporation.

   (1) Received cash of $500,000 for the issuance of 5,000 shares of common stock.

   (2) Purchased land for $50,000 in cash and a note payable of $200,000.

   (3) Purchased $2,400 of supplies on account.

   (4) Rendered services worth $30,000 to clients on account.

   (5) Rendered services to clients for $10,000 in cash.

   (6) Paid $1,000 on account for the supplies previously purchased.

   (7) Collected $20,000 on accounts receivable.

   (8) Declared and paid a dividend of $5,000.

2. Given the following trial balance, prepare (1) an income statement for the year ended December 31, 2005, (2) a statement of retained earnings for the year ended December 31, 2005, and (3) a balance sheet as of December 31, 2005.

Young Corporation
Trial Balance
December 31, 2005

Account Title	Debit	Credit
Cash	15,000	
Accounts Receivable	33,000	
Supplies	10,500	
Land	168,000	
Accounts Payable		19,000
Note Payable		11,000
Common Stock		100,000
Retained Earnings		23,000
Dividends	5,000	
Service Revenue		244,000
Salary Expense	83,000	
Rent Expense	72,000	
Utilities Expense	7,500	
Repairs Expense	3,000	
Totals	$397,000	$397,000

SOLUTIONS

Matching

1	C	5	I	9	Q	13	R	17	D
2	N	6	F	10	K	14	L	18	E
3	J	7	M	11	G	15	A	19	H
4	B	8	S	12	T	16	O	20	P

Multiple Choice

1	B
2	A
3	D
4	C
5	B
6	D
7	A
8	B
9	B
10	A
11	C
12	A
13	C
14	B
15	C

Completion

1. future
2. account
3. cash
4. T-account
5. increases
6. net income
7. Cash
8. capital
9. uses
10. dividends
11. nine
12. chronological
13. ledger
14. transaction
15. accrued

True/False

1. F   The income statement reports a company's operating performance in terms of revenue and expenses.
2. T
3. T
4. T
5. F   If the total debits do not equal the total credits on the trial balance and the difference is divisible by two, the likely cause is an entry for half of the difference on the side with the higher total that should be on the side with the lower total.
6. F   A note receivable is more binding than is an account receivable because a note receivable must be in writing and comply with certain legal requirements.
7. F   Most business failures result from a shortage of cash.
8. T
9. F   Many companies have multiple revenue accounts, which are allowed by generally accepted accounting principles.
10. F   When a company purchases office supplies for cash, its total assets do not change because office supplies are an asset. Only when the company uses the office supplies do they become an expense.
11. T
12. T
13. F   Accounts Receivable is an asset.
14. T
15. F   Posting is copying the record of a transaction from a journal to the ledger.

Exercises

1.

(1) Increased. The asset Accounts Receivable increased $10,000 and the stockholders' equity account Retained Earnings increased $10,000 because Service Revenue increased.

(2) Did not affect. The asset Cash increased $6,000, and the asset Accounts Receivable decreased $6,000. Therefore, total assets remained the same.

(3) Increased. The asset Supplies increased $1,500, and the liability Accounts Payable increased $1,500.

(4) Decreased. The asset Cash decreased $800, and the liability Accounts Payable decreased $800.

(5) Decreased. The asset Cash decreased $1,000, and the stockholders' equity account Retained Earnings decreased $1,000.

2.

(1) Debit
(2) Debit
(3) Debit
(4) Credit
(5) Credit
(6) Credit
(7) Credit
(8) Debit

3.

(1)	Cash...	250,000	
	Common Stock.....................		250,000
	Issued common stock.		
(2)	Land...	100,000	
	Cash..............................		100,000
	Purchased land.		
(3)	Supplies...................................	11,000	
	Accounts Payable................		11,000
	Purchased supplies on account.		
(4)	Cash..	10,000	
	Service Revenue..................		10,000
	Rendered services to clients for cash.		
(5)	Accounts Payable.........................	900	
	Cash...............................		900
	Paid accounts payable.		
(6)	Accounts Receivable.....................	25,000	
	Service Revenue..................		25,000
	Rendered services to clients on account.		
(7)	Cash.......................................	16,000	
	Accounts Receivable............		16,000
	Received cash from clients on account.		
(8)	Rent Expense.............................	4,000	
	Cash...............................		4,000
	Paid rent expense.		
(9)	Utilities Expense.........................	850	
	Cash...............................		850
	Paid utilities expense.		
(10)	Dividends.................................	2,000	
	Cash...............................		2,000
	Paid dividends to stockholders.		

4.

Williams Company
Trial Balance
January 31, 2006

Account Title	Debit	Credit
Cash	26,000	
Accounts Receivable	14,000	
Supplies	5,000	
Land	509,000	
Accounts Payable		19,000
Common Stock		509,000
Retained Earnings		29,000
Service Revenue		18,000
Dividends	2,000	
Salary Expense	6,000	
Rent Expense	3,000	
Utilities Expense	1,000	
Totals	$566,000	$566,000

5.

Estimated increase in Service Revenue		$50,000
Estimated increase in Advertising Expense	$10,000	
Estimated increase in Salary Expense	20,000	
Total estimated increases in expenses		30,000
Estimated increase in net income		$20,000

Critical Thinking

The $9,000 difference could be caused by the failure to include an account on the trial balance with a credit balance of $9,000. Because the $9,000 difference is divisible by two, a possible cause of the error is an entry of $4,500 on the debit side that should be on the credit side. A third possible cause of the error is a transposition error because the $9,000 difference is divisible by nine. For example, a debit balance of $45,000 might have been incorrectly written as $54,000.

Demonstration Problems

1.

(1)	Cash..	500,000	
	Common Stock...........................		500,000
	Issued common stock.		

(2)	Land..	250,000	
	Cash.....................................		50,000
	Note Payable...........................		200,000
	Purchased land by making a downpayment and signing a note for the balance.		

(3)	Supplies...	2,400	
	Accounts Payable.......................		2,400
	Purchased supplies on account.		

(4)	Accounts Receivable............................	30,000	
	Service Revenue........................		30,000
	Rendered services on account.		

(5)	Cash...	10,000	
	Service Revenue........................		10,000
	Rendered services for cash.		

(6)	Accounts Payable...............................	1,000	
	Cash.....................................		1,000
	Paid on accounts payable.		

(7)	Cash...	20,000	
	Accounts Receivable..................		20,000
	Received payments on accounts.		

(8)	Dividends.......................................	5,000	
	Cash.....................................		5,000
	Paid dividends to stockholders.		

2.

Young Corporation
Income Statement
For the Year Ended December 31, 2005

Revenue

Service Revenue $244,000

Expenses

Salary Expense	$83,000	
Rent Expense	72,000	
Utilities Expense	7,500	
Repairs Expense	3,000	
Total Expenses		165,500
Net Income		$ 78,500

Young Corporation
Statement of Retained Earnings
For the Year Ended December 31, 2005

Retained Earnings, January 1, 2005	$23,000
Add: Net Income	78,500
Sub-Total	$101,500
Less: Dividends	(5,000)
Retained Earnings, December 31, 2005	$96,500

Young Corporation
Balance Sheet
December 31, 2005

Assets		Liabilities	
Cash	$15,000	Accounts Payable	$19,000
Accounts Receivable	33,000	Note Payable	11,000
Supplies	10,500	Total Liabilities	$30,000
Land	168,000		
		Stockholders' Equity	
		Common Stock	$100,000
		Retained Earnings	96,500
		Total Stockholders' Equity	$196,500
		Total Liabilities and	
Total Assets	$226,500	Stockholders' Equity	$226,500

Chapter 3

USING ACCRUAL ACCOUNTING TO MEASURE INCOME

CHAPTER OBJECTIVES

The learning objectives for this chapter are as follows:

1. Relate accrual accounting and cash flows
2. Apply the revenue and matching principles
3. Update the financial statements by adjusting the accounts
4. Prepare the financial statements
5. Close the books
6. Use the current ratio and the debt ratio to evaluate a business

CHAPTER OVERVIEW

This chapter shows how investors and creditors use accrual accounting to evaluate a company's operating performance. The two basic accounting methods are the cash basis and the accrual basis. A company that uses accrual accounting records the effect of every transaction when it occurs. In cash-basis accounting, a company records transactions only when it receives cash or pays cash. Generally accepted accounting principles (GAAP) require companies to use accrual accounting because it provides more complete information than cash-basis accounting. Better information enables investors, creditors, and managers to make better financial decisions.

CHAPTER REVIEW

Objective 1—Relate accrual accounting and cash flows

Cash-basis accounting records only transactions that include the receipt of cash or the payment of cash. For example, cash-basis accounting would record sales for cash, collections from customers from credit sales, and the payment of operating expenses. Accrual accounting also records transactions involving cash. In addition, accrual accounting records transactions that do not involve the receipt or payment of cash. For example, accrual accounting records sales on account, purchases on account, and expenses incurred but not yet paid.

The time-period concept requires a company to prepare financial statements at regular intervals. The basic accounting period is one year. Many companies use the calendar year as their accounting year. Some companies use a fiscal year for their accounting period. A fiscal year is a year that ends on a date other than December 31.

The users of a company's financial statements cannot wait until the end of the year to evaluate a company's performance. Managers, investors, and creditors also need accounting information on an interim basis, such as monthly or quarterly.

Objective 2—Apply the revenue and matching principles

The basic difference between cash-basis accounting and accrual accounting is when to record revenues and expenses. In cash-basis accounting, a company records revenue when it receives cash from the sale of its products and services. Cash-basis accounting distorts the reported amounts on the income statement and the balance sheet. In accrual accounting, the revenue principle governs when to record revenue and how much revenue to record. The matching principle controls the recording of expenses.

A company should record revenue when it earns it. A company earns revenue when it delivers products or provides services to a customer. Exhibit 3-1 illustrates when to record revenue. The amount of revenue to record is the cash value of the goods sold or the services provided to the customer. The cash value of the sale is the amount of cash the company expects to receive from the transaction, excluding any interest that the company might earn on the account. The cash value might differ from the list price or estimated value of the goods or services.

Expenses are costs that have expired in the process of earning revenue. Expenses are costs that provide no future benefit to the company. The matching principle states that a company should identify the expenses incurred during the accounting period, measure the expenses, and match the expenses incurred with the related revenue earned during the accounting period. To match the expenses with the related revenue earned means to subtract the expenses from the revenues to compute the net income or the net loss. Exhibit 3-2 illustrates the matching principle.

> **Study Tip:** When a company incurs a cost, it can be an asset or an expense. The cost is an asset if it will provide future benefits to the company. The cost is an expense if it will not provide future benefits to the company. Over time, however, assets can become expenses as a company uses or consumes them.

A company can incur an expense by making a payment. For example, when a company makes a payment for its monthly rent, it would recognize the rent expense at that time. A second way a company can incur an expense is by using up an asset. For example, when a company uses supplies, the cost of the supplies used becomes supplies expense. A third way a company can incur an expense is to create a liability for a cost that no longer has value to the company. For example, a company receives a bill for its monthly electric bill that it has not yet paid. The main thing to remember is that a company can incur an expense whether or not it makes a payment.

Because accrual accounting recognizes expenses when a company incurs them rather than when a company makes payments, the recognition of expenses can present ethical issues. Management might be tempted to recognize expenses in the period that would be more beneficial to the company. Some companies attempt to smooth their net income over time by manipulating the timing of expenses. The companies manage earnings in this way because they believe that investors prefer a smooth trend in reported earnings over time. One way to manipulate expenses is to overstate an estimated expense and its corresponding estimated liability during the adjusting process in a year when profits are high. The overstatement is called a "cookie-jar reserve." When profits are low, the company reduces the amount of the estimated liability (the reserve), which also reduces the related expense for that year.

Objective 3—Update the financial statements by adjusting the accounts

---

Study Tip: The adjusting process involves three basic steps:

1. Know what the account balances are.
2. Carefully analyze the accounts to determine what the account balances should be. This step is the most difficult.
3. Prepare adjusting journal entries to change the account balances from what they are to what they should be.

Before a business can prepare its financial statements at the end of the accounting period, it must adjust its accounts. The process begins with a trial balance, which is a listing of all the accounts in the general ledger with their respective debit and credit balances. Exhibit 3-3 shows an example of a trial balance. The balances of some accounts will not need any adjustment, but other accounts will have balances that do not reflect all transactions. For example, the Supplies account will not be correct because recording supplies used each time the business uses them would be impractical.

The three basic categories of adjustments are deferrals, depreciation, and accruals. Each adjustment involves an account that appears on the income statement and an account that appears on the balance sheet.

One type of deferral adjustment involves an adjustment of an asset account for a cost that was an asset at the time of purchase that has since become an expense. For example, when a company purchases supplies, the company records the cost of the supplies purchased in the Supplies account, which is an asset. At the end of the period, the company must record the cost of the supplies that it has used. The supplies the company has used are an expense. The company debits the Supplies Expense account and credits the Supplies account. For example, assume that the balance in Supplies is $9,000, but a count of supplies at the end of the year shows that only $4,000 of supplies are on hand. The company has used $5,000 ($9,000 – $4,000) of supplies. The company would record the use of the supplies by debiting Supplies Expense $5,000 and crediting Supplies $5,000. The journal entry would appear as follows:

Dec. 31   Supplies Expense....................5,000
                          Supplies......................   5,000
                     To record supplies used.

Other prepaid expense accounts that require a similar adjustment include Prepaid Insurance and Prepaid Rent.

Depreciation is the systematic allocation of the cost of a plant asset to expense over its useful life. Assets that a company must depreciate are called depreciable assets. Depreciable assets include buildings, furniture, and equipment.

> **Study Tip:** Land is a plant asset, but it is not a depreciable asset. Therefore, no adjustment to the Land account is necessary.

Plant assets are also called fixed assets. The adjustment process is similar to a deferral adjustment. The company debits Depreciation Expense, but the entry does not decrease the plant asset directly. Instead, the adjustment credits a contra asset account called Accumulated Depreciation. For example, assume that depreciation on equipment of $12,000 has not been recorded. The company would record the depreciation by debiting Depreciation Expense—Equipment $12,000 and crediting Accumulated Depreciation—Equipment $12,000. The journal entry would appear as follows:

Dec. 31   Depreciation Expense—Equipment.................12,000
                          Accumulated Depreciation—Equipment....   12,000
                     To record depreciation on equipment.

> **Study Tip:** Depreciation is a cost allocation concept. The fair market value of the plant asset is not relevant to the calculation of depreciation.

A contra account always has a normal balance that is the opposite of its companion account in the general ledger. The Accumulated Depreciation account has a normal credit balance because assets have a normal balance of debit and the Accumulated Depreciation account is opposite to its related plant asset account. The balance in the Accumulated Depreciation account equals the sum of all the depreciation on the related asset from the date the company acquired it. The difference between the cost of a plant asset and its related accumulated depreciation is called the book value or carrying value of the plant asset. Exhibit 3-4 shows how a company would report the book value of its plant assets. Exhibit 3-5 gives an example of how a company would report its property, plant, and equipment in its annual report.

Another type of deferral involves an adjustment of a liability account for revenue that the company received before it earned it. A company may not recognize revenue until it has delivered a product or provided a service. Revenue received in advance is a liability.

> **Study Tip:** Any account title that begins with the word *Unearned* is a liability. Unearned Revenue is a liability account, not a revenue account.

At the end of the period, the company credits a revenue account to reflect the revenue earned and debits the liability account. For example, assume that a law firm received a retainer of $10,000 in November. The law firm recorded the transaction by debiting Cash $10,000 and crediting Unearned Revenue $10,000. At the end of its accounting period on December 31, the law firm has earned $6,000 of the retainer. The law firm would debit Unearned Revenue $6,000 and credit Fees Revenue $6,000. The journal entry would appear as follows:

Dec. 31   Unearned Revenue..................6,000
                    Fees Revenue.................   6,000
                    To record the $6,000 of unearned fees that have since been earned.

An accrual is the opposite of a deferral. An accrued expense involves the incurrence of an expense before the business pays it.

> **Study Tip:** Accrued expenses are also called accrued liabilities because an accrued expense is a liability for an expense that the business has not yet paid.

A common example of an accrued expense is Salary Payable. A company normally pays its employees at set intervals such as weekly or monthly, but the accounting period might end between the regular pay dates. This situation would require the business to recognize the accrued Salary Expense and the related Salary Payable at the end of the accounting period.

For example, assume that a business normally pays its employees total salaries of $25,000 each week for the five-day work week ending on Friday. Also assume that the accounting period ends on Wednesday, December 31. The company would record the $15,000 ($25,000 x 3/5) in accrued salaries by debiting Salary Expense $15,000 and crediting Salary Payable $15,000. The journal entry would appear as follows:

Dec. 31   Salary Expense.......................15,000
                    Salary Payable...............   15,000
                  To record accrued salaries ($25,000 x 3/5)

An adjustment for accrued revenue involves the recording of revenue before the business collects any cash by debiting a receivable and crediting a revenue account. For example, assume that a consulting firm has performed $3,000 of services for a client, but it has not sent the client a bill or recorded the revenue on its books on December 31, the end of its accounting period. The consulting firm would record the accrued revenue by debiting Accounts Receivable $3,000 and crediting Fees Revenue $3,000. The journal entry would appear as follows:

Dec. 31   Accounts Receivable…….…….3,000
                          Fees Revenue……………   3,000
                 To record fees earned that have not been recorded.

For prepaids, the cash transaction occurs before the adjustment. For accruals, the adjustment occurs before the cash transaction. Exhibit 3-6 shows a diagram of prepaids and accruals.
The adjustment process serves to measure income and update the balance sheet. Therefore, each adjusting entry involves a revenue account or expense account and an asset or liability account. Exhibit 3-7 summarizes common adjustments. Exhibit 3-8 illustrates the adjusting entries for a sample company.

Another adjustment that corporations must make is for income tax expense. Corporations usually accrue income tax expense and the related income tax payable as the last adjusting entry at the end of the accounting period. Assume that a corporation has an estimated income tax liability of $20,000 on December 31, the end of its accounting period. The corporation would record the accrued income tax expense by debiting Income Tax Expense $20,000 and crediting Income Tax Payable $20,000. The journal entry would appear as follows:

Dec. 31   Income Tax Expense…………………….20,000
                          Income Tax Payable……………   20,000
                 To record accrued income tax expense.

After the company has recorded all of the adjusting entries in the journal and posted them to the accounts in the general ledger, the company should prepare an adjusted trial balance. The adjusted trial balance lists each account in the general ledger with its adjusted balance. Exhibit 3-9 illustrates the preparation of an adjusted trial balance using a worksheet. The first two columns show the unadjusted trial balance; the next two columns show the adjustments; and the final two columns show the adjusted trial balance.

Study Tip: In calculating the adjusted balances, the following rules apply:

1. Add the debit adjustments to unadjusted debit balances
2. Subtract credit adjustments from unadjusted debit balances
3. Add the credit adjustments to unadjusted credit balances
4. Subtract the debit adjustments from unadjusted credit balances

---

Objective 4—Prepare the financial statements

A company prepares its financial statements using the account balances from the adjusted trial balance. Exhibit 3-10 illustrates an income statement, where a company reports the balances in its revenue and expense accounts. Exhibit 3-11 illustrates a statement of retained earnings, where a company reports the changes in its retained earnings. Exhibit 3-12 illustrates a balance sheet, where a company reports its assets, liabilities, and stockholders' equity.

A company must prepare its income statement first. Next, a company prepares its statement of retained earnings. Net income from the income statement goes on the statement of retained earnings because net income increases retained earnings. A net loss would decrease retained earnings. Then a company prepares its balance sheet. The ending balance of retained earnings from the statement of retained earnings goes in the stockholders' equity section of the balance sheet.

Objective 5—Close the books

> **Study Tip:** To close an account means to make a journal entry to cause its balance to become zero.

Closing the books involves transferring the balances in the temporary accounts to Retained Earnings. The closing entries cause the balances in the temporary accounts to become zero and their balances to be transferred to Retained Earnings. The temporary accounts are the revenue accounts, the expense accounts, and the Dividends account. Another name for temporary account is nominal account. Nominal means in name only. The revenue, expense, and Dividends accounts are nominal accounts because they reflect the changes in the permanent account Retained Earnings. Exhibit 3-13 illustrates closing entries.

The permanent accounts are not closed. Permanent accounts are also called real accounts or balance sheet accounts because they are the assets, liabilities, and stockholders' equity accounts that appear on the balance sheet.

Closing entries include the following three steps:

1. Debit each revenue account for its balance and credit Retained Earnings for the total revenues.
2. Credit each expense account for its balance and debit Retained Earnings for the total expenses.
3. Credit Dividends for its balance and debit Retained Earnings.

On the balance sheet, a company classifies its assets as current assets or long-term assets based on their relative liquidity. Liquidity refers to how quickly a company can convert an asset to cash. Current assets are assets that a company can convert to cash, sell, or consume within 12 months or the operating cycle of the business, whichever is longer. The operating cycle begins when a company pays cash for goods and services and ends when the company receives cash from the sale of goods and services. Cash is a current asset, and it is the most liquid asset. Other current assets include accounts receivable, merchandise inventory, and prepaid expenses. Long-term assets are all assets other than current assets. Long-term assets include plant assets, often shown on a balance sheet under the category Property, Plant, and Equipment. Plant assets include land, buildings, furniture and fixtures, and equipment. Other categories of long-term assets include Intangible Assets, such as patents and copyrights, and Other Assets.

A balance sheet shows liabilities in the order in which a company must pay them. The two classifications of liabilities are current liabilities and long-term liabilities. Current liabilities are debts that a company must pay within one year or the company's operating cycle, whichever is longer. Examples of current liabilities are Accounts Payable, Notes Payable if due within one year, Salary Payable, Interest Payable, Unearned Revenue, and Income Tax Payable.

All other liabilities are long-term liabilities. Many notes payable are long-term liabilities because they are not due until after one year from the date of the balance sheet. Some notes payable, such as mortgages, call for installment payments. They have some payments due within one year, which are current liabilities. The payments due after one year are long-term liabilities.

A classified balance sheet shows assets grouped into current assets and long-term assets and liabilities grouped into current liabilities and long-term liabilities. Exhibit 3-14 illustrates a classified balance sheet.

A company can prepare its balance sheet in one of two formats—the report format or the account format. The report format shows assets on top with liabilities and stockholders' equity below the assets. The account format shows assets on the left and liabilities and stockholders' equity on the right.

A company can also prepare its income statement using one of two formats—the multi-step income statement or the single-step income statement. A multi-step income statement has a number of subtotals that emphasize important relationships between revenues and expenses. Examples of subtotals include gross profit, income from operations, and income before tax. Exhibit 3-15 illustrates a multi-step income statement. A single-step income statement groups all revenues together and all expenses together. It then shows net income or net loss.

Objective 6—Use the current ratio and the debt ratio to evaluate a business

The current ratio is equal to total current assets divided by total current liabilities.

$$\text{Current Ratio} = \frac{\text{Total Current Assets}}{\text{Total Current Liabilities}}$$

The current ratio is one indicator of how well a company can pay its current liabilities. A current ratio of 1.50 is generally considered good, but a current ratio of 1.00 would be considered poor.

Another important financial ratio is the debt ratio, which equals the total liabilities divided by the total assets.

$$\text{Debt Ratio} = \frac{\text{Total Liabilities}}{\text{Total Assets}}$$

The debt ratio shows the percentage of a company's assets it has financed with debt. The debt ratio is a measure of a company's ability to pay its liabilities. A low debt ratio is less risky than a high debt ratio because a business with a low debt ratio has low required payments on its liabilities. A company with a high debt ratio has high required payments on its liabilities, which can lead to bankruptcy during a downturn in sales.

Study Tip: In general, the debt ratio cannot be more than 1.00. If the debt ratio were higher than 1.00, the company's liabilities would be greater than its assets. In that case, the company would be insolvent.

Business transactions affect a company's current ratio and debt ratio. The textbook shows how various transactions affect a company's current ratio and its debt ratio. For example, issuing stock for cash will increase a company's current ratio and decrease its debt ratio. The purchase of a building for cash will decrease a company's current ratio, but it will have no effect on its debt ratio. Making a sale increases a company's current ratio and decreases its debt ratio. Collecting an account receivable has no effect on the current ratio or on the debt ratio. Incurring an accrued expense decreases the current ratio and increases the debt ratio. Recording depreciation expense has no effect on the current ratio, but it increases the debt ratio. Recording the supplies used or paying an immediate expense with cash decreases the current ratio and increases the debt ratio.

> **Study Tip:** If a company's current ratio is greater than 1.00, the payment of a current liability will cause the current ratio to increase.

Assume that a company has current assets of $200,000 and current liabilities of $100,000, which means that its current ratio is 2.00 ($200,000 / $100,000). If the company pays $40,000 of its current liabilities, its current ratio will increase to 2.67 ($160,000 / $60,000). If the current ratio is greater than 1.00 and the company increases its current assets and current liabilities by the same amount, such as by purchasing merchandise inventory on account, the company's current ratio will decrease. For example, if the company purchases $50,000 of merchandise inventory on account, its current ratio will decrease to 1.67 ($250,000 / $150,000).

> **Study Tip:** If a company's current ratio is less than 1.00, the payment of a current liability will cause the company's current ratio to decrease.

Assume that a company has current assets of $40,000 and current liabilities of $50,000, which means that its current ratio is 0.80 ($40,000 / $50,000). If the company pays $10,000 of its current liabilities, its current ratio will decrease to 0.75 ($30,000 / $40,000). If the current ratio is less than 1.00 and the company increases its current assets and current liabilities by the same amount, such as by purchasing merchandise inventory on account, the company's current ratio will increase. For example, if the company purchases $50,000 of merchandise inventory on account, its current ratio will increase to 0.90 ($90,000 / $100,000).

TEST YOURSELF

Matching

Match each numbered term with its lettered definition.

_____	1. accrual accounting		_____	11. report format
_____	2. current assets		_____	12. liquidity
_____	3. depreciation		_____	13. classified balance sheet
_____	4. revenue principle		_____	14. deferral
_____	5. matching principle		_____	15. operating cycle
_____	6. cash-basis accounting		_____	16. single-step income statement
_____	7. prepaid expense		_____	17. permanent accounts
_____	8. unearned revenue		_____	18. long-term assets
_____	9. closing entries		_____	19. accumulated depreciation
_____	10. contra account		_____	20. multi-step income statement

A. accounting that records only transactions in which cash is received or paid.

B. category of miscellaneous assets that typically expire or get used up in the near future or cash received before the company earns revenue.

C. cumulative sum of all depreciation expense from the date of acquiring a plant asset.

D. directs accountants to identify all expenses incurred during the period, to measure the expenses, and to match them against the revenues earned during that same period.

E. shows current assets separate from long-term assets, and current liabilities separate from long-term liabilities.

F. recognizes (records) the impact of a business event as it occurs, regardless of whether the transaction affected cash.

G. an asset that is not a current asset.

H. is expected to be converted to cash, sold, or consumed during the next 12 months, or within the business' normal operating cycle if longer than a year.

I. measure of how quickly an asset can be converted to cash.

J. contains subtotals to highlight important relationships between revenues and expenses.

K. tells accountants when to record revenue and the amount of revenue to record.

L. time span between the time a company pays cash for goods and the company collects cash from the sale of goods and services.

M. lists all the revenues together under a heading such as Revenues or Revenues and Gains; Expenses appear in a separate category called Expenses, Costs and Expenses, or Expenses and Losses.

N. liability created when a business collects cash from customers in advance of rendering services or delivering products to them. The obligation is to provide a product or a service in the future.

O. asset, liability, and stockholders' equity accounts that a company does not close at the end of the period.

P. a balance-sheet format that lists assets at the top, followed by liabilities and stockholders' equity below.

Q. an account that has a companion account and whose normal balance is opposite that of the companion account.

R. an expense paid in advance, which is an asset because it provides a future benefit for the owner.

S. expense associated with spreading (allocating) the cost of a plant asset over its useful life.

T. entries that transfer the revenue, expense, and dividends balances from these respective accounts to Retained Earnings.

Multiple Choice

Circle the best answer.

1. In accrual accounting, a company records the transactions, even if it receives or pays no cash, when it:
   a. performs a service
   b. makes a sale
   c. incurs an expense
   d. all of the above

2. In cash-basis accounting, a company records a transaction only when it:
   a. receives cash
   b. pays cash
   c. either receives or pays cash
   d. neither receives nor pays cash

3. A calendar year ends on:
   a. December 31
   b. May 31
   c. January 31
   d. a date other than December 31

4. Companies prepare financial statements for a basic accounting period of:
   a. three or six months
   b. three months
   c. six months
   d. one year

5. An example of an account that is a deferral is:
   a. Service Revenue
   b. Prepaid Rent
   c. Accumulated Depreciation
   d. Salary Payable

6. The current ratio uses information from the:
   a. income statement
   b. statement of retained earnings
   c. income statement and the statement of retained earnings
   d. balance sheet

7. An example of a temporary account is:
   a. Accounts Receivable
   b. Accounts Payable
   c. Dividends
   d. Cash

8. GAAP stands for:
   a. generally accepted accounting practices
   b. generally accepted accounting principles
   c. generally accepted accrual practices
   d. globally accepted accounting principles

9. An example of a plant asset is:
   a. equipment
   b. merchandise inventory
   c. prepaid insurance
   d. cash

10. The only way for a business to know for certain how well it performed is to:
    a. perform an inventory
    b. ask the accountant
    c. liquidate
    d. prepare a tax return

11. The basis for recording expenses is called the:
    a. matching principle
    b. revenue principle
    c. accounting principle
    d. time-period concept

12. Which financial statement shows total stockholders' equity?
    a. income statement
    b. statement of retained earnings
    c. balance sheet
    d. income statement and statement of retained earnings

13. Which financial statement shows the net income or net loss?
    a. income statement
    b. statement of retained earnings
    c. balance sheet
    d. income statement and statement of retained earnings

14. An example of a long-term asset is:
    a. furniture
    b. merchandise inventory
    c. accounts receivable
    d. cash

15. At the end of the accounting period, net income is transferred to:
    a. Cash
    b. Retained Earnings
    c. Common Stock
    d. Dividends

Completion

Complete each of the following statements.

1. The current ratio is the ratio of total current assets divided by _____.
2. The debt ratio is the ratio of _____ divided by total assets.
3. Investors want to invest in companies whose stock price will increase and that pay _____.
4. Accrual accounting requires a company to record revenues as they are _____.
5. If a company fails to record a sale on account, the balance sheet will not report an _____.
6. All but the _____ businesses use the accrual basis of accounting.
7. The process of _____ means going out of business.
8. Prepaid Rent is a(n) _____.
9. An accrual is the opposite of a(n) _____.
10. The process of allocating the cost of a plant asset to expense is called _____.
11. The cost of a plant asset minus its _____ is called its book value.
12. An unearned revenue account is a(n) _____.
13. The measure of how quickly a company can convert an asset into cash is called _____.
14. A multi-step income statement contains a number of _____ that highlight important relationships between revenues and expenses.
15. The report form of the balance sheet lists assets at the _____.

True/False

For each of the following statements, circle T *for true or* F *for false.*

1. T F In cash-basis accounting, a company does not record anything unless cash changes hands.
2. T F The higher the current ratio, the weaker is a company's financial position.
3. T F Generally accepted accounting principles require that a business use accrual accounting.
4. T F Most retailers use the calendar year as their basic accounting period.
5. T F The critical event for recording an expense is the payment of cash.
6. T F Financial statements prepared for less than one year are interim financial statements.
7. T F All plant assets, including land, decline in usefulness as they age.
8. T F A business carries an accumulated depreciation account for each depreciable asset.
9. T F The collection of an account receivable will increase the current ratio.
10. T F A company reports prepaid expenses on the income statement.
11. T F To close the revenue accounts, a company debits each revenue account for its balance and credits Retained Earnings for the sum of the revenues.
12. T F A company shows unearned revenue as a liability on the balance sheet.
13. T F Like individual taxpayers, corporations are subject to income tax.
14. T F The balance sheet lists current liabilities below long-term liabilities.
15. T F Most successful businesses operate with current ratios between 1.20 and 1.50.

Exercises

1. Given the following unadjusted trial balance and other information, prepare the adjusting journal entries.

Treybig Corporation
Unadjusted Trial Balance
December 31, 2005

Cash	50,246	
Accounts Receivable	154,148	
Prepaid Insurance	24,000	
Supplies	11,500	
Equipment	400,000	
Accumulated Depreciation—Equipment		80,000
Accounts Payable		68,765
Income Tax Payable		0
Note Payable (due in five years)		100,000
Common Stock		200,000
Retained Earnings		59,771
Dividends	18,000	
Service Revenue		854,691
Advertising Expense	14,100	
Insurance Expense	6,000	
Depreciation Expense	0	
Interest Expense	9,000	
Salary Expense	575,888	
Rent Expense	48,000	
Supplies Expense	0	
Income Tax Expense	52,345	
Totals	1,363,227	1,363,227

Other Information:

1. The supplies on hand on at the end of the year were $7,400.
2. The Prepaid Insurance represents the cost of a two-year policy purchased on July 1, 2005.
3. The company has not recorded depreciation on equipment in the amount of $40,000.
4. The company had performed $10,000 of services for a client late in December 2005. The company has not yet recorded the services performed on its books.
5. The company has not yet recorded additional income tax expense that it owes in the amount of $90,000.
6. There are no accrued salaries because the company pays the employees every Friday for the five-day work week ending on that day, and December 31, 2005, is on a Friday.

Use the following adjusted trial balance for Exercises 2, 3, and 4.

Bates Corporation
Adjusted Trial Balance
December 31, 2005

Cash	180,464	
Accounts Receivable	231,678	
Prepaid Insurance	34,000	
Supplies	5,510	
Equipment	500,000	
Accumulated Depreciation—Equipment		120,000
Accounts Payable		68,765
Income Tax Payable		24,143
Note Payable (due in five years)		100,000
Common Stock		500,000
Retained Earnings		82,582
Dividends	18,000	
Service Revenue		854,691
Advertising Expense	14,100	
Depreciation Expense	60,000	
Insurance Expense	6,000	
Interest Expense	10,000	
Salary Expense	604,090	
Rent Expense	48,000	
Supplies Expense	14,196	
Income Tax Expense	24,143	
Totals	1,750,181	1,750,181

2. Prepare the closing journal entries.

3. (1) Prepare an income statement using the single-step format for the year ended December 31, 2005. (2) Prepare the statement of retained earnings for the year ended December 31, 2005.

4. Prepare a classified balance sheet as of December 31, 2005.

5. Given the following information, calculate (1) the current ratio and (2) the debt ratio.

Cash	$70,000
Accounts Receivable	30,000
Merchandise Inventory	80,000
Prepaid Expenses	20,000
Property, Plant, and Equipment (net)	400,000
Total Assets	$600,000
Accounts Payable	$100,000
Note Payable (due in 10 years)	140,000
Common Stock	160,000
Retained Earnings	200,000
Total Liabilities and Stockholders' Equity	$600,000

Critical Thinking

If a company fails to record services rendered on account to a customer, what are the effects on (1) net income, (2) retained earnings, (3) total stockholders' equity (4) total assets, (5) the current ratio, and (6) the debt ratio?

Demonstration Problems

1. Given the following unadjusted trial balance and other information, prepare the following: (1) adjusting journal entries, and (2) an adjusted trial balance

Rios Company
Unadjusted Trial Balance
December 31, 2005

Cash	36,814	
Accounts Receivable	152,490	
Prepaid Insurance	14,400	
Supplies	8,625	
Equipment	695,000	
Accumulated Depreciation—Equipment		100,000
Accounts Payable		48,560
Interest Payable		0
Income Tax Payable		0
Note Payable (due in five years)		120,000
Common Stock		300,000
Retained Earnings		108,232
Dividends	12,000	
Service Revenue		908,362
Advertising Expense	25,046	
Depreciation Expense	0	
Insurance Expense	0	
Interest Expense	0	
Salary Expense	562,779	
Rent Expense	60,000	
Supplies Expense	0	
Income Tax Expense	18,000	
Totals	1,585,154	1,585,154

Other Information:

1. The company had $2,960 of supplies on hand at the end of the year.
2. The amount in Prepaid Insurance represents a 24-month policy purchased on October 1, 2005.
3. The company has not recorded depreciation on equipment in the amount of $50,000.
4. The company has not recorded interest due on the note payable at the rate of 11 percent per year for the year. The company made the note in 2004.
5. The company has not yet recorded additional income tax expense of $82,000 that is due to the IRS and the state.

2. Given the following adjusted trial balance, prepare the following: (1) income statement for the year ended December 31, 2005, (2) statement of retained earnings for the year ended December 31, 2005, (3) classified balance sheet as of December 31, 2005, and (4) the closing entries. (5) In addition, calculate the current ratio and the debt ratio.

Eagle Corporation
Adjusted Trial Balance
December 31, 2005

Cash	297,995	
Accounts Receivable	145,913	
Prepaid Insurance	52,000	
Supplies	8,598	
Equipment	450,000	
Accumulated Depreciation—Equipment		180,000
Accounts Payable		28,444
Income Tax Payable		8,000
Note Payable (due in five years)		100,000
Common Stock		300,000
Retained Earnings		141,638
Dividends	6,000	
Service Revenue		772,112
Advertising Expense	27,400	
Depreciation Expense	45,000	
Insurance Expense	9,000	
Interest Expense	20,000	
Salary Expense	367,831	
Rent Expense	36,000	
Supplies Expense	4,457	
Income Tax Expense	60,000	
Totals	1,530,194	1,530,194

(1) Prepare the income statement for the year ended December 31, 2005.

(2) Prepare the statement of retained earnings for the year ended December 31, 2005.

(3) Prepare the classified balance sheet as of December 31, 2005.

(4) Prepare the closing entries.

(5) Calculate the current ratio and the debt ratio.

SOLUTIONS

Matching

1	F	5	D	9	T	13	E	17	O
2	H	6	A	10	Q	14	B	18	G
3	S	7	R	11	P	15	L	19	C
4	K	8	N	12	I	16	M	20	J

Multiple Choice

1	D
2	C
3	A
4	D
5	B
6	D
7	C
8	B
9	A
10	C
11	A
12	C
13	D
14	A
15	B

Completion

1. total current liabilities
2. total liabilities
3. high dividends
4. earned
5. account receivable
6. smallest
7. liquidation
8. asset
9. deferral
10. depreciation
11. accumulated depreciation
12. liability
13. liquidity
14. subtotals
15. top

True/False

1. T
2. F   A higher current ratio means that a company can more easily pay its short-term obligations.
3. T
4. F   Most retailers use a fiscal year that ends on January 31 because the low point in their business activity occurs in January.
5. F   The critical event for recording an expense is when a company incurs it, not necessarily when the company makes a payment.
6. T
7. F   Land is the only plant asset that is not subject to depreciation.
8. T
9. F   The collection of an account receivable has no effect on the current ratio because the current asset Cash increases and the current asset Accounts Receivable decreases by the same amount.
10. F Prepaid expenses are assets that a company reports on the balance sheet.
11. T
12. T
13. T
14. F The balance sheet lists long-term liabilities below current liabilities.
15. T

Exercises

1.

(1)	Supplies Expense		4,100	
	Supplies			4,100
	To record supplies used ($11,500 – $7,400).			

(2)	Insurance Expense		6,000	
	Prepaid Insurance			6,000
	To record expired insurance [($24,000 / 24) x 6].			

(3)	Depreciation Expense—Equipment		40,000	
	Accumulated Depreciation—Equipment			40,000
	To record depreciation on equipment.			

(4)	Accounts Receivable		10,000	
	Service Revenue			10,000
	To record services performed but not yet billed.			

(5)	Income Tax Expense		90,000	
	Income Tax Payable			90,000
	To record accrued income tax expense.			

2.

Service Revenue	854,691	
Retained Earnings		854,691
To close the revenue account.		

Retained Earnings	780,529	
Advertising Expense		14,100
Depreciation Expense		60,000
Insurance Expense		6,000
Interest Expense		10,000
Salary Expense		604,090
Rent Expense		48,000
Supplies Expense		14,196
Income Tax Expense		24,143
To close the expense accounts.		

Retained Earnings	18,000	
Dividends		18,000
To close Dividends.		

3.

Bates Corporation
Income Statement
For the Year Ended December 31, 2005

Service Revenue		854,691
Expenses:		
Advertising Expense	14,100	
Depreciation Expense	60,000	
Insurance Expense	6,000	
Rent Expense	48,000	
Salary Expense	604,090	
Supplies Expense	14,196	
Interest Expense	10,000	
Income Tax Expense	24,143	
Total Expenses		780,529
Net Income		74,162

Bates Corporation
Statement of Retained Earnings
For the Year Ended December 31, 2005

Retained Earnings, January 1, 2005	82,582
Add: Net Income	74,162
Sub-Total	156,744
Less: Dividends	(18,000)
Retained Earnings, December 31, 2005	138,744

4.

Bates Corporation
Balance Sheet
December 31, 2005

Assets

Current Assets
Cash	$180,464	
Accounts Receivable	231,678	
Prepaid Insurance	34,000	
Supplies	5,510	
Total Current Assets		$451,652

Equipment	$500,000	
Less: Accumulated Depreciation	(120,000)	
Total Equipment		380,000

Total Assets		$831,652

Liabilities and Stockholders' Equity

Liabilities

Current Liabilities:
Accounts Payable	$68,765	
Income Tax Payable	24,143	
Total Current Liabilities		$ 92,908

Long-Term Liabilities		
Note Payable (due in five years)		100,000
Total Liabilities		$192,908

Stockholders' Equity

Common Stock	$500,000	
Retained Earnings	138,744	

Total Stockholders' Equity		638,744

Total Liabilities and Stockholders' Equity		$831,652

5. The current ratio equals total current assets divided by total current liabilities. The total current assets are $200,000, calculated as follows:

Cash	$70,000
Accounts Receivable	30,000
Merchandise Inventory	80,000
Prepaid Expenses	20,000
Total Current Assets	$200,000

The only current liability is Accounts Payable in the amount of $100,000. Therefore, the current ratio is 2.00 ($200,000 / $100,000).

The debt ratio equals total liabilities divided by total assets. The total liabilities are calculated as follows:

Accounts Payable	$100,000
Note Payable (due in 10 years)	140,000
Total Liabilities	$240,000

Therefore, the debt ratio is 0.40 or 40% ($240,000 / $600,000).

Critical Thinking

When a company renders services to customer on account, it should record the transaction by debiting Accounts Receivable and crediting Service Revenue. Failure to record this transaction (1) understates net income, (2) understates retained earnings, (3) understates total stockholders' equity, (4) understates total assets, (5) understates the current ratio, and (6) overstates the debt ratio.

If a company fails to record this transaction, then net income would be understated because the failure to record the transaction will understate total revenues and have no effect on total expenses. Because the failure to record the transaction understates net income, retained earnings would also be understated because a company transfers net income to Retained Earnings through the closing process. Because retained earnings are a part of total stockholders' equity, total stockholders' equity would be understated. The failure to record the receivable would cause total assets to be understated. Because Accounts Receivable is a current asset, total current assets would be understated. The current ratio would be understated because the current ratio equals total current assets divided by current liabilities. The debt ratio, which equals total liabilities divided by total assets, would be overstated because total assets would be understated.

Demonstration Problems

1.

(1)

Supplies Expense	5,665	
Supplies		5,665
To record supplies used ($8,625 – $2,960).		
Insurance Expense	1,800	
Prepaid Insurance		1,800
To record expired insurance [($14,400 / 24) x 3].		
Depreciation Expense—Equipment	50,000	
Accumulated Depreciation—Equipment		50,000
To record depreciation on equipment.		
Interest Expense	13,200	
Interest Payable		
To record accrued interest ($120,000 x 11%).		13,200
Income Tax Expense	82,000	
Income Tax Payable		82,000
To record accrued income taxes.		

(2)

Rios Company
Adjusted Trial Balance
December 31, 2005

Cash	36,814	
Accounts Receivable	152,490	
Prepaid Insurance	12,600	
Supplies	2,960	
Equipment	695,000	
Accumulated Depreciation—Equipment		150,000
Accounts Payable		48,560
Interest Payable		13,200
Income Tax Payable		82,000
Note Payable (due in five years)		120,000
Common Stock		300,000
Retained Earnings		108,232
Dividends	12,000	
Service Revenue		908,362
Advertising Expense	25,046	
Depreciation Expense	50,000	
Insurance Expense	1,800	
Interest Expense	13,200	
Salary Expense	562,779	
Rent Expense	60,000	
Supplies Expense	5,665	
Income Tax Expense	100,000	
Totals	1,730,354	1,730,354

2.

(1)

Eagle Corporation
Income Statement
For the Year Ended December 31, 2005

Service Revenue		$772,112
Expenses:		
Advertising Expense	$ 27,400	
Depreciation Expense	45,000	
Insurance Expense	9,000	
Interest Expense	20,000	
Salary Expense	367,831	
Rent Expense	36,000	
Supplies Expense	4,457	
Income Tax Expense	60,000	
Total Expenses		569,688
Net Income		$202,424

(2)

Eagle Corporation
Statement of Retained Earnings
For the Year Ended December 31, 2005

Retained Earnings, January 1, 2005	$141,638
Add: Net Income	202,424
Sub-Total	$344,062
Less: Dividends	(6,000)
Retained Earnings, December 31, 2005	$338,062

(3)

Eagle Corporation
Balance Sheet
December 31, 2005

Asset

Current Assets:

Cash	$297,995	
Accounts Receivable	145,913	
Prepaid Insurance	52,000	
Supplies	8,598	
Total Current Assets		$504,506

Equipment	$450,000	
Less: Accumulated Depreciation	(180,000)	
Total Equipment		270,000

Total Assets		$774,506

Liabilities and Stockholders' Equity

Liabilities

Current Liabilities

Accounts Payable	$28,444	
Income Tax Payable	8,000	
Total Current Liabilities		$36,444

Long-Term Liabilities

Note Payable (due in five years)		100,000

Total Liabilities		$136,444

Stockholders' Equity

Common Stock	$300,000	
Retained Earnings	338,062	
Total Stockholders' Equity		638,062

Total Liabilities and Stockholders' Equity		$774,506

(4)

Service Revenue	772,112	
Retained Earnings		772,112
To close the revenue account		

Retained Earnings	569,688	
Advertising Expense		27,400
Depreciation Expense		45,000
Insurance Expense		9,000
Interest Expense		20,000
Salary Expense		367,831
Rent Expense		36,000
Supplies Expense		4,457
Income Tax Expense		60,000
To close the expense accounts		

Retained Earnings	6,000	
Dividends		6,000
To close the Dividends account		

(5)

Current Ratio = Current Assets / Current Liabilities
         = \$504,506 / \$36,444
         = 13.84

Debt Ratio = Total Liabilities / Total Assets
         = \$136,444 / \$774,506
         = 0.18 or 18%

Chapter 4

INTERNAL CONTROL & CASH

CHAPTER OBJECTIVES

The learning objectives for this chapter are as follows:

1. Set up an effective system of internal control
2. Use a bank reconciliation as a control device
3. Apply internal controls to cash receipts and cash payments
4. Use a budget to manage cash
5. Weigh ethical judgments in business

CHAPTER OVERVIEW

Internal control is the responsibility of an organization's top managers. Internal control is the organizational plan and related measures that an organization adopts to safeguard assets, ensure accurate and reliable accounting records, encourage adherence to company policies, and promote operational efficiency. Exhibit 4-1 is an excerpt from an annual report that illustrates how management must acknowledge its responsibility for internal control and overall financial responsibility.

Congress passed the Sarbanes-Oxley Act (often abbreviated SOX) in response to the scandals at Enron and WorldCom (now MCI). Arthur Andersen had audited both of these companies and issued clean (unqualified) audit opinions. The Sarbanes-Oxley Act created a new board called the Public Company Accounting Oversight Board to oversee the work of auditors of public companies. The Sarbanes-Oxley Act also provides that an auditor of a public company may not provide consulting services for the same company. In addition, the lead auditor for a public client may serve no more than seven years, but the individual may serve as the lead auditor again after a two-year period. Further, public companies must issue an internal control report, and the independent auditor must evaluate the internal controls of the company. Finally, the Sarbanes-Oxley Act provides for stiff penalties for violations for securities fraud and for a CEO or CFO who makes false statements.

CHAPTER REVIEW

Objective 1—Set up an effective system of internal control

An effective internal control system has several characteristics. Management should hire employees who are competent, ethical, and reliable. Paying good salaries is important in attracting competent employees. Training and supervising employees serve to increase their abilities. Rotating employees makes them more valuable to the organization because they develop more skills.

Management must assign each employee specific responsibilities. Exhibit 4-2 shows an organizational chart of a corporation. The treasurer of an organization manages its cash. The chief accounting officer is the controller.

A good internal control system requires proper authorization for business transactions. For example, management should approve all expenditures. If the expenditure is above a certain amount, company policy may require that a manager at a higher level in the organization approve it.

Supervision of employees is essential to a good internal control system. Without adequate supervision, even the most trusted employees might be tempted to steal from the company.

One of the most important characteristics of a good internal control system is separation of duties. Managers should divide the responsibility for transactions between two or more individuals. Separation of duties minimizes the opportunity for fraud and helps to ensure accurate accounting records. The accounting department should be separate from the company's operating departments. In addition, the custody of assets should be separate from accounting.

Internal and external audits are a part of a good internal control system. An audit is an examination of a company's financial statements, accounting system, and internal controls. An internal auditor is an employee of the company who should report to the company's audit committee of the board of directors. The chief internal auditor may also report to the president or chief executive officer on a regular basis. Internal auditors primarily examine the segments of a company to ensure that the employees are following company policies. External auditors are independent CPA firms that are primarily interested in the fairness of a company's financial statements. Exhibit 4-2 shows where the auditing function fits in a corporation's organizational chart.

Adequate documents and records are important parts of internal control. They include invoices, receipts, checks, and the accounting journals. All documents should be prenumbered to ensure that no document is missing. Prenumbered sales invoices discourage theft by cashiers or the sales staff. The total cash collected should be checked against the cash shown as collected on the sales invoices. If sales invoices are not prenumbered, the cashier could destroy the receipt and steal the cash.

Companies use electronic devices such as cash registers, computers, and electronic sensors to safeguard assets. If an individual attempts to remove merchandise with an electronic sensor from a store, an alarm sounds.

Special internal controls protect the information that drives e-commerce. Companies must protect the information from hackers and system failures. To prevent fraud in e-commerce, experts in information technology have created the onion model of system security illustrated in Exhibit 4-3. The layers of this security system include encryption, firewalls, intrusion detection devices, incident response procedures, and audits by external specialists.

Encryption transforms data into a form that is not readable without a secret decryption key. If a hacker intercepts an encrypted message, the hacker will likely not be able to interpret it without the decryption key. Exhibit 4-4 illustrates the encryption process.

A firewall limits access to hardware, software, or data to individuals within a network. A firewall must keep out intruders without denying access to legitimate users. Most companies use a series of firewalls as shown in Exhibit 4-5.

Intrusion detection devices are electronic monitors that identify unauthorized entries to the system. When an intrusion detection device identifies an unauthorized entry into the system, incident response procedures begin to apprehend hackers and remove them from the system. Some companies pay for audits by external specialists such as WebTrust, SysTrust, and CPA firms to test their e-commerce systems. Their logos often appear on e-commerce Web sites.

Companies use other controls to safeguard their assets. Examples include the use of fireproof vaults for storing important business contracts and titles to properties. Companies protect buildings and their contents with burglar alarms. Point-of-sale terminals protect cash and record each sales transaction. Companies often purchase fidelity bonds on cashiers. If the cashier embezzles money, the insurance company will reimburse the company for the loss. Mandatory vacations and job rotations can help to discover fraud.

A good internal control system provides a company with many benefits, but it also has its limitations. Employees can overcome any internal control system by collusion, which is working together to defraud the company. A good internal control system is costly. An internal control system that is too complex can unnecessarily impede the operations of the business. Managers should make sure that the benefits of the internal control system outweigh its cost.

Cash is the most liquid asset. It is easy to conceal and relatively easy to steal. Therefore, most companies have extensive controls to safeguard cash.

Keeping cash in a bank account is one of the most important internal control devices. The bank account also provides a company with an independent record of cash transactions. A company should deposit all cash receipts in a bank account. A company should pay all expenses by check, except for small expenses paid by petty cash.

A check has three parties: (1) the maker, who signs the check, (2) the payee, to whom the check is written, and (3) the bank, on which the check is drawn. Checks should be prenumbered with the name of the maker and bank printed on them. A remittance advice is an optional part of a check that shows the reason for the payment. Exhibit 4-6 illustrates a check with a remittance advice.

A bank sends a monthly bank statement to the depositor. Electronic funds transfer (EFT) relies on electronic communications rather than paper documents to transfer cash. EFT is becoming more popular because it is less expensive than writing checks. A bank statement shows EFT cash receipts and EFT cash payments along with the other cash transactions on the bank statement. Exhibit 4-7 illustrates a bank statement that includes transactions by EFT.

Objective 2—Use a bank reconciliation as a control device

The two records of a company's cash are the company's books and the bank statement. Exhibit 4-8 illustrates a company's cash records. Seldom does the cash balance on the company's books equal the balance on the bank statement. The company might have made deposits that are not yet shown on the bank statement. The company might have written checks that have not yet cleared the bank.

To ensure an accurate record of all cash transactions, an accountant prepares a bank reconciliation. Exhibit 4-9 illustrates a bank reconciliation. The bank reconciliation explains the reasons for the difference between the cash balance according to the bank and the cash balance according to the company's records.

To the balance according to the bank statement, the company must add deposits in transit. These are deposits that appear on the company's books, but which do not appear on the bank statement. The bank reconciliation then shows a subtotal. From this subtotal, the company subtracts all outstanding checks. Outstanding checks are checks the company has written, which the bank has not yet paid. If the bank has made an error, the company makes an adjustment to the balance according to the bank statement. The adjustment can be positive or negative. Such an error is rare.

To the balance according to the company's records, the company adds any amounts collected by the bank on behalf of the company. Many companies use a lockbox system in which customers send their payments directly to the company's bank account. The company also adds deposits received by electronic funds transfer that the company has not yet recorded on its books and any interest revenue earned on the account. The company subtracts any electronic funds transfer payments that it has not yet recorded on its books from the balance according to the company's records. The company also subtracts any bank service charges, charges for printed checks, and checks deposited but returned for not sufficient funds (NSF) from the balance according to the company's books. If the company has made an error, the company makes an adjustment to the balance according to the company's records. The adjustment can be positive or negative.

The bank reconciliation is a powerful internal control device, but it has no effect on a company's books. Based on the items that affected the balance according to the company's records, the company must prepare and post journal entries. No journal entries are required for adjustments to the balance according to the bank.

Study Tip: The following summary shows how to treat various items on a bank reconciliation.

Bank Balance	**Book Balance**
Add deposits in transit.	*Add* bank collection items, interest revenue, and EFT receipts.
Subtract outstanding checks.	*Subtract* service charges, NSF checks, and EFT payments.
Add or *subtract* corrections of bank errors, as appropriate.	*Add* or *subtract* corrections of book errors, as appropriate.

Objective 3—Apply internal controls to cash receipts and cash payments

The goal of internal control over cash receipts is to ensure that the company deposits all cash receipts into its bank account. Each source of cash receipts has its own security measures.

A point-of-sale system or cash register provides internal control over cash receipts in a retail store. The cash drawer opens only when an employee enters an amount on the keypad. The system records each transaction. Exhibit 4-10 illustrates a point-of-sale system. At the end of the day, a manager compares the cash on hand to the machine's record of the cash received from sales. The treasurer deposits the cash in the bank, and the total amount of cash receipts is transmitted electronically to the accounting department.

Many companies use a lockbox system for receiving cash in the mail. Customers send their checks directly to the company's bank using a special address. The cash goes directly into the company's bank account without any handling by the company's employees.

If the company receives cash by mail, a mail room employee opens the mail and compares the check received with the attached remittance advice. At the end of the day, another employee verifies the total remittance advices and cash received. The treasurer receives the checks and prepares the bank deposit. The mail room employee sends the remittance advices to the accounting department. The controller then compares the control total from the mail room, the bank deposit amount from the cashier, and the debit to Cash from the accounting department. Exhibit 4-11 illustrates the processing of checks received by mail.

Paying all expenses, except for small amounts paid from petty cash, is an important part of internal control. The check provides a record of each payment, and an authorized official must sign each check.

To purchase merchandise a company prepares a purchase request or purchase requisition. The purchasing department then prepares a purchase order and sends it to the supplier. When the supplier ships the goods on account, the supplier also sends an invoice or bill. Exhibit 4-12 illustrates the purchasing/paying process.

When the goods arrive, the receiving department inspects them for any damage and prepares a list of the merchandise received on a document called a receiving report. The accounting department then compares the purchase order, the receiving report, and the invoice and forwards this payment packet to the designated officers for approval and payment. Exhibit 4-13 shows the documents included in the payment packet.

Before approving the payment of the invoice, the controller or treasurer should examine the packet to make sure that all of the documents agree. The company wants to ensure that it received the goods it ordered and pays only for the goods it received. After the treasurer signs the check for payment, the treasurer should mark the invoice as paid or punch a hole through the packet to indicate that the company has paid the invoice.

Companies maintain a petty cash fund to pay for small expenses such as for coffee, postage, and small amounts of office supplies. A company establishes a petty cash fund by writing a check payable to petty cash and exchanging it for currency and coins. For each petty cash payment, the custodian prepares a petty cash ticket to list the item purchased and its amount. The sum of the petty cash on hand and the petty cash tickets should equal the amount of the petty cash fund. When the amount in the petty cash fund becomes too low, the company will write a check to replenish it. Maintaining the Petty Cash account in this manner is called an imprest system.

Study Tip: If the amount of petty cash on hand differs from the amount of petty cash that should be in the fund, the company accounts for the difference in the Cash Short or Over account.

Objective 4—Use a budget to manage cash

A budget expresses management's plans in quantitative terms. Managers compare actual results to the budget as a part of the control function. A cash budget helps managers plan cash receipts and cash payments for a future period. The cash budget starts with the beginning balance of cash, which is the same amount as the ending balance for the prior period. Next, it adds the expected cash receipts to the beginning balance and then subtracts the expected cash payments to arrive at the budgeted ending balance of cash. If the actual cash on hand at the end of the period is greater than the budgeted cash balance at the end of the period, the company can invest the excess cash. If the actual cash on hand at the end of the period is less than the budgeted cash balance, the company may need to borrow money to meet its financial needs. Exhibit 4-14 illustrates a cash budget.

Most companies have numerous cash accounts, but they combine them into one total called "Cash and Cash Equivalents" on the balance sheet. Cash equivalents are liquid assets such as certificates of deposit and money market accounts.

The amount reported as Cash on the balance sheet is available for the company's daily use. If the company has pledged any cash as collateral, the company must report this amount separately because it is not available for daily use.

A bank often loans money to a company, but the bank requires the company to maintain a minimum balance in a checking account at the bank at all times. This minimum balance is called a compensating balance. It allows the bank to earn a higher effective interest rate on the loan. The company reports the compensating balance on its balance sheet as a long-term asset because it is not available for daily use.

Objective 5—Weigh ethical judgments in business

Practicing good ethics is not only the right thing to do, but it is also good business. Unethical behavior leads to bad results. Most large companies have codes of ethics to encourage their employees to act in an ethical manner. Managers must also set an example of adhering to high ethical conduct and clearly inform subordinates that the company will not tolerate unethical conduct.

Accountants must adhere to higher ethical standards than society in general. Members of the American Institute of Certified Public Accountants (AICPA) must abide by the AICPA Code of Professional Conduct. Members of the Institute of Management Accountants (IMA) must follow the Standards of Ethical Conduct for Management Accountants.

In many cases, the ethical choice is clear. A conflict of interest, however, creates an ethical dilemma. A conflict of interest occurs when an individual has two responsibilities that directly compete. For example, a judge may not decide a case in which a relative is a party to the case. In such cases, judges recuse themselves to avoid a conflict of interest between their duty to be impartial and their duty to be loyal to their family. Likewise a CPA may not perform an independent audit of a company unless the CPA is independent of the company. Exhibit 4-15 illustrates a conflict of interest between Enron Corporation and its former CFO Andrew Fastow. In accounting, the main ethical responsibility is to ensure that accounting information provided to the public is complete and accurate. Five general guidelines for making ethical decisions are as follows:

1. Identify the ethical issues.
2. Specify the alternatives.
3. Identify the people involved.
4. Assess the possible consequences.
5. Make the decision.

TEST YOURSELF

Matching

Match each numbered term with its lettered definition.

_____ 1. controller	_____ 11. budget
_____ 2. petty cash	_____ 12. external auditors
_____ 3. internal auditors	_____ 13. check
_____ 4. bank reconciliation	_____ 14. audit
_____ 5. electronic funds transfer (EFT)	_____ 15. separation of duties
_____ 6. firewall	_____ 16. encryption
_____ 7. imprest system	_____ 17. internal control
_____ 8. bank statement	_____ 18. bank collections
_____ 9. outstanding checks	_____ 19. collusion
_____ 10. deposits in transit	_____ 20. nonsufficient funds (NSF) check

A. recorded by the company but not yet by its bank.

B. issued by the company and recorded on its books but not yet paid by its bank.

C. quantitative expression of a plan that helps managers coordinate the entity's activities.

D. organizational plan and related measures adopted by an entity to safeguard assets, encourage adherence to company policies, promote operational efficiency, and ensure accurate and reliable accounting records.

E. system that transfers cash by electronic communication rather than by paper documents.

F. collection of money by the bank on behalf of a depositor.

G. a way to account for petty cash by maintaining a constant balance in the petty cash account, supported by the fund (cash plus disbursement tickets) totaling the same amount.

H. fund containing a small amount of cash that is used to pay minor expenditures.

I. chief accounting officer of a business.

J. periodic examination of a company's financial statements and the accounting systems, controls, and records that produce them.

K. document explaining the reasons for the difference between a depositor's records and the bank's records about the depositor's bank account.

L. check for which the payer's bank account has insufficient money to pay the check.

M. document instructing a bank to pay the designated person or business the specified amount of money.

N. document showing the beginning and ending balances of a particular bank account listing the month's transactions that affected the account.

O. not employees of the companies; hired by a company to audit the entity as a whole; concerned mainly with the financial statements.

P. two or more employees working together to defraud a firm.

Q. limits the chances for fraud and promotes the accuracy of accounting records by dividing responsibilities for transactions between two or more people.

R. the transformation of data by a mathematical process into a form that is unreadable by those without the secret decryption key.

S. limits access to hardware, software, or data to persons within a network; allows legitimate users to enter the system while denying access to intruders.

T. employees of the business who examine various segments of the organization to ensure that employees follow company policies.

Multiple Choice

Circle the best answer.

1. The Sarbanes-Oxley Act created a new organization called the:
   a. Financial Accounting Standards Board
   b. Public Company Accounting Oversight Board
   c. Auditing Standards Board
   d. American Institute of Certified Public Accountants

2. An examination of a company's financial statements, accounting system, and internal controls is called a(n):
   a. audit
   b. firewall
   c. encryption
   d. intrusion detection device

3. What transforms data into a form that is not readable without a secret decryption key?
   a. audit
   b. firewall
   c. encryption
   d. intrusion detection device

4. What limits access to hardware, software, or data within a network?
   a. audit
   b. firewall
   c. encryption
   d. intrusion detection devices

5. What are electronic monitors that identify unauthorized entries to a system?
   a. point-of-sale terminals
   b. firewall
   c. encryption
   d. intrusion detection devices

6. What do companies often purchase on cashiers?
   a. fidelity bonds
   b. life insurance
   c. corporate bonds
   d. treasury bonds

7. Working together to defraud a company is called:
    a. fidelity bond
    b. encryption
    c. collusion
    d. decryption

8. What is the most liquid asset?
    a. merchandise inventory
    b. cash
    c. accounts receivable
    d. equipment

9. The one who signs a check is called the:
    a. maker
    b. payee
    c. bank
    d. drawee

10. In a bank reconciliation, outstanding checks should be:
    a. added to the bank balance
    b. subtracted from the bank balance
    c. added to the book balance
    d. subtracted from the book balance

11. In a bank reconciliation, deposits in transit should be:
    a. added to the bank balance
    b. subtracted from the bank balance
    c. added to the book balance
    d. subtracted from the book balance

12. In a bank reconciliation, interest earned on the bank account should be:
    a. added to the bank balance
    b. subtracted from the bank balance
    c. added to the book balance
    d. subtracted from the book balance

13. When a company needs merchandise, what does the purchasing department send to the supplier?
    a. purchase request
    b. purchase order
    c. receiving report
    d. payment packet

14. The cash budget starts with the:
    a. Expected cash receipts.
    b. Expected ending balance of cash.
    c. Beginning balance of cash.
    d. Expected cash payments.

15. Who must abide by the Standards of Ethical Conduct for Management Accountants?
    a. Members of the American Institute of Certified Public Accountants
    b. Members of the Institute of Management Accountants
    c. Members of the American Accounting Association
    d. Members of the Institute of Internal Auditors

Completion

Complete each of the following statements.

1. Internal control is the responsibility of an organization's _____ _____.
2. Management should hire good employees who are competent, ethical, and _____.
3. The chief accounting officer is the _____.
4. One of the most important characteristics of a good internal control system is _____ _____ _____.
5. A hacker would need the _____ _____ to interpret an intercepted encrypted message.
6. Companies often store important business documents in a _____ _____.
7. Keeping cash in a _____ _____ is one of the most important internal control devices.
8. In a bank reconciliation, the bank service charge should be subtracted from the _____ balance.
9. The person to whom a check is written is called the _____.
10. A system in which customers send their payments directly to the company's bank account is called a _____ system.
11. No journal entries are required for adjustments to the _____ balance.
12. When goods arrive from a supplier, the company should prepare a _____ _____.
13. A budget expresses management's plans in _____ terms.
14. Cash equivalents are liquid assets such as certificates of _____.
15. In accounting, the main ethical responsibility is to ensure that accounting information provided to the public is complete and _____.

True/False

For each of the following statements, circle T *for true or* F *for false.*

1.   T   F   Most businesses have few controls to safeguard cash.
2.   T   F   Paying good salaries, training employees, and supervising their work help to build a competent staff.
3.   T   F   If one employee has both cash-handling and accounting duties, the employee will be more useful to the company.
4.   T   F   Auditors must be independent of the operations they examine.
5.   T   F   Two or more employees working together can defraud a company.
6.   T   F   Paying employees by issuing payroll checks is much cheaper than paying them by EFT (direct deposit).
7.   T   F   Cash equivalents include liquid assets such as time deposits and certificates of deposit.
8.   T   F   Seldom does a business use a budget for cash.
9.   T   F   Any restricted amount of cash should be reported as Cash on the balance sheet.
10.   T   F   A conflict of interest occurs when someone plays two roles that directly compete.
11.   T   F   To prevent electronic fraud, experts in information technology have devised the onion model of system security.
12.   T   F   Separation of duties limits the chances for fraud and promotes the accuracy of accounting records.
13.   T   F   Internal control over cash receipts ensures that all cash is deposited in the bank and that no collections are lost.
14.   T   F   The cash balance on the books rarely equals the balance shown on the bank statement, but both the books and the bank may be correct.
15.   T   F   The company's top managers are not responsible for internal controls.

Exercises

1. Given the following bank reconciliation, prepare all necessary journal entries.

Woodruff Company
Bank Reconcilation
June 30, 2006

Bank Balance	$44,692.77	Book Balance	$50,189.40
Add: Deposit in transit	20,000.00	Add: Interest revenue	41.25
Sub-total	$64,692.77	Sub-total	$50,230.65
Less: Outstanding checks	(18.587.12)	Less: Service charge	(25.00)
		Less: NSF check	(4,100.00)
Adjusted balance	$46,105.65	Adjusted balance	$46,105.65

2. Given the following information, calculate the amount that would appear on the balance sheet as cash and cash equivalents.

Petty cash	$500
Checking account at First National Bank	$25,641
Money market account at Merrill Lynch	$10,000
Certificate of deposit at First National Bank	$8,500
Savings account at First National Bank pledged as collateral for a loan	$5,000

3. Cooper Company wants to maintain a minimum cash balance of $15,000 at all times. For the next year, the company expects to have a beginning cash balance of $23,200. It expects its cash receipts to be $289,400. The company expects its cash payments to be $300,000. How much will the company have to borrow to maintain its desired minimum cash balance?

4. While preparing a bank reconciliation, Taylor Company discovered that a check for $494 for utilities expense had been incorrectly recorded on the company's books as $944. Calculate the amount of the error and explain how it would appear on the company's bank reconciliation. Prepare the journal entry to correct the error on the company's books.

5. The bank statement shows that the bank had collected a note on behalf of Griggs Company. The principal amount of the note was $5,000 and the interest was $600. The bank statement also shows a collection on an account receivable of $1,000 by electronic funds transfer (EFT). The company has not recorded these transactions on its books. Prepare journal entries to record these transactions on the company's books.

Critical Thinking

A trusted employee named Janice opens all of the mail at Breaux Company. She prepares a deposit slip for all of the checks received from customers and deposits them in the company's bank account. Janice then records all of the payments in the customers' accounts and prepares a journal entry to record the bank deposit for the total amount received. Janice has worked for the company for five years and enjoys her work so much that she has never taken a vacation. Because the general manager of the company trusts Janice so much, he feels that taking out a fidelity bond on Janice would be a waste of money. What changes would you recommend to improve the internal control over customers' payments at Breaux Company?

Demonstration Problems

1. Given the following information, prepare a bank reconciliation for Morgan Company as of April 30, 2006.

Balance per the bank statement	$42,561.78
Balance per books	$39,359.74
Deposit in transit	$3,655.00
Outstanding checks	$4,287.24
Service charge	$25.00
NSF check	$360.00
EFT payment for utilities	$255.20
Note collected by the bank	$3,300.00

2. Given the following information, prepare a cash budget for Thompson Company for the month ending May 31, 2006.

Beginning cash balance	$65,789
Expected cash collections from sales	$430,000
Expected interest and dividends on investments	$15,000
Expected cash payments:	
Merchandise	$250,000
Salaries	$100,000
Payroll taxes	$10,000
Rent	$5,000
Utilities	$1,000
Supplies	$12,000

SOLUTIONS

Matching

1	I	5	E	9	B	13	M	17	D
2	H	6	S	10	A	14	J	18	F
3	T	7	G	11	C	15	Q	19	P
4	K	8	N	12	O	16	R	20	L

Multiple Choice

1	B
2	A
3	C
4	B
5	D
6	A
7	C
8	B
9	A
10	B
11	A
12	C
13	B
14	C
15	B

Completion

1. top managers
2. reliable
3. controller
4. separation of duties
5. decryption key
6. fireproof vault
7. bank account
8. book
9. payee
10. lockbox
11. bank
12. receiving report
13. quantitative
14. deposit
15. accurate

True/False

1. F   Most businesses have elaborate controls to safeguard cash because it is easy to conceal and relatively easy to steal.
2. T
3. F   If the same person has cash-handling and accounting duties, that person can steal cash and conceal the theft by making a false entry in the accounting records.
4. T
5. T
6. F   Paying employees by direct deposit using electronic funds transfer (EFT) is much cheaper than paying them by payroll checks.
7. T
8. F   Companies budget cash more than any other item on the financial statements.
9. F   A company separately reports cash that is restricted, such as a bank account that serves as collateral for a loan, because such cash is not available for daily use.
10. T
11. T
12. T
13. T
14. T
15. F   Top managers are responsible for internal control. Managers of a public company must acknowledge this responsibility in the annual report.

Exercises

1.

Cash	41.25	
Interest Revenue		41.25

To record interest earned on the bank account.

Miscellaneous Expense	25.00	
Cash		25.00

To record the bank service charge.

Accounts Receivable	4,100.00	
Cash		4,100.00

To record NSF check returned by the bank.

2.

Petty cash	$ 500
Checking account at First National Bank	25,641
Money market account at Merrill Lynch	10,000
Certificate of deposit at First National Bank	8,500
Cash and cash equivalents	$ 44,641

The savings account of $5,000 at First National Bank that the company has pledged as collateral for a loan would not appear on the balance sheet under cash and cash equivalents because it is not available for daily use. The company would report the savings account on its balance sheet as cash pledged as collateral.

3.

Beginning cash balance	$ 23,200
Add: Budgeted cash receipts	289,400
Cash available	$312,600
Less: Budgeted cash payments	300,000
Ending cash balance before financing	$ 12,600

To maintain its minimum cash balance of $15,000, Cooper Company will have to borrow $2,400 ($15,000 – $12,600).

4.

Taylor Company has overstated its utilities expense by $450 ($944 – $494) and understated its cash balance by the same amount because of this transposition error.

The error would appear on the company's bank reconciliation as a $450 addition to the cash per books. The cash per the bank statement is not affected because the bank paid the $494 check as written. The error was in recording the check for $450 too much on the company's books.

The journal entry to correct this error is as follows:

Cash   450.00
    Utilities Expense   450.00
To correct error in recording check for utilities expense.

5.

Cash   5,600
    Notes Receivable   5,000
    Interest Revenue   600
To record a collection of a note receivable by the bank.

Cash   1,000
    Accounts Receivable   1,000
To record the collection of an account receivable by EFT.

Critical Thinking

Breaux Company could improve its internal control by separating the duties of the custody of the checks received from customers and the accounting for the receipt of such checks. The company could also improve its internal control by requiring employees to take vacations. Companies can discourage embezzlements by requiring vacations because an employee must often be present to take actions to conceal the embezzlement. Many companies discover embezzlement when a dishonest employee is on vacation. Regardless of how good an employee Janice is and how much the general manager of the company trusts her, the company could improve its internal control by obtaining a fidelity bond on Janice.

Demonstration Problems

1.

Morgan Company
Bank Reconciliation
April 30, 2006

Bank		Books	
Balance, April 30	$42,561.78	Balance, April 30	$39,359.74
Add: Deposit in transit	3,655.00	Add: Note collection	3,300.00
	$46,306.78		$42,659.74
Less: Outstanding checks	4,287.24		
		Less:	
		Service charge $ 25.00	
		NSF check 360.00	
		EFT payment	
		for utilities 255.20	640.20
Adjusted bank balance	$42,019.54	Adjusted book balance	$42,019.54

2.

Thompson Company
Cash Budget
For the Month Ending May 31, 2006

Cash balance, May 1, 2006		$65,789
Budgeted cash receipts:		
Collections from sales	$430,000	
Interest and dividends on investments	15,000	445,000
Cash available		$510,789
Budgeted cash payments:		
Merchandise	$250,000	
Salaries	100,000	
Payroll taxes	10,000	
Rent	5,000	
Utilities	1,000	
Supplies	12,000	378,000
Cash balance, May 31, 2006		$132,789

Chapter 5

SHORT-TERM INVESTMENTS & RECEIVABLES

CHAPTER OBJECTIVES

The learning objectives for this chapter are as follows:

1. Account for short-term investments
2. Apply internal controls to receivables
3. Use the allowance method for uncollectible receivables
4. Account for notes receivable
5. Use days' sales in receivables and the acid-test ratio to evaluate financial position

CHAPTER OVERVIEW

This chapter focuses on accounting for receivables. Receivables include accounts receivable, notes receivable, and other receivables. This chapter also explains how to account for short-term investments, which are also known as marketable securities. Short-term investments are the next most liquid asset after cash. Accounts receivable are the third most liquid asset.

Understanding certain terms is vital to understanding accounts receivable and short-term investments. A creditor is a person to whom money is owed. When a company sells goods or services on account, the company becomes a creditor and has an account receivable from the customer. A debtor is the person who owes money. The customer who buys goods or services on account is a debtor and has an account payable. A debt instrument is usually some form of note. An equity security is a stock certificate that represents ownership in a company. Maturity is the date on which a debtor must pay a note. The length of time from inception to the maturity of a debt instrument is known as term.

CHAPTER REVIEW

Objective 1—Account for short-term investments

Short-term investments are also known as marketable securities, and they are investments that a company plans to hold for one year or less. They allow a company to earn a return on cash reserves until the company needs the cash.

Short-term investments are second only to cash in terms of liquidity. Therefore, a company reports short-term investments on the balance sheet below cash and above receivables. A company classifies short-term investments into one of three categories: (1) trading investments, (2) available-for-sale investments, or (3) held-to-maturity investments. This chapter discusses trading investments. Held-to-maturity investments have the same accounting treatment as notes receivable, which this chapter covers. Chapter 10 discusses available-for-sale investments.

All trading investments are current assets because by definition a company plans to hold them for only a few months at most. Available-for-sale investments and held-to-maturity investments can appear on the balance sheet under current assets or long-term investments depending on how long management plans to hold them.

A company purchases a trading investment with the goal of selling it for more than its cost. A company records trading investments at their cost. For example, assume that a company purchased 1,000 shares of another company's common stock at $40 per share. The company would record the transaction as follows:

Short-Term Investments.................................40,000
     Cash..   40,000
Purchased trading investment.

Assume that the company received a $1,000 dividend on this investment. The company would record the receipt of the dividend as follows:

Cash... 1,000
     Dividend Revenue...............................   1,000
Received cash dividend.

A company reports trading investments on the balance sheet at their current market value. Therefore, a company must adjust the cost of the trading investments to their current market value at the end of the accounting period. If the current market value of the trading investment is greater than its cost, the company has an unrealized gain. The company would debit Short-Term Investments and credit Unrealized Gain on Investments for the excess of the current market value of the investment over its cost. A gain has the same effect as revenue.

For example, assume that the trading investment purchased for $40,000 is worth $43,000 at the end of the accounting period. The company would record this increase in value as follows:

Short-Term Investments................................ 3,000
     Unrealized Gain on Investments...............   3,000
To adjust investment to market value.

If the current market value of the trading investment is less than its cost, the company has an unrealized loss. The company would debit Unrealized Loss on Investments and credit Short-Term Investments for the excess of the cost of the investment over its current market value. A loss has the same effect as an expense.

For example, assume that the investment purchased for $40,000 was worth only $39,000 at the end of the accounting period instead of $43,000. The company would record the decrease in value as follows:

Unrealized Loss on Investments........................... 1,000
          Short-Term Investments...........................   1,000
To adjust investment to market value.

Short-term investments are current assets. They are almost as liquid as cash. Therefore, they immediately follow cash on the balance sheet because assets appear on the balance sheet in decreasing order of liquidity. The interest revenue, dividend revenue, gains, and losses from short-term investments appear on the income statement under other revenue, gains and losses. Exhibit 5-1 shows how a company reports short-term investments on the balance sheet and how a company reports the revenue, gains, and losses from short-term investments on the income statement.

A realized gain or loss usually occurs when a company sells an investment. A realized gain is the excess of the sales price over the carrying value of the investment.

For example, assume that a company sold a short-term investment that had a carrying value of $100,000 for $104,000. The company would record the transaction as follows:

Cash..104,000
          Short-Term Investments........................   100,000
          Gain on Sale of Investments...................   4,000
Sold investment and realized a gain.

A realized loss is the excess of the carrying value of the investment over its sales price.

For example, assume that a company sold a short-term investment that had a carrying value of $200,000 for $195,000. The company would record the transaction as follows:

Cash..195,000
Loss on Sale of Investments........................... 5,000
          Short-Term Investments........................   200,000
Sold investment and realized a loss.

The word *realized* does not appear in the account title of realized gains or losses because the users of the financial statements understand that a gain or loss is realized unless it contains the word *unrealized*. The carrying value of the investment is its original cost as adjusted for any unrealized gain or loss the company recorded at the end of the accounting period.

Receivables are amounts that others owe the company. Most receivables result from the sale of goods or services. The two major types of receivables are accounts receivable and notes receivable. Accounts receivable, sometimes called trade receivables, are current assets.

Most accounts receivable arise from the sale of goods or services on account. For example, assume that a company made a sale on account for $9,000. It would record the sale as follows:

Accounts Receivable...9,000
      Sales Revenue...   9,000
Made sale on account.

The Accounts Receivable account in the general ledger serves as a control account that summarizes the total amount owed the company by all of its customers. Companies also keep a subsidiary record, often called the accounts receivable subsidiary ledger, which shows how much each customer owes the company.

> **Study Tip:** The total of the balances in the subsidiary record should equal the balance in the Accounts Receivable account in the general ledger.

Notes receivable are more formal than are accounts receivable because notes receivable are written agreements in which the debtor (also known as the maker) promises to pay the amount due the company at the maturity date. In addition, notes receivable usually bear interest. The note may require the debtor to provide security for the payment of the note. Assets that secure the payment of a debt are known as collateral.

Notes receivable that are due within one year are current assets. Notes that are due beyond one year are long-term receivables and appear on the balance sheet as long-term assets. Some notes receivable call for periodic installment payments. The installment payments due within one year are current assets, and the payments due beyond one year are long-term receivables.

Other receivables include payroll advances or other loans to employees. Loans to subsidiary companies are also shown on the balance sheet under other receivables. Other receivables due within one year are current assets. Other receivables due beyond one year are long-term receivables.

Objective 2—Apply internal controls to receivables

Companies that sell on credit receive most of their cash collections by mail in the form of checks. The separation of cash-handling and cash-accounting duties is a critical element of internal control over the collection of receivables. If the same individual has access to the cash and to the accounts, the individual could steal the customer's check and write off the account as uncollectible. The customer is satisfied because the company has credited the account, but the company would not have the cash. The employee would forge the company's endorsement on the checks and deposit them in his or her own account.

To prevent theft, the company should have one employee open the mail and deposit the checks. The company would forward the remittance advices to the bookkeeper so that the bookkeeper can update the customers' accounts and the Cash and Accounts Receivable accounts in the general ledger.

The use of a bank lockbox also achieves the same separation of duties. Customers send their payments directly to the company's bank. The bank records the cash as it goes into the company's account. The bank then forwards the remittance advices to the company's bookkeeper. The bookkeeper then updates the customers' accounts and the Cash and Accounts Receivable accounts in the general ledger.

Objective 3—Use the allowance method for uncollectible receivables

When a company sells on credit, it receives the benefit of higher revenues and profits. Many customers who cannot pay the full amount in cash can afford payments on their accounts or pay the balance in full at a later date. The company also incurs an increase in expenses because some customers will not pay the company the amounts they owe on their accounts. Accountants often call this expense uncollectible-account expense, doubtful-account expense, or bad-debt expense.

To ensure a proper matching of revenues with the related uncollectible-account expense, generally accepted accounting principles require companies to use the allowance method to account for uncollectible-account expense. In rare cases, a company may use the direct write-off method. It does not recognize uncollectible-account expense until the company writes off a customer's account as uncollectible.

Under the allowance method, the company records uncollectible-account expense as an adjusting entry at the end of the accounting period. Because the amount of the uncollectible-account expense is an estimate and the company does not know which customers' accounts will be uncollectible, the company sets up an account called Allowance for Uncollectible Accounts. This account is also known as Allowance for Doubtful Accounts, Allowance for Uncollectible Receivables, or Allowance for Bad Debts.

This allowance account is a contra asset account to Accounts Receivable. It shows the amount of the receivables the company does not expect to collect. The balance sheet shows the accounts receivable and then a reduction for the allowance for uncollectible accounts. The difference between the total amount of accounts receivable and the allowance for uncollectible accounts is known as the net realizable value of the accounts receivable, the net accounts receivable, or the carrying value of the accounts receivable. The balance sheet might show the net amount of accounts receivable with the amount of the allowance for uncollectible accounts disclosed in parentheses or next to the net amount.

The two ways to estimate the uncollectible accounts are the percent-of-sales method and the aging-of-receivables method. The percent-of-sales method estimates uncollectible-account expense as a percent of sales revenue. This method emphasizes the income statement and the proper matching of revenues and expenses. The debit to Uncollectible-Account Expense and the related credit to Allowance for Uncollectible Accounts is the estimated percent multiplied by the sales revenue. The company disregards the previous balance in the Allowance for Uncollectible Accounts.

For example, assume that at the end of its accounting period a company has a credit balance of $6,000 in its Allowance for Uncollectible Accounts. The company estimates that 6% of its $300,000 of sales revenue realized during the year will be uncollectible. Therefore, the company's uncollectible-account expense is $18,000 ($300,000 x 6%). The company ignores the $6,000 credit balance in Allowance for Uncollectible Accounts. The new balance in Allowance for Uncollectible Accounts will be $24,000 ($6,000 + $18,000). The entry to record uncollectible-account expense is as follows:

Uncollectible-Account Expense..............................18,000
       Allowance for Uncollectible Accounts..............   18,000
To record uncollectible-account expense as 6% of sales revenue ($300,000 x 6%).

The aging-of-receivables method emphasizes the balance sheet and the net realizable value of the receivables. The company analyzes the receivables from individual customers based on how long the account has been outstanding. The longer that an account has been outstanding, the higher is the percent of the receivable that is likely to be uncollectible. Exhibit 5-2 illustrates an aging schedule. The aging-of-receivables method calculates the balance that should be in the Allowance for Uncollectible Accounts. The company subtracts the amount of the previous credit balance in the Allowance for Uncollectible Accounts or adds the amount of its previous debit balance to calculate the debit to Uncollectible-Account Expense and the credit to Allowance for Uncollectible Accounts. A debit balance in Allowance for Uncollectible Accounts occurs if the amount of the accounts written off exceeds the sum of the beginning balance and any recoveries of accounts written off.

For example, assume that a company estimates that 10% of its accounts receivable will be uncollectible. Accounts Receivable has a balance of $500,000, and Allowance for Uncollectible Accounts has a balance of $20,000. Therefore, the company's uncollectible-account expense is $30,000 [($500,000 x 10%) – $20,000]. The company must take into account the $20,000 credit balance in Allowance for Uncollectible Accounts. The new balance in Allowance for Uncollectible Accounts will be $50,000 ($20,000 + $30,000). The entry to record uncollectible-account expense is as follows:

Uncollectible-Account Expense..............................30,000
      Allowance for Uncollectible Accounts..............   30,000
To record uncollectible-account expense as 10% of accounts receivable [($500,000 x 10%) – $20,000].

If Allowance for Uncollectible Accounts had a debit balance of $10,000 instead of a credit balance of $20,000, the entry to record uncollectible-account expense would be as follows:

Uncollectible-Account Expense...........................60,000
      Allowance for Uncollectible Accounts...........   60,000
To record uncollectible-account expense as 10% of accounts receivable [($500,000 x 10%) + $10,000].

Some companies use the percent-of-sales method for interim financial statements and the aging-of-receivables method for the annual financial statements. Exhibit 5-3 compares these two methods.

To write off an account as uncollectible, a company debits Allowance for Uncollectible Accounts and credits Accounts Receivable and the customer's account in the subsidiary record. This entry has no effect on total assets because the entry reduces the asset Accounts Receivable and reduces the contra asset Allowance for Uncollectible Accounts. For example, assume that a company decides to write off Tim Young's account of $7,000 as uncollectible. The entry to record the write-off is as follows:

Allowance for Uncollectible Accounts.................. 7,000
      Accounts Receivable—Tim Young.............   7,000
To write off the account as uncollectible.

The direct write-off method of recognizing uncollectible-account expense is acceptable only when the amount of the uncollectible accounts is so low that it does not differ significantly from the uncollectible-account expense the company would report under the allowance method. Under the direct write-off method, a company debits Uncollectible-Account Expense and credits Accounts Receivable and the customer's account in the subsidiary record at the time it identifies a customer's account as uncollectible. For example, assume that a company that uses the direct write-off method decides to write off the account of Sue Fong in the amount of $2,500 as uncollectible. The entry to record the write-off is as follows:

Uncollectible-Account Expense......................... 2,500
   Accounts Receivable—Sue Fong...............   2,500
To write off the account as uncollectible.

A company does not maintain an allowance account when it uses the direct write-off method. The direct write-off method overstates assets on the balance sheet because not all of a company's receivables will be collected. The direct write-off method also results in a mismatching of sales revenue and uncollectible-account expense on the income statement.

A company can analyze its Accounts Receivable account in the general ledger to calculate the cash collections from customers. A company can calculate the cash collections from customers using the following formula:

Beginning balance of Accounts Receivable
Add: Debits to Accounts Receivable for sales on account
Less: Credits to Accounts Receivable for write-offs of uncollectible accounts
Less: Ending balance of Accounts Receivable
Equals: Cash collections from customers

Study Tip: The credits to Accounts Receivable for write-offs of uncollectible accounts should be the same as the debits to Allowance for Uncollectible Accounts.

Objective 4—Account for notes receivable

Notes receivable are more formal contracts than are accounts receivable. The creditor is the one to whom the note is due. The creditor has a note receivable. The debtor is the maker of the note, and the debtor has a note payable. Notes are also known as promissory notes because the debtor makes a formal promise to pay the amount due. Exhibit 5-4 illustrates a typical promissory note.

The principal of the note is the original amount borrowed. Most notes bear interest. Interest is revenue to the lender and an expense to the borrower. Interest rates are always for a year unless otherwise stated. The following formula determines the amount of interest due on a note: Principal x Interest Rate x Time. Time is expressed in terms of the fraction of a year that the note has been in force. For example, the interest due on a $10,000 note that bears interest at 12% that is due in five months would be $500 ($10,000 x 12% x 5/12). A company must prepare an adjusting entry to record the accrued interest due on a note receivable at the end of the year. The adjusting entry involves a debit to Interest Receivable and a credit to Interest Revenue.

Sometimes a company will accept a note receivable in payment of a customer's account receivable. For example, assume that on November 30, 2006, a company accepted a $5,000 note from Frank Smith that bears interest at 12% and is due in six months in payment of his account. The company would record the transaction as follows:

Note Receivable—Frank Smith.........................5,000
      Account Receivable—Frank Smith............   5,000
Accepted a note in payment of the customer's account.

On December 31, 2006, the end of the company's accounting period, the company would record the accrued interest as follows:

Interest Receivable.......................................   50
      Interest Revenue.................................   50
To record accrued interest on note receivable from Frank Smith ($5,000 x 12% x 1/12). The company would record the collection of the note from Frank Smith on May 31, 2006, as follows:

Cash..5,300
      Note Receivable—Frank Smith...............   5,000
      Interest Receivable...........................   50
      Interest Revenue..............................   250
To record the collection of Frank Smith's note at maturity.

Many companies now accept credit cards. This strategy can increase sales because customers can pay the credit card company over time. In addition, the company does not have to bill the customer and engage in other collection activities. The company incurs a cost for the benefits of accepting credit cards. This cost is known as financing expense or bank charges. This expense is similar to interest expense. It is a percent of the amount charged on the credit card. Assume that the financing expense is 2% and that a company deposited $50,000 in sales charged to Visa and MasterCard. The company would record the sales as follows:

Cash..49,000
Financing Expense................................... 1,000
      Sales Revenue   50,000
To record sales made on credit cards.

Some companies also sell their accounts receivable to obtain cash quickly. The company that buys the accounts receivable is called a factor. The factor earns revenue by buying the receivables at a discount and then hopefully collecting the full amount due from the customers. The company debits the discount to Financing Expense. Some companies might use the account title Factor's Margin. Assume that a company sold $200,000 of accounts receivable to a factor at a discount of 6%. The company would record the transaction as follows:

Cash.. 188,000
Financing Expense.................................... 12,000
      Accounts Receivable..........................   200,000
Sold accounts receivable at a discount of 6% to a factor.

Objective 5—Use days' sales in receivables and the acid-test ratio to evaluate financial position

Investors, creditors, and other users of financial statements use ratios to evaluate the financial health of a company. One ratio often used to assess a company's liquidity is the current ratio, which is equal to current assets divided by current liabilities. Other ratios used to measure a company's liquidity include the days' sales in receivables and the acid-test ratio. The acid-test ratio is also known as the quick ratio.

When a business makes a credit sale, it expects to collect the receivable within the period allowed by the company's credit terms. The ratio days' sales in receivables, which is also known as the collection period, indicates how long the company takes to collects its average receivables. A business prefers a short collection period so that it will have the necessary cash available to pay bills and to expand the business.

Calculating the days' sales in receivables involves two steps. The first step is to calculate one day's sales by dividing the sales revenue by 365 days. The second step is to divide the average net receivables by one day's sales. A company should compare its days' sales in receivables to its credit terms. The days' sales in receivables should be less than or equal to the number of days the company allows for payment in its credit terms. The average net receivables are equal to the sum of the beginning balance of net receivables and the ending balance of net receivables divided by two.

> **Study Tip:** The term *net receivables* refers to the balance in Accounts Receivable minus the balance in Allowance for Uncollectible Accounts.

The acid-test ratio (also known as the quick ratio) is a more robust measure of a company's liquidity than is the current ratio. The acid-test ratio is equal to the sum of the company's cash, short-term investments, and net current receivables, divided by its total current liabilities. The higher the acid-test ratio, the easier a company can pay its current liabilities. An acid-test ratio of 1.0 or higher is generally considered acceptable.

> **Study Tip:** The basic difference between the current ratio and the acid-test ratio is that the acid-test ratio does not include inventory or prepaid expenses in the numerator.

TEST YOURSELF

Matching

Match each numbered item with its lettered definition.

_____ 1. debtor
_____ 2. principal
_____ 3. securities
_____ 4. interest
_____ 5. bad-debt expense
_____ 6. acid-test ratio
_____ 7. equity securities
_____ 8. maturity
_____ 9. receivables
_____ 10. direct write-off method

_____ 11. percent-of-sales method
_____ 12. aging-of-accounts receivable
_____ 13. debt instrument
_____ 14. creditor
_____ 15. held-to-maturity investments
_____ 16. days' sales in receivables
_____ 17. allowance method
_____ 18. marketable securities
_____ 19. trading investments
_____ 20. Allowance for Uncollectible Accounts

A. computes uncollectible-account expense as a percent of net sales.

B. amount borrowed by a debtor and lent by a creditor.

C. ratio of average net accounts receivable to one day's sales.

D. method of accounting for bad debts in which the company waits until the credit department decides that a customer's account receivable is uncollectible and then debits Uncollectible-Account Expense and credits the customer's Account Receivable.

E. notes payable or stock certificates that entitle the owner to the benefits of an investment.

F. contra account, related to Accounts Receivable, that holds the estimated amount of collection losses.

G. stock certificates that represent the investor's ownership in a corporation.

H. bonds and notes that an investor intends to hold until maturity.

I. the date on which a debt instrument must be paid.

J. stock investments that are to be sold in the near future with the intent of generating profits on the sale.

K. method of recording collection losses based on estimates of how much money the business will not collect from its customers.

L. tells whether the entity can pay all its current liabilities if they come due immediately.

M. investments that a company plans to hold for one year or less.

N. the party who owes money.

O. a payable, usually some form of note or bond payable.

P. arises from the failure to collect from credit customers.

Q. monetary claims against a business or an individual, acquired mainly by selling goods and services and by lending money.

R. the party to whom money is owed.

S. the borrower's cost of renting money from a lender.

T. a way to estimate bad debts by analyzing individual accounts receivable according to the length of time they have been receivable from the customer.

Multiple Choice

Circle the best answer.

1. Short-term investments are also known as:
   a. accounts receivable
   b. notes receivable
   c. finance receivables
   d. marketable securities

2. Accounts receivable are also known as:
   a. notes receivable
   b. trade receivables
   c. long-term receivables
   d. other receivables

3. A critical element of internal control concerning procedures for cash receipts is:
   a. paying all expenses from petty cash
   b. requiring the bookkeeper to handle all incoming cash only once
   c. allowing the bookkeeper to write off accounts as uncollectible
   d. the separation of cash-handling and cash-accounting duties

4. A company reports trading securities on the balance sheet at their:
   a. original cost
   b. current market value
   c. original cost plus one-half of their increase in value or minus one-half of their decrease in value
   d. current market value or original cost, whichever is lower

5. A contra account to Accounts Receivable is:
   a. Uncollectible-Account Expense
   b. Allowance for Uncollectible Accounts
   c. Notes Receivable
   d. Short-Term Investments

6. Short-term investments are investments that a company plans to hold:
   a. for at least five years
   b. for one year or less
   c. for more than one year
   d. indefinitely

7. When a company writes off an account receivable against the Allowance for Uncollectible Accounts, total current assets:
   a. decrease
   b. increase
   c. remain the same
   d. may increase or decrease depending on the size of the account written off

8. Uncollectible-Account Expense is a(n):
   a. current asset
   b. contra asset
   c. current liability
   d. expense

9. The percent-of-sales method computes uncollectible-account expense as a percent of:
   a. revenue
   b. accounts receivable
   c. allowance for uncollectible accounts
   d. the previous year's uncollectible-account expense

10. The aging-of-receivables method of estimating uncollectibles is a(n):
    a. income statement approach
    b. balance sheet approach
    c. statement of cash flows approach
    d. statement of retained earnings approach

11. If a company uses the direct write-off method:
    a. total assets are overstated
    b. total assets are understated
    c. total liabilities are overstated
    d. total liabilities are understated

12. What is the single most important source of cash for any business?
    a. sales of marketable securities
    b. interest revenue
    c. dividend revenue
    d. collections from customers

13. Unless otherwise stated, interest rates are always for a(n):
    a. daily period
    b. monthly period
    c. quarterly period
    d. annual period

14. A gain has the same effect as a(n):
    a. loss
    b. expense
    c. revenue
    d. asset

15. The Accounts Receivable account in the general ledger serves as a:
    a. control account
    b. subsidiary record
    c. short-term investment
    d. contra account

Completion

Complete each of the following statements.

1. Selling accounts receivable is known as _____.
2. The days' sales in receivables is also known as the _____ _____.
3. The balance sheet lists _____ in the order of relative liquidity.
4. The party to whom money is owed is a(n) _____.
5. A realized gain or loss usually occurs when the investor _____ an investment.
6. Gain or Loss on the Sale of Investments would be reported in the _____ items of the income statement.
7. Certain assets that secure the payment of a note receivable are known as _____.
8. Companies keep a _____ _____ of accounts receivable with a separate account for each customer.
9. A company reports loans to employees under the category of _____ _____.
10. Companies that sell on credit receive most of their cash receipts through the _____.
11. When a company writes off an account as uncollectible, it _____ Allowance for Uncollectible Accounts.
12. The direct write-off method results in a poor _____ of uncollectible-account expense against revenue.
13. The _____ is the amount borrowed by a debtor.
14. Collections of accounts receivable are reported as cash received from _____ activities on the statement of cash flows.
15. When the market value of an investment is greater than its cost, the company has a(n) _____ gain.

True/False

For each of the following statements, circle T *for true or* F *for false.*

1. T F The purpose of owning a trading investment is to sell it for more than its cost.
2. T F A company reports trading investments on the balance sheet at their original cost.
3. T F A time lag occurs between earning sales revenue from a credit sale and collecting the cash.
4. T F Accounts receivable are more formal contracts than are notes receivable.
5. T F Long-term investments are current assets.
6. T F Receivables are the third most liquid asset.
7. T F The bookkeeper should not be allowed to handle the cash.
8. T F Using a bank lockbox does not result in separation of duties.
9. T F The aging-of-receivables method focuses on the uncollectible-account expense.
10. T F At the end of the year, companies use the aging method to ensure that Accounts Receivable are reported at their net realizable value.
11. T F A company may accept a note receivable from a trade customer whose account receivable is past due.
12. T F Accounts receivable are sometimes called current receivables.
13. T F An equity security is usually some form of note.
14. T F Investments can earn interest revenue or dividend revenue.
15. T F A loss has the same effect as an expense.

Exercises

1. Prepare journal entries to record each of the following.

(1) The purchase for cash of $200,000 of common stock to be held as a trading investment.

(2) The receipt of $3,000 in dividends on the common stock purchased as a trading investment.

(3) On the balance sheet date, the current value of the common stock was $210,000.

2. Prepare the journal entry to record uncollectible-account expense for each of the following independent cases.

(1) Murphy Company uses the allowance method and estimates its uncollectible-account expense using the percent-of-sales method. The company makes all sales on credit. Sales for the year were $758,000. The company estimates that 4% of its sales will be uncollectible. The balance in the Allowance for Uncollectible Accounts before recording the uncollectible-account expense for the year was a credit balance of $5,200.

(2) Harris Company uses the allowance method and estimates its uncollectible-account expense using the aging-of-receivables method. Based on the aging schedule, the company estimates that 8% of its $100,000 in accounts receivable will be uncollectible. The balance in the Allowance for Uncollectible Accounts before recording the uncollectible-account expense for the year was a credit balance of $1,400.

3. Foster Company had a beginning balance in Accounts Receivable of $40,000, and an ending balance in Accounts Receivable of $120,000. The debits to Accounts Receivable during the year were $500,000. The debits to the Allowance for Uncollectible Accounts were $12,000. What were Foster Company's collections from customers during the year?

4. Prepare journal entries to record the all the necessary journal entries for Maxwell Company. The company's accounting year ends on December 31.

(1) On October 31, 2006, the company received a $10,000 note from Gina Courtney in payment of her account. The note is due on April 30, 2007, and it bears interest at 12%.

(2) Record any necessary adjusting entry on December 31.

(3) On April 30, 2007, Gina Courtney paid the note, including the interest.

5. Reynolds Company had net sales of $28,999,980 for 2006. The company makes all sales on account. Given the following additional information, calculate (1) the days' sales in receivables as of December 31, 2006, and (2) the acid-test ratio as of December 31, 2006.

	December 31, 2005	December 31, 2006
Cash	$200,000	$250,000
Short-term investments	900,000	800,000
Accounts receivable	2,200,000	2,650,000
Allowance for uncollectible accounts	(100,000)	(150,000)
Inventory	2,600,000	2,800,000
Prepaid expenses	200,000	230,000
Total current assets	6,000,000	6,580,000
Current liabilities	3,200,000	3,400,000

Critical Thinking

Ross Corporation began its business operations on December 1, 2006. The corporation has adopted the calendar year as its accounting period. The company makes all of its sales on account with credit terms of net 60 days. In the industry in which Ross Corporation operates, all companies have a small percentage of their accounts that are uncollectible. Explain the effect on (1) the acid-test ratio, (2) total assets, (3) net income, and (4) retained earnings if Ross Corporation fails to record a journal entry to estimate its uncollectible accounts as of December 31, 2006.

Demonstration Problems

1. Davidson Company had a balance in Accounts Receivable of $200,000 and a credit balance in Allowance for Uncollectible Accounts of $16,000 as of December 31, 2006. Prepare journal entries to record the following during 2006.

(1) Made sales on account of $1,600,000.

(2) Received collections on its customers' accounts of $1,587,000.

(3) Wrote off the accounts of customers in the amount of $22,000 as uncollectible.

(4) Purchased common stock as a trading investment for $300,000

(5) Sold the common stock purchased for $300,000 as a trading investment for $283,000.

(6) Purchased common stock as a trading investment in the amount of $400,000.

(7) Received a cash dividend of $10,000 on the common stock held as a trading investment.

(8) At the end of the accounting period, the market value of the common stock purchased for $400,000 and held as a trading investment was $412,000.

(9) Recorded uncollectible-account expense based on eight percent of sales on account.

2. Prepare journal entries to record the following for McAllister Corporation:

(1) On October 31, 2006, received a $20,000 note from Larry Abel in payment of his account. The note bears interest at 6% and is due on January 31, 2007.

(2) Sold accounts receivable of $400,000 at a discount of 8% to a factor.

(3) Recorded sales of $900,000 made by customers using a Visa or MasterCard. The bank charged the company a 3% financing charge.

(4) The accrued interest on the note from Larry Abel as of December 31, 2006, the end of McAllister Corporation's accounting period.

(5) On January 31, 2007, Larry Abel paid his note, including the interest.

SOLUTIONS

Matching

1	N	5	P	9	Q	13	O	17	K
2	B	6	L	10	D	14	R	18	M
3	E	7	G	11	A	15	H	19	J
4	S	8	I	12	T	16	C	20	F

Multiple Choice

1	D
2	B
3	D
4	C
5	B
6	B
7	C
8	D
9	A
10	B
11	A
12	D
13	D
14	C
15	A

Completion

1. factoring
2. collection period
3. assets
4. creditor
5. sells
6. other
7. collateral
8. subsidiary record
9. other receivables
10. mail
11. debits
12. matching
13. principal
14. operating
15. unrealized

True/False

1. T
2. F   A company reports trading investments on the balance sheet at their current market value.
3. T
4. F   Notes receivable are more formal contracts than are accounts receivable. The maker of a note makes a formal promise to pay the amount due, and notes usually bear interest.
5. F   Short-term investments are current assets.
6. T
7. T
8. F   Using a bank lockbox achieves separation of duties because customers send their payments directly to the company's bank. The bank records the cash received and sends the remittance advices to the company's bookkeeper.
9. F   The aging-of-receivables method of estimating uncollectible accounts focuses on the accounts receivable.
10. T
11. T
12. T
13. F   A debt security is usually some form of note. An equity security is a stock certificate that represents the investor's ownership in a corporation.
14. T
15. T

Exercises

1.

(1)

Short-Term Investments......................   200,000
          Cash...................................   200,000
Purchased investment.

(2)

Cash..   3,000
          Dividend Revenue......................   3,000
Received cash dividend.

(3)

```
Short-Term Investments......................... 10,000
        Unrealized Gain on Investments..........            10,000
Adjusted investment to market value.
```

2.

(1)

```
Uncollectible-Account Expense.................. 30,320
        Allowance for Uncollectible Accounts......            30,320
To record uncollectible-account expense for the year ($758,000 x 4%).
```
(2)

```
Uncollectible-Account Expense...........................6,600
        Allowance for Uncollectible Accounts...........            6,600
To record uncollectible-account expense for the year [($100,000 x 8%) – $1,400].
```

3.

Beginning balance in Accounts Receivable		$ 40,000
Add: Debits to Accounts Receivable		500,000
		$540,000
Less: Accounts Receivable written off as uncollectible	$ 12,000	
Less: Ending balance in Accounts Receivable	120,000	132,000
Collections from customers		$408,000

4.

(1)

```
Notes Receivable—Gina Courtney......................10,000
        Accounts Receivable—Gina Courtney.........            10,000
Received a note receivable on account.
```

(2)

```
Interest Receivable...................................... 200
        Interest Revenue...................................            200
To record accrued interest ($10,000 x 12% x 2/12).
```

(3)

```
Cash.............................................................10,600
        Notes Receivable—Gina Courtney..............          10,000
        Interest Receivable.................................          200
        Interest Revenue ($10,000 x 12% x 4/12).........          400
To record the collection of a note at maturity.
```

5.

(1) One day's sales = $28,999,980 / 365 days = $79,452 per day

Net accounts receivable as of December 31, 2005 = $2,200,000 – $100,000 = $2,100,000

Net accounts receivable as of December 31, 2006 = $2,650,000 – $150,000 = $2,500,000

Average net accounts receivable = ($2,100,000 + $2,500,000) / 2 = $2,300,000

Days' sales in receivables = $2,300,000 / $79,452 = 28.95 days or approximately 29 days

(2)

Cash	$250,000
Short-term investments	800,000
Accounts receivable	2,650,000
Allowance for uncollectible accounts	(150,000)
Total quick assets	$3,550,000

Acid-test ratio = $3,550,000 / $3,400,000 = 1.04

Critical Thinking

If Ross Corporation fails to record a journal entry to estimate its uncollectible accounts as of December 31, 2006, the allowance for uncollectible accounts will be understated, which will cause the quick assets, the current assets, and the total assets to be overstated. Because total quick assets will be overstated, the acid-test ratio will be overstated because the acid-test ratio is equal to quick assets divided by current liabilities. The uncollectible-account expense will be understated. Therefore, total expenses will be understated and net income will be overstated. Retained earnings will also be overstated because net income flows to retained earnings.

Demonstration Problems

1.

(1)

Accounts Receivable..............................1,600,000
        Sales Revenue.............................   1,600,000
To record sales on account.

(2)

Cash.. 1,587,000
        Accounts Receivable.....................   1,587,000
To record collections on customers' accounts.

(3)

Allowance for Uncollectible Accounts............ 22,000
        Accounts Receivable..........................   22,000
To write off accounts as uncollectible.

(4)

Short-Term Investments............................300,000
        Cash...   300,000
Purchased trading investment.

(5)

Cash..283,000
Loss on Sale of Investment........................... 17,000
        Short-Term Investments.......................   300,000
Sold trading investment at a loss.

(6)

Short-Term Investments............................ 400,000
        Cash...   400,000
Purchased trading investment.

(7)

Cash.. 10,000
        Dividend Revenue.............................   10,000
Received cash dividend on trading investment.

(8)

Short-Term Investments.................................	12,000	
Unrealized Gain on Investments..............		12,000

To adjust trading investment to market value.

(9)

Uncollectible-Account Expense........................	128,000	
Allowance for Uncollectible Accounts........		128,000

To record uncollectible-account expense ($1,600,000 x 8%).

2.
(1)

Note Receivable—Larry Abel..........................	20,000	
Accounts Receivable—Larry Abel............		20,000

Received note on account.

(2)

Cash..	368,000	
Financing Expense.....................................	32,000	
Accounts Receivable...........................		400,000

Sold accounts receivable to a factor at a discount of 8%.

(3)

Cash..	873,000	
Financing Expense.....................................	27,000	
Sales Revenue...................................		900,000

To record sales made on credit cards.

(4)

Interest Receivable.....................................	200	
Interest Revenue................................		200

To record accrued interest on the note receivable from Larry Abel ($20,000 x 6% x 2/12).

(5)

Cash..	20,300	
Notes Receivable...............................		20,000
Interest Receivable............................		200
Interest Revenue...............................		100

To record collection of note receivable from Larry Abel at maturity.

Chapter 6

MERCHANDISE INVENTORY AND COST OF GOODS SOLD

CHAPTER OBJECTIVES

The learning objectives for this chapter are as follows:

1. Account for inventory transactions
2. Analyze the various inventory methods
3. Identify the income and tax effects of the inventory methods
4. Use the gross profit percentage and inventory turnover to evaluate a business
5. Estimate inventory by the gross profit method
6. Show how inventory errors affect cost of goods sold and income

CHAPTER OVERVIEW

Merchandise inventory is often one of the largest assets a firm owns. Identifying and tracking merchandise costs is a vital component of a firm's ability to report the relative success or failure of their operations (profit). Merchandise Inventory's opposite account on the income statement is known as Cost of Goods Sold. This account, though not labeled as an expense, has the same effect as an expense. Cost of Goods Sold is reported in a separate segment of the income statement, distinct from Operating Expenses. Several methods of estimating and reporting merchandise inventory are also covered.

CHAPTER REVIEW

Introduction

Merchandise inventory (an asset) represents products that are ready for sale to customers. Cost of goods sold is exactly what it sounds like: the expired cost (expense) of the products that have been sold to customers. Net income is a commonly used indicator of the relative success or failure of a firm's operations. However, there are equally important measures of success or failure that can be found on the income statement. One of these is gross profit, defined as follows:

$$
\begin{aligned}
&\text{Sales} \\
-\ &\text{Cost of Goods Sold} \\
=\ &\text{Gross Profit}
\end{aligned}
$$

Gross profit is a preliminary evaluation of success of the firm's sales efforts. It is preliminary in that it includes only product costs in its determination: operating expenses are reported separately and handled later on in the income statement. Gross profit is also sometimes referred to as gross margin.

Objective 1—Account for inventory transactions

To account for inventories, a firm must make a decision between two approaches for maintaining the accounting records: perpetual or periodic.

Periodic inventory systems are used for inexpensive products. The accounting records are adjusted only periodically, such as monthly, quarterly, or annually. A sale will generate only one entry: the sale itself.

Accounts Receivable or Cash	XX	
Sales		XX

Perpetual inventory systems can be used with any product, but are frequently associated with computerized tracking systems, often using bar codes. The accounting records are updated with every transaction completed. A sale generates two entries: the sale, and the reduction of inventory (expense).

Accounts Receivable or Cash	XX	
Sales		XX
Cost of Goods Sold	X	
Merchandise Inventory		X

The differences between periodic and perpetual are summarized below:

Perpetual Inventory System	Periodic Inventory System
Keeps a running record of all goods bought and sold	Does not keep a running record of all goods bought and sold
Used for all types of goods	Used for inexpensive goods

The purchase price of a good is only the starting point for determining the final (net) cost of purchases for a given period of time:

  Purchase Price of the Inventory
+ Freight-in (the cost to transport the goods from seller to buyer)
− Purchase Returns (for credit due to unsuitable goods physically rejected)
− Purchase Allowances (price reductions due to unsatisfactory goods
− Purchase Discounts (price reduction due to early invoice payment)
= Net Purchases of Inventory

Objective 2—Analyze the various inventory methods

Consider the Cost of Goods Sold section of the income statement:

Beginning Merchandise Inventory balance (i.e., January 1)
+ Net Purchases
= Cost of Goods Available for Sale
− Ending Merchandise Inventory balance (i.e., December 31)
= Cost of Goods Sold

The four inventory methods (FIFO, LIFO, weighted average and specific identification) all value the ending inventory, or conversely the cost of goods sold. At least initially, the beginning balance and the purchases will be the same regardless of the method selected.

Specific identification tracks costs and movement by each individual, unique unit. It is the most accurate method of accounting for inventory, but the most complex and expensive. Few products are capable of being tracked individually, physically and economically.

Consider the following set of information common to all three of our examples for inventory estimation.

Description	Units	$/unit	Total $ Cost
Beginning Balance	10	1	10
Purchase #1	20	2	40
Purchase #2	30	3	90
Available for Sale	60		140

Note that for any of the three inventory estimation methods (FIFO, LIFO, average cost), goods available for sale is the same: 60 units for a total of $140. This is the starting point for inventory estimation.

Assuming that our sample firm sold 45 units at $10 each, that leaves 15 units in ending inventory. Our goal in inventory estimation is to attach a dollar value to both ending inventory and to cost of goods sold.

Average Costing is probably the simplest of the three to use, so let's begin there.

Step 1: Calculate an average cost per unit, using this formula:

> Cost of Goods Available for Sale ÷ Units of Goods Available for Sale

In our example, the calculation would be $140 ÷ 60 = $2.33 per unit

Step 2: Use the cost per unit figure to allocate costs between ending inventory and cost of goods sold.

Description	Units	$/unit	Total $ Cost (rounded)
Ending Inventory	15	2.33	35
Cost of Goods Sold	45	2.33	105
Total Allocated in this step	60		140
Available for Sale (these should equal)	60		140

Let's evaluate FIFO next.

Our basic process will be to identify the ending inventory layer. Under FIFO, the first (oldest) items or layers of items will be sold first. That leaves the last items (newest) sitting in ending inventory. This is what we will identify. Recall the information previously displayed, as well as the ending inventory count of 15.

Description	Units	$/unit	Total $ Cost
Beginning Balance	10	1	10
Purchase #1	20	2	40
Purchase #2	30	3	90
Available for Sale	60		140

Our ending inventory will come out of this last layer:
We only need 15 units.

Our ending inventory will be 15 units, valued at the last layer's cost per unit of $3, for a total $45. Cost of goods sold is still 45 units valued at a simple remainder: $140 – $45 = $95.

Let's evaluate LIFO next.

Our basic process will still be to identify the ending inventory layer. Under LIFO, the last (newest) items or layers of items will be sold first. That leaves the first items (oldest) sitting in ending inventory. This is what we will identify. Recall the information previously displayed, as well as the ending inventory count of 15.

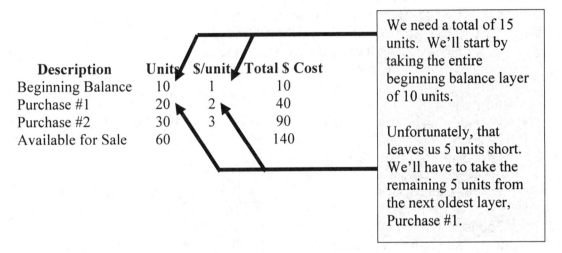

Description	Units	$/unit	Total $ Cost
Beginning Balance	10	1	10
Purchase #1	20	2	40
Purchase #2	30	3	90
Available for Sale	60		140

We need a total of 15 units. We'll start by taking the entire beginning balance layer of 10 units.

Unfortunately, that leaves us 5 units short. We'll have to take the remaining 5 units from the next oldest layer, Purchase #1.

Our ending inventory will be 15 units, valued at the older layer's cost of $20 ([10x1] + [5x2]). Cost of goods sold is still 45 units valued at a simple remainder: $140 − $20 = $120.

Objective 3—Identify the income and tax effects of the inventory methods

The following table summarizes the effects of the three inventory methods on gross profit:

Description	FIFO	LIFO	Average
Sales	450	450	450
Cost of Goods Sold:			
Beginning Merchandise Inventory	10	10	10
+Purchases	130	130	130
=Goods Available for Sale	140	140	140
− Ending Merchandise Inventory	45	20	35
=Cost of Goods Sold	95	120	105
Gross Profit	355	330	345

Note that all rows are identical in amount regardless of the method, up to the Goods Available for Sale line.

Observations:

FIFO results in the highest Ending Inventory, therefore....
> the lowest Cost of Goods Sold, therefore....
> the highest Gross Profit, which will lead to....
> the highest Net Income Before Taxes, therefore
> the highest Income Tax Expense, therefore....
> the highest Net Income.

LIFO results in the lowest Ending Inventory, therefore....
> the highest Cost of Goods Sold, therefore....
> the lowest Gross Profit, which will lead to....
> the lowest Net Income Before Taxes, therefore
> the lowest Income Tax Expense, therefore....
> the lowest Net Income.

Average costing, by definition, will fall somewhere in between the high and low.

In summary, review the following table:

Description	FIFO	LIFO	Average
Sales	450	450	450
Cost of Goods Sold:			
Beginning Merchandise Inventory	10	10	10
+Purchases	130	130	130
=Goods Available for Sale	140	140	140
- Ending Merchandise Inventory	45	20	35
=Cost of Goods Sold	95	120	105
Gross Profit	355	330	345
Operating Expenses (not related to method)	10	10	10
Income before Income Taxes	345	320	335
Income Tax Expense (40%)	138	128	134
Net Income	207	192	201

LIFO is a legal approach to minimizing corporate taxes.

Supplementary Definitions:

Consistency Principle – businesses should use the same accounting methods and procedures from one period to the next.

Disclosure Principle – a firm's financial statements should report enough information for outsiders to make informed decisions about the company.

Conservatism – financial statements portray the "worst case scenario" of the firm. The idea is to avoid any unmet expectations or negative "surprises." This includes the lower of cost or market principle.

Objective 4—Use the gross profit percentage and inventory turnover to evaluate a business

Gross Profit Percentage	Gross Profit ÷ Net Sales Revenue	Interpretation: Higher Is Better
Inventory Turnover Ratio	Cost of Goods Sold ÷ Average Inventory	Interpretation: Higher (faster) Is Better

Note: Average inventory is calculated by adding the beginning and ending inventory balances and dividing the sum by two. Generally speaking, average *anything* is calculated in this manner.

Objective 5—Estimate inventory by the gross profit method

The gross profit method of estimating inventory is used for unusual circumstances, such as the destruction of accounting records due to fire, tornado, etc. Do not make this method harder than it is. This method simply folds the gross profit percentage calculated previously, with a small modification of the income statements above.

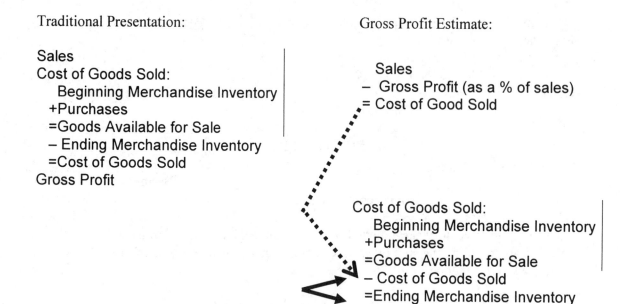

Traditional Presentation:

Sales
Cost of Goods Sold:
    Beginning Merchandise Inventory
  +Purchases
  =Goods Available for Sale
  – Ending Merchandise Inventory
  =Cost of Goods Sold
Gross Profit

Gross Profit Estimate:

Sales
– Gross Profit (as a % of sales)
= Cost of Good Sold

Cost of Goods Sold:
    Beginning Merchandise Inventory
  +Purchases
  =Goods Available for Sale
  – Cost of Goods Sold
  =Ending Merchandise Inventory

Objective 6—Show how inventory errors affect cost of goods sold and income

Ending inventory errors flow (roll) down the income statement, they affect every major subtotal, ending with net income. Since one period's ending inventory becomes the beginning inventory for the next, errors affect at least two periods. Consider the following ending inventory error of $100 understatement (undercount). For simplicity's sake, all unaffected amounts are left at zero (blank).

Description	Period 1	Period 2	Period 3
Sales			
Cost of Goods Sold:			
Beginning Merchandise Inventory		–10	
+Purchases			
=Goods Available for Sale		–10	
– Ending Merchandise Inventory	–10		
=Cost of Goods Sold	+10	–10	
Gross Profit	–10	+10	
Operating Expenses (not related to method)			
Income before Income Taxes	–10	+10	
Income Tax Expense (40%)	–4	+4	
Net Income	–6	+6	

TEST YOURSELF

Matching

Match each numbered item with its lettered definition.

_____ 1. gross profit
_____ 2. disclosure principle
_____ 3. inventory turnover
_____ 4. periodic inventory system
_____ 5. cost of goods sold
_____ 6. purchase return
_____ 7. inventory profit
_____ 8. consistency principle
_____ 9. gross profit percentage
_____ 10. purchase discount

_____ 11. weighted average cost method
_____ 12. perpetual inventory system
_____ 13. lower-of-cost-or-market rule
_____ 14. conservatism
_____ 15. average cost method
_____ 16. gross profit method
_____ 17. specific-unit-cost method
_____ 18. first-in, first-out method (FIFO)
_____ 19. last-in, first-out method (LIFO)
_____ 20. inventory

A. inventory costing method based on the weighted average cost of inventory during the period.
B. the cost of the inventory that the business has sold to customers.
C. based on accounting conservatism and requires that inventory be reported in the financial statements at whichever is lower.
D. a way to estimate ending inventory by using the cost-of-goods-sold model.
E. ratio of cost of goods sold to average inventory.
F. inventory costing method by which the last costs into inventory are the first costs out to cost of goods sold.
G. gross profit divided by net sales revenue.
H. based on the average cost of inventory during the period.
I. difference between gross margin figured on the FIFO basis and gross margin figured on the LIFO basis.
J. inventory cost method based on the specific cost of particular units of inventory.
K. states that businesses should use the same accounting methods and procedures from period to period.
L. the merchandise that a company sells to customers.
M. holds that a company's financial statements should report enough information for outsider to make informed decisions about the company.
N. system in which the business keeps a continuous record for each inventory item to show the inventory on hand at all times.
O. decrease in the cost of purchases because the buyer returned the goods to the seller.
P. inventory costing method by which the first costs into inventory are the first costs out to cost of goods sold.
Q. sales revenue minus cost of goods sold.
R. a decrease in the cost of purchases earned by making an early payment to the vendor.
S. accounting concept by which the least favorable figures are presented in the financial statements.
T. system in which the business makes a physical count of the inventory on hand and applies the appropriate unit costs to determine the cost of the ending inventory.

Multiple Choice

Circle the best answer.

1.   The largest expense category on the income statement of most merchandising companies is:
     a.   cost of goods sold
     b.   other expenses
     c.   selling expenses
     d.   administrative expenses

2.   Which of the following would **not** be included in the Inventory account on a merchandising company's balance sheet?
     a.   customs duties
     b.   sales taxes received
     c.   shipping costs from the manufacturer to the merchandising company
     d.   insurance on the merchandise while in transit from the manufacturer

3.   Which of the following would be included in the Cost of Goods Sold account on a merchandising company's income statement?
     a.   shipping costs from the manufacturer to the merchandiser
     b.   sales commissions
     c.   costs of advertising
     d.   sales taxes

4.   In a merchandising business, gross profit is equal to sales revenue minus:
     a.   the sum of cost of goods sold, operating expenses, and prepaid expenses
     b.   the sum of cost of goods sold and operating expenses
     c.   cost of goods sold
     d.   the sum of cost of goods sold and sales commissions

5.   A perpetual inventory system offers all the following advantages **except**:
     a.   inventory balances are always current
     b.   it enhances internal control
     c.   it is less expensive than a periodic system
     d.   it helps salespeople determine whether there is a sufficient supply of inventory on hand to fill customer orders

6.   Perpetual inventory records provide information helpful in making all the following decisions **except**:
     a.   whether immediate delivery of merchandise is possible
     b.   when to reorder
     c.   how quickly items of merchandise are selling
     d.   whether to extend credit to a customer

7. Technological advances in computers and inventory tracking have:
   a. made perpetual inventory records less expensive to maintain
   b. completely eliminated the need to physically count inventory
   c. made journal entries unnecessary for inventory purchases
   d. made perpetual inventory records more expensive to maintain

8. If a company uses a perpetual inventory system, it will maintain all of the following accounts except:
   a. Cost of Goods Sold
   b. Purchases
   c. Sales
   d. Inventory

9. Using a perpetual inventory system, which of the following entries would record the cost of merchandise sold on credit?
   a. Sales
          Accounts Receivable
   b. Cost of Goods Sold
          Purchases
   c. Cost of Goods Sold
          Inventory
   d. Inventory
          Cost of Goods Sold

10. Under a perpetual inventory system, which of the following entries would record the purchase of merchandise on credit?
    a. Inventory
           Accounts Payable
    b. Purchases
           Cost of Goods Sold
    c. Sales
           Accounts Receivable
    d. Purchases
           Accounts Payable

11. If a company is using a perpetual inventory system, the balance in its Inventory account three-quarters of the way through an accounting period would be equal to:
    a. the total of the beginning inventory plus goods purchased during the accounting period
    b. the inventory on hand at the beginning of the period
    c. the amount of inventory on hand at that date
    d. the amount of goods purchased during the period

12.   If a company is using a perpetual inventory system, the balance in its Inventory account three-quarters of the way through an accounting period would be equal to:
   a.   the inventory on hand at the beginning of the period
   b.   the inventory on hand at the beginning of the period plus goods purchased during the accounting period minus goods sold during the period
   c.   the total of the beginning inventory plus goods purchased during the accounting period
   d.   the amount of goods purchased during the period

13.   Given the following data, what is the cost of goods sold?

   Sales revenue $1,980,000
   Beginning inventory   380,000
   Ending inventory   340,000
   Purchases   1,250,000

   a. $690,000
   b. $770,000
   c. $1,290,000
   d. $1,210,000

14.   Given the following data, what is the cost of beginning inventory?

   Sales revenue $1,450,000
   Cost of goods sold   845,000
   Ending inventory   310,000
   Purchases   950,000

   a. $1,485,000
   b. $415,000
   c. $1,035,000
   d. $205,000

15.   Given the following data, what is the cost of purchases?

   Sales revenue $725,000
   Cost of goods sold   345,000
   Ending inventory   250,000
   Beginning inventory   120,000

   a. $370,000
   b. $465,000
   c. $595,000
   d. $475,000

Completion

Complete each of the following statements.

1. The largest current asset for most retailers is_____.
2. The largest single expense for most retailers is_____.
3. The inventory system that maintains continuous records of items in the inventory is called_____.
4. Which inventory system(s) require(s) a physical count of inventory?_____
5. LIFO stands for _____.
6. The lower-of-cost-or-market rule for inventory is an example of the _____ principle.
7. During periods of rising prices, the _____ method of accounting for inventories results in the highest cost of goods sold.
8. The _____ method would not be appropriate for a retailer selling a large number of units each with low prices.
9. FIFO stands for _____.
10. A seller's request for payment is called a(n) _____.
11. A company debits the Purchases account when goods are acquired. It is using a _____ inventory system.
12. Sales minus cost of goods sold is called _____.
13. A company credits the Merchandise Inventory account when merchandise is sold. It is using a _____ inventory system.
14. The formula for the gross profit percentage is: _____.
15. The formula for inventory turnover is:_____.

True/False

For each of the following statements, circle T *for true or* F *for false.*

1.   T F   Gross profit is entitled as such because operating expenses have not yet been subtracted.
2.   T F   The physical count establishes the correct amount of ending inventory for the financial statements and also serves as a check on the periodic systems.
3.   T F   Freight-out is accounted for as part of the cost of inventory.
4.   T F   Weighted average, FIFO, and LIFO do not use the specific cost of a particular unit.
5.   T F   Advertising and sales commissions are included as the cost of inventory.
6.   T F   When prices are rising, LIFO results in the lowest taxable income and thus the lowest incomes taxes.
7.   T F   Consistency enables investors to compare a company's financial statements from one period to the next.
8.   T F   Beginning inventory and ending inventory have the same effects on cost of goods sold.
9.   T F   The inventory turnover statistic shows how many times the company sold its average level of inventory during the year.
10.   T F   Businesses such as restaurants and hometown nurseries use the perpetual inventory system because the accounting cost is low.
11.   T F   Freight-in is the transportation cost, paid by the buyer, to move goods from the seller to the buyer.
12.   T F   Sales taxes paid by a merchandising company on its sales are normally included in the Cost of Goods Sold account.
13.   T F   A purchase allowance is a decrease in the cost of purchases because the purchaser returned goods to the supplier.
14.   T F   In a perpetual inventory system, businesses maintain a continuous record for each inventory item.
15.   T F   Historically, perpetual inventory systems have been used to account for inventory items with a low unit cost.

Exercises

1. The following information is given for Stephanie's Beach Shoes for the month of March:

		Pairs of shoes	Unit Cost
3/1	Inventory	600	$40
3/7	Purchase	800	44
3/13	Purchase	1,400	48
3/22	Purchase	1,400	50
3/29	Purchase	400	46

During the month, 3,800 pairs of shoes were sold.

A. How many shoes should be in the inventory at the end of March?

B. Using the weighted-average cost method, what are the cost of ending inventory and cost of goods sold?

C. Using the FIFO method, what are the cost of ending inventory and cost of goods sold?

D. Using the LIFO method, what are the cost of ending inventory and cost of goods sold?

2. The Beckham Co.'s inventory was destroyed by a fire. The company's records show net sales of $720,000, beginning inventory of $160,000, net purchase of $600,000, and a gross profit rate of 50%. What is the estimated value of ending inventory?

3. Assume the following:

	X1	X2	X3
Beginning Inventory	$ 8,000	$15,000	$12,000
Net Purchases	45,000	50,000	55,000
Goods Available for Sale	53,000	65,000	67,000
Ending Inventory	15,000	12,000	8,000
Cost of Goods Sold	38,000	53,000	59,000

You discover the following errors:
a. Ending inventory XI was overstated by $6,000
b. Ending inventory X2 was understated by $4,000
Considering these errors, recalculate cost of goods sold for all three years.

4. The following information is available for Lasky Co. for 2006:

Beginning Inventory	$ 4,000
Ending Inventory	2,400
Operating Expenses	3,150
Cost of Goods Sold	19,225
Sales Discounts	360
Sales	28,610
Sales Returns and Allowances	205

Required:
1. What is net sales for 2006?

2. What is gross profit for 2006?

3. What is net income for 2006?

4. What is the gross profit rate?

5. What is the inventory turnover rate?

5. The following information is given for Will's Wraps for 2006:

Beginning Inventory	$ 12,250
Gross Margin	7,500
Operating Expenses	3,100
Purchase Returns & Allowances	600
Purchase Discounts	550
Purchases	39,250
Sales Discounts	500
Sales	51,500
Sales Returns & Allowances	1,700

Required:

1. Compute net sales.

2. Compute net purchases.

3. Compute cost of goods sold.

4. Compute ending inventory.

5. Compute net income.

6. What is the inventory turnover rate?

7. What is the gross profit rate?

Critical Thinking

Re-examine the facts presented in Exercise 1. A physical count was taken, and ending inventory was determined to be 700 pairs. In re-checking the sales, you verify that 3,800 pairs were sold. How would you explain the 100 pair difference (800 pairs you expected to be on hand less the actual count of 700 pairs), and how would you "account" for it?

Demonstration Problems

1.

Andrew's Appliance has the following records relating to its May 2006 inventory:

Date	Item	Quantity	Unit Cost	Sales Price
5/1	Beginning Inventory	25	10	
5/3	Purchase	40	11	
5/9	Sale	45		18
5/11	Purchase	50	13	
5/18	Sale	30		21
5/22	Purchase	20	14	
5/28	Sale	30		25

Company accounting records indicate that the related operating expense for the month of May was $960.

Required:
1. Assume that Andrew uses a periodic inventory system and a FIFO cost flow assumption, record the May 3 through May 28 transactions (omit explanations).

2. Assume Andrew uses a perpetual inventory system and a FIFO cost flow assumption, record the May 3 through May 28 transactions (omit explanations).

Requirement 1 (Periodic Inventory System):

Date	Accounts and Explanation	PR	Debit	Credit

Requirement 2: Perpetual Inventory System

Date	Accounts and Explanation	PR	Debit	Credit

2.

Refer to the information in Demonstration Problem #1. Assuming Andrew uses a periodic system, complete the income statement columns below. (Round income statement figures to whole dollar amounts.)

	LIFO	FIFO	Weighted-Average
Sales			
Cost of Goods Sold:			
Beginning Inventory			
Net Purchases			
Cost of Goods Available for Sale			
Ending Inventory			
Cost of Goods Sold			
Gross Margin			
Operating Expenses			
Operating Income (Loss)			

SOLUTIONS

Matching

1	Q	5	B	9	G	13	C	17	J
2	M	6	O	10	R	14	S	18	P
3	E	7	I	11	A	15	H	19	F
4	T	8	K	12	N	16	D	20	L

Multiple Choice

1	A
2	B
3	A
4	C
5	C
6	D
7	A
8	B
9	C
10	A
11	C
12	B
13	C
14	D
15	D

Completion

1. merchandise inventory
2. cost of goods sold
3. perpetual
4. Both systems require a physical count. In a perpetual inventory system, this verifies that the inventory listed in the accounting records actually exists.
5. Last-In, First-Out.
6. conservatism (The LCM rule ensures that a business reports its inventory at its replacement cost if that is lower than its original cost. This rule ensures that assets are not overstated and that declines in inventory value are reported on the income statement in the period of the decline.)
7. LIFO (The oldest and therefore lower prices are used to value ending inventory.)
8. specific unit cost
9. First-In, First-Out.
10. invoice (To the seller, the invoice results in a sale being recorded. To the purchaser, the same invoice results in a purchase being recorded.)
11. periodic (In a periodic system, Purchases is debited and Cash (or Accounts Payable) is credited.)
12. Gross margin or gross profit (The basic income statement formula for a merchandising company is:
Sales
– Cost of Goods Sold
Gross margin
– Operating expenses
13. perpetual (Under the perpetual system, all merchandise is debited to the Inventory account
    when acquired and credited to the Inventory account when sold.)
14. gross margin divided by net sales
15. cost of goods sold divided by average inventory

True/False

I. T

2. F A LIFO reserve will be present only when the company uses LIFO costing.

3. F Inventory and Cost of Goods Sold accounts are features of a perpetual inventory system.

4. T

5. T

6. F While gross margin and gross profit are synonymous terms, the denominator in the calculation for the gross margin rate is net sales revenue, not cost of goods sold.

7. T

8. F Inventory transactions are operating activities, not investing activities.

9. T

10. T

11. F With rising costs, FIFO results in the highest value for ending inventory because FIFO assigns the most recent costs (and therefore the highest) to ending inventory.

12. T

13. F LIFO reports old cost amounts for ending inventory because it assigns the most recent costs to cost of goods sold.

14. F It would be virtually impossible for a grocery store to trace each item on hand (a large grocery store will have thousands of items on hand) with its actual cost.

15. F From a historical perspective, perpetual inventory systems were costly and labor-intensive, used only for relatively high dollar items. The most common inventory method was the periodic method, at least prior to the introduction of bar codes, scanners, and inventory-tracking software.

Exercises

Exercise 1:

A. Beginning inventory 600
   + Purchases* 4,000
   Shoes available for sale 4,600
   − Shoes sold 3,800
   Ending inventory <u>800</u>
   *Sum of purchases on 3/7 (800), 3/13 (1,400), 3/22 (1,400), and 3/29 (400).

B. 3/1 600 pairs at $40 $ 24,000
   3/7 800 44 35,200
   3/13 1,400 48 67,200
   3/22 1,400 50 70,000
   3/29 <u>400</u> 46 <u>18,400</u>
   Goods available <u>4,600</u> <u>$214,800</u>
   Average unit cost = $214,800 ÷ 4,600 = $46.70 (rounded)
   Ending inventory = 800 pairs $46.70 = $37,360

Cost of goods sold = 3,800 pairs x $46.70 = $177,460
Merchandise Inventory, Cost of Goods Sold, and Gross Profit 159

C. Ending inventory will be the last 800 pairs purchased.

3/29 400 pairs at $46	$18,400
3/22 400 pairs at $50	20,000
Ending inventory	$38.400
Cost of goods available for sale	$ 214,800
– Ending inventory –	38,400
Cost of goods sold	$176,400

D. Ending inventory will be the 800 pairs that have been in inventory the longest.

Beginning inventory 600 pairs at $40	$24,000
3/7 200 pairs at $44	8,800
Ending inventory	32,800
Cost of goods available for sale	$214,800
– Ending inventory –	32,800
Cost of goods sold	$182,000

Exercise 2:

Beginning inventory $160,000
+ Purchases 600,000
Cost of goods available for sale 760,000
– Cost of goods sold [$720,000 x (1 – .50)] 360,000
Ending inventory $400,000

Exercise 3:

For Xl, ending inventory decreases to $9,000, so cost of goods sold will increase to $44,000

For X2, beginning inventory decreases to $9,000, and ending inventory increases to $16,000, so:

Beginning inventory $ 9,000
+ Net purchases 50,000
Goods available for sale 59,000
– Ending inventory 16,000
Cost of goods sold $43,000

For X3, beginning inventory increases to $16,000, so cost of goods sold increases to $63,000

Exercise 4:

Requirement 1
Sales – Sales Returns & Allowances – Sales Discount = Net Sales
$28,610 – $205 – $360 = $28,045

Requirement 2
Net Sales – Cost of Goods Sold = Gross Profit (or Gross Margin)
$28,045 – $19,225 = $8,820

Requirement 3
Gross Margin – Operating Expenses = Net Income
$8,820 – $3,150 = $5,670

Requirement 4
Gross Margin + Net Sales
$8,820 ÷ $28,045 = 31.4%

Requirement 5
Cost of Goods Sold ÷ Average Inventory
Average Inventory = ($4,000 + $2,400) ÷ 2 $3,200
$19,225 ÷ $3,200 = 6 times

Exercise 5:

Requirement 1
Sales – Sales Discounts – Sales Returns & Allowances = Net Sales
$51,500 – $500 – $1,700 = $49,300

Requirement 2
Purchases – Purchase Discounts – Purchase Returns & Allowances = Net Purchases
$39,250 – $550 – $600 = $38,100

Requirement 3
Net Sales – Cost of Goods Sold = Gross Profit
Cost of Goods Sold $49,300 – $7,500 = $41,800

Requirement 4
Beginning Inventory + Net Purchase - Ending Inventory = Cost of Goods Sold
Therefore, Ending Inventory = Beginning Inventory + Net Purchase – Cost of Goods Sold
Ending Inventory = $12,250 + $38,100 – $41,800 = $8,550
Merchandise Inventory, Cost of Goods Sold, and Gross Profit 161

Requirement 5
Gross Profit – Operating Expenses = Net Income
$7,500 – $3,100 = $4,400

Requirement 6
Inventory Turnover Rate = Cost of Goods Sold + Average Inventory
Average Inventory ($12,250 + $8,550) ÷ 2 = $10,400
Inventory Turnover Rate = $41,800 ÷ $10,400 = 4 times
Requirement 7
Gross Margin Rate = Gross Margin ± Net sales
Gross Margin Rate = $7,500 ÷ $49,300 = 15.2%

Critical Thinking

The 100-pair difference is called inventory shrinkage. Since the figure that appears on the balance sheet for ending inventory must represent the actual amount on hand (700 pairs), the shrinkage is accounted for by a larger cost of goods sold figure on the income statement. Possible explanations for the shrinkage are errors in the physical count, theft, and/or errors in recording purchases during the period. Internal control requires that the cause of the difference be investigated and appropriate corrective procedures taken.

Demonstration Problems

1. Solved and Explained

Requirement 1 (Periodic Inventory System)

Date	Accounts and Explanation	PR	Debit	Credit
5/3	Purchases		440	
	Account Payable			440
5/9	Account Receivable		810	
	Sales			810
5/I1	Purchases		650	
	Account Payable			650
5/18	Account Receivable		630	
	Sales			630
5/22	Purchases		280	
	Account Payable			280
5/28	Account Receivable		750	
	Sales			750

These six journal entries are pretty straightforward. With a periodic system, the Purchase account is debited as merchandise for resale is acquired, but is not affected when goods are sold.

Study Tip: In a periodic system, the cost flow assumption (in this case FIFO) is irrelevant as far as these transactions are concerned. It becomes important only when you need to determine the value of ending inventory.

Requirement 2 (Perpetual Inventory System)

Date	Accounts and Explanation	PR	Debit	Credit
5/3	Inventory		440	
	Account Payable			440
5/9	Account Receivable		810	
	Sales			810
	Cost of Goods Sold		470	
	Inventory			470
	(25 $10 + 20 x $11)			
5/11 —	Inventory		650	
	Account Payable			650
5/18	Account Receivable		630	
	Sales			630
	Cost of Goods Sold		350	
	Inventory			350
	(20 x $11 + 10 x $13)			
5/22	Inventory		280	
	Account Payable			280
5/28	Account Receivable		750	
	Sales			750
	Cost of Goods Sold		390	
	Inventory			390
	(30 x $13)			

In a perpetual system, goods for resale are debited to the Inventory account. When a sale occurs, the entry is identical to those recorded in a periodic system. However, a second entry is required for each sale. This entry transfers the cost of the sale from the Inventory account to a Cost of Goods Sold Account. The amount of the entry is determined by the cost flow assumption used. In this problem, FIFO is assumed. Therefore, the cost of each sale is assigned using the oldest costs in the inventory. For instance, the 5/9 sale was 45 units. How much did these units cost the business? Assuming FIFO, 25 of the units cost $10 each (these are the units from the beginning inventory, i.e., the first units (oldest) in the inventory), and the next 20 units (45-25) cost $11 each (the purchase on 5/3). This same analysis applies to the 5/18 and 5/28 sales. The details for each entry are provided following each entry.

2.

Requirement 1

Andrew's Appliance
Income Statement
Month Ended May 31, 2005

	LIFO	FIFO	Weighted-Average
Sales revenue	$2, 190	$2,190	$2,190
Cost of goods sold:			
Beginning inventory	250	250	250
Net purchases	1,370	1,370	1,370
Cost of goods available for sale	1,620	1,620	1,620
Ending inventory	305	410	360
Cost of goods sold	1,315	1,210	1,260
Gross margin	875	980	930
Operating expenses	960	960	960
Operating income (loss)	$ (85)	$ 20	$ (30)

Computations:

Sales Revenue:

Sale Date	Quantity	Price	Total
5/9	45	$18	$ 810
5/18	30	21	630
5/28	30	25	750
	105		$2,190

Sales revenue is unaffected by the firm's method of accounting for inventory costs. Quantity

^{x} Price = Total. Beginning inventory: 5/1 quantity (25 units) x unit cost ($10) = $250

Purchase Date	Quantity	Price	Total
5/3	40	$ 11	$ 440
5/11	50	13	650
5/22	20	14	280
	110		$1,370

Computation for beginning inventory, purchases, and goods available for sale are identical under the three methods.

	Beginning inventory in units	25
+	Total May purchases in units	110
	Units available for sale	135
−	Units sold	105
	Ending inventory in units	30

Valued at LIFO:

Purchase Date	Quantity	Price	Total
Beginning inventory	25	$10	$250
5/3	5	11	55
	30		$305

LIFO attains the best matching of current expense with current revenue. The most recently acquired costs (the last items in) are deemed sold first (the first ones out). Logically, ending inventory should consist of the oldest layers of cost.

Valued at FIFO:

Purchase Date	Quantity	Price	Total
5/22	20	$14	$280
5/1I	10	13	130
	30		$410

FIFO reports the ending inventory at its most recent cost. The oldest costs are expensed as cost of goods sold. Note that net income under FIFO is larger than that reported under LIFO. In a period of rising prices, LIFO will generally produce a lower net income. The potential tax savings achieved under a LIFO valuation has made it an increasingly popular valuation method in recent years.

Valued at weighted-average cost:

Purchase Date	Quantity	Price	Total
Beginning inventory	25	$10	$ 250
Purchases in May	110	Various	1,370
	135		$1,620

$1,620 inventory cost / 135 units = $12 per unit (rounded)

30 ending inventory units ^{x} $12 weighted-average cost per unit = $360

The weighted-average cost method reports ending inventory and produces operating income that falls between the results of FIFO and LIFO. It is not used as a valuation method by as many firms as LIFO and FIFO.

Chapter 7

PLANT ASSETS, NATURAL RESOURCES, & INTANGIBLES

CHAPTER OBJECTIVES

The learning objectives for this chapter are as follows:

1. Determine the cost of a plant asset
2. Account for depreciation
3. Select the best depreciation method
4. Analyze the effect of a plant asset disposal
5. Account for natural resources and depletion
6. Account for intangible assets and amortization
7. Report plant asset transactions on the statement of cash flows

CHAPTER OVERVIEW

Accounting for so-called "capital assets" is a very important part of a firm's financial statement. Capital assets is a broad term that includes both plant (or fixed) assets and intangible assets. Fixed assets are tangible, long-lived assets. Tangible means that they can be seen and touched, and their value is derived from this trait. Intangible assets have little or no physical form. For the most part, they can't be seen or touched, nor do they derive any value from their physical form. They derive value from having some special (often legal) right. This category includes patents, copyrights and trademarks. Goodwill is a special type of intangible asset.

The costs of capital assets are reflected in two different financials statements, as outlined below:

Asset Account (Balance Sheet)	Expense Account (Income Statement)
Plant Assets	
Land	None
Buildings, Machinery, and Equipment	Depreciation
Furniture and Fixtures	Depreciation
Land Improvements	Depreciation
Natural Resources	Depletion
Intangibles	
Legal Rights (copyrights, trademarks, etc.)	Amortization
Goodwill	Loss

CHAPTER REVIEW

Objective 1—Determine the cost of a plant asset

General Rule: The cost of any asset is the sum of all the costs incurred to bring the asset to its intended use.

Land – includes
1. the purchase price,
2. brokerage commission,
3. survey fees, legal fees,
4. back property taxes,
5. land grading and clearing costs,
6. the cost of removing or demolishing unwanted structures.

Buildings – includes
New:
1. architectural fees
2. building permits
3. contractors' charges
4. payments for materials, labor and overhead
5. interest on money borrowed to finance construction

Purchased:
1. purchase price
2. brokerage commission
3. sales and other taxes
4. repair and renovation costs

Land Improvements include
1. paving
2. driveways
3. signs
4. fences
5. sprinkler systems

Equipment includes
1. purchase price
2. transportation costs
3. insurance
4. sales and other taxes
5. purchase commission
6. installation costs
7. equipment testing costs
8. special platforms

Lump-Sum (Basket) Purchases of Assets
Sometimes purchases of assets are done in a group, not individually. In these cases, it is necessary to estimate the cost of the individual assets. The cost is allocated on a simple percentage basis of their relative sales values. This method is called the Relative Sales Value Method. Here is a simple example of a purchase of $10,000 of assets for only $7,500 (a bargain!):

Asset	Sales Value		Market Value		Percentage of Total Market Value		Total Cost		Allocated Cost of Each Asset
Land	$ 1,000	÷	$ 10,000	=	10% X	$	7,500	= $	750
Building	$ 9,000	÷	$ 10,000	=	90% X	$	7,500	= $	6,750
Total	$10,000	÷	$ 10,000	=	100% X	$	7,500	= $	7,500

Capital Expenditures are disbursements that increase the asset's capacity or extend its useful life. They are added to the cost of the asset on the balance sheet. They are not directly expensed.

Repair and Maintenance Expenses are disbursements that do *not* extend the asset's capacity or extend its useful life. They are *never* added to the cost of the asset on the balance sheet. They are *always* directly expensed.

Depreciation is the process of allocating an asset's cost over its useful life. This is an estimated cost of doing business due to physical wear and tear, and obsolescence of the asset.
1. Depreciation is only an estimate – does not reflect reality
2. Depreciation is not a representation of market value
3. Depreciation does not mean cash is "set aside" for later use or replacement

Depreciation methods require three figures are available:
1. The cost of the asset
2. The estimated useful life of the asset – a guess as to how long the asset will remain in service
3. The estimated residual value of the asset – also know as the salvage or scrap value, this is an estimate of how much cash the firm will receive at the end of the asset's useful value and is sold. This number may be zero.

Book Value = Asset – Accumulated Depreciation (a contra-asset)

Objective 2—Account for depreciation

Depreciation Methods
1. Straight-Line
2. Units-of-Production
3. Double-Declining-Balance (Accelerated Depreciation)

Depreciation formulas:

Straight-line depreciation per year	=	$\dfrac{\text{Cost} - \text{Residual Value}}{\text{Useful life, in years}}$		

Units-of-Production depreciation Expense per unit of output	=	$\dfrac{\text{Cost} - \text{Residual Value}}{\text{Useful life, in units of production}}$		

Double-Declining-Balance Depreciation Expense per year	=	$\dfrac{2}{\text{Estimated Useful Life}}$	X	Book Value

Comparative example of using different depreciation methods:

Common information of equipment purchased on January 1, 2006:

Description	Amounts
Cost of Equipment	$11,000
Less Estimated Residual Value	(1,000)
Depreciable Cost	$10,000
Estimated Useful Life:	
Years	5
Units of Production	10,000 units

Straight-line:

Date	Depreciation Rate: 1/5 = 20%		Depreciable Cost		Depreciation Expense		Accumulated Depreciation		Asset Book Value
1/1/2006									$11,000
12/31/2006	0.2	X	$10,000	=	$ 2,000	$	2,000	$	9,000
12/31/2007	0.2	X	$10,000	=	$ 2,000	$	4,000	$	7,000
12/31/2008	0.2	X	$10,000	=	$ 2,000	$	6,000	$	5,000
12/31/2009	0.2	X	$10,000	=	$ 2,000	$	8,000	$	3,000
12/31/2010	0.2	X	$10,000	=	$ 2,000	$	10,000	$	1,000

Units-of-Production:

Date	Depreciation per Unit: $1		Number of Units		Depreciation Expense	Accumulated Depreciation	Asset Book Value
1/1/2006							$ 11,000
12/31/2006	$	1 X	500	= $	500	$ 500	$ 10,500
12/31/2007	$	1 X	1,500	= $	1,500	$ 2,000	$ 9,000
12/31/2008	$	1 X	3,000	= $	3,000	$ 5,000	$ 6,000
12/31/2009	$	1 X	2,000	= $	2,000	$ 7,000	$ 4,000
12/31/2010	$	1 X	3,000	= $	3,000	$ 10,000	$ 1,000

Double-Declining-Balance:

Date	January 1 Book Value		DDB Rate = 2÷5		Depreciation Expense	Accumulated Depreciation	December 31 Book Value
1/1/2006	$ 41,000						$ 41,000
12/31/2006	$ 41,000	X	40%	=	$ 16,400	$ 16,400	$ 24,600
12/31/2007	$ 24,600	X	40%	=	$ 9,840	$ 26,240	$ 14,760
12/31/2008	$ 14,760	X	40%	=	$ 5,904	$ 32,144	$ 8,856
12/31/2009	$ 8,856	X	40%	=	$ 3,542	$ 35,686	$ 5,314
12/31/2010					$ 4,314	$ 40,000	$ 1,000

Note: Depreciation Expense in last year is a "plug" or a force figure to ensure that the ending book value equals the needed residual value.

Objective 3—Select the best depreciation method

Accelerated depreciation methods, such as the double-declining-balance method, maximize depreciation expense in the early years of an asset's life. This is a legitimate income tax deduction that will minimize income taxes in those early years.

Depreciation for mid-year asset purchases (partial year) – multiply the depreciation expense for the whole year by the portion of the year the asset is actually held. For example, an asset purchased on October 1 of a given year would use 25% (3 months owned ÷ 12 months in a whole year).

Changing the useful life of an asset is referred to as a change in accounting estimate. This means that the change will be reflected prospectively only. The firm will not change previously issued financial statements. Rather, the firm will make the change in the current year, and adjust only the current and all future financial statements to reflect the change.

Fully depreciated assets are those assets that have a book value of zero. In other words, the cost of the asset is perfectly balanced by an equal amount of depreciation. Such an asset is left on the books until it is physically disposed of.

Objective 4—Analyze the effect of a plant asset disposal

Disposing of long-term assets may result in a gain or a loss. This gain or loss is determined by comparing the amount of cash received, if any, to the current book value of the assets. For instance, consider the above example of any of the depreciation methods. If the asset is sold on January 1, 2011, for $3,000, the firm would recognize a gain of $2,000 ($3,000 cash - $1,000 book value). On the other hand, if the asset is sold on January 1, 2011, for $250 cash, the firm would recognize a loss of $750 ($250 cash - $1,000 book value). If the asset is simply disposed of on that date (hauled to the trash dump), no cash would be received, and a full $1,000 loss would be recorded.

Exchanging similar assets will result in no gain or loss on the transaction.

Objective 5—Account for natural resources and depletion

Natural (consumable) resources are expensed through depletion. Depletion is calculated using the same units-of-production method found in the depreciation section.

Objective 6—Account for intangible assets and amortization

Intangible assets representing legal rights are expensed through an amortization account. The most common approach used for allocating expenses is the straight-line method. Legal right intangible assets include patents (20-year life), copyrights (70-year life), trademarks (various lives), and franchises and licenses (various lives).

A special type of intangible is Goodwill. Goodwill is recorded only when one company buys another company, and pays more than the value of the "net assets" (assets – liabilities) for the other firm. Goodwill has an indefinite life, but must be evaluated annually. This annual evaluation is conducted for the express purpose of determining whether goodwill has been "impaired" (lost some or all of its future value). An immediate write-off (to an income statement loss account) is done for the amount of any impairment uncovered.

Objective 7—Report plant asset transactions on the statement of cash flows

Operating Activities Section:
- Depreciation expense is always added back to net income, as depreciation reduced net income, but never uses cash.

Investing Activities Section:
- Capital expenditures are reported as a use of cash (a negative cash flow, or an outflow).
- Disposals (sales) of capital assets are reported as a source of cash (a positive cash flow, or an inflow).

TEST YOURSELF

Matching

Match each numbered item with its lettered definition.

_____ 1. trademark
_____ 2. goodwill
_____ 3. depreciable cost
_____ 4. intangible asset
_____ 5. estimated residual value
_____ 6. amortization
_____ 7. plant asset
_____ 8. capital expenditure
_____ 9. franchises and licenses
_____ 10. patent

_____ 11. units-of-production method
_____ 12. estimated useful life
_____ 13. accelerated depreciation method
_____ 14. straight-line (SL) method
_____ 15. double-declining-balance method
_____ 16. copyright
_____ 17. depletion expense
_____ 18. brand name
_____ 19. natural resources
_____ 20. Modified Accelerated Cost Recovery System (MACRS)

A. depreciation method that writes off a relatively larger amount of the asset's cost nearer the start of its useful life than the straight-line method does.
B. has no physical form, a special right to current and expected future benefits.
C. length of a service that a business expects to get from an asset.
D. expense that applies to intangible assets in the same way depreciation applies to plant assets and depletion applies to natural resources.
E. exclusive right to reproduce and sell a book, musical composition, film, other work of art, or computer program; extends 50 years beyond the author's life.
F. depreciation method used only for income tax purposes; assets are grouped into classes, and for a given class deprecation is computed by the double-declining-balance method, the 150%-declining-balance method, or, for most real estate, the straight-line method.
G. excess of the cost of an acquired company over the sum of the market values of its net assets.
H. depreciation method in which an equal amount of depreciation expense is assigned to each year (or period) of asset use.
I. a distinctive identification of a product or service.

J. expected cash value of an asset at the end of its useful life.

K. plant assets of a special type, such as iron ore, petroleum (oil), and timber which are expensed through depreciation (depletion).

L. cost of a plant asset minus its estimated residual value.

M. that portion of the cost of a natural resource that is used up in a particular period.

N. privileges granted by a private business or a government to sell product or service in accordance with specified conditions.

O. depreciation method by which a fixed amount of depreciation is assigned to each unit of output produced by the plant asset.

P. expenditure that increases an asset's capacity or efficiency or extends its useful life.

Q. a federal government grant giving the holder the exclusive right for 20 years to produce and sell an invention.

R. distinctive identification of a product or service.

S. depreciation method that computes annual depreciation by multiplying the asset's decreasing book value by a constant percentage.

T. long-lived assets, such as land, buildings, and equipment, used in the operation of the business.

Multiple Choice

Circle the best answer.

1. Which of the following is **not** a plant asset?
    a. supplies
    b. furniture
    c. buildings
    d. land

2. All amounts paid to acquire a plant asset and to get it ready for its intended use are referred to as:
    a. immediate expenses
    b. capital expenditures
    c. salvage value
    d. the cost of an asset

3. The cost of land would include all of the following except:
    a. purchase price
    b. back property taxes
    c. clearing the land
    d. sidewalks and curbs

4. Which of the following is **not** an intangible asset?
    a. accounts receivable
    b. patent
    c. copyright
    d. goodwill

5. The cost of paving a parking lot should be charged to:
   a. land
   b. land improvements
   c. immediate expense
   d. repairs and maintenance expense

6. A lump-sum acquisition of assets requires an allocation of the purchase price among the assets acquired. This allocation is called the:
   a. cost method
   b. allocation method
   c. relative sales value method
   d. book-value method

7. Which of the following would **not** be included in the Land account?
   a. brokerage commissions connected with the purchase of the land
   b. survey fees connected with the purchase of the land
   c. paving costs for a driveway
   d. back property taxes paid

8. Land, buildings, and equipment are acquired for a lump sum of $950,000. The market values of the three assets are respectively, $200,000, $500,000, and $300,000. What is the cost assigned to the building?
   a. $190,000
   b. $475,000
   c. $500,000
   d. $555,556

9. Land is purchased for $60,000. Back taxes paid by the purchaser were $2,400, clearing and grading costs were $3,000, fencing costs were $2,500, and lighting costs were $500. What is the cost of the land?
   a. $60,000
   b. $65,400
   c. $66,700
   d. $67,200

10. Which of the following would **not** be included in the Machinery account?
    a. cost of transporting the machinery to its setup location
    b. cost of a maintenance insurance plan after the machinery is up and running
    c. cost of installing the machinery
    d. cost of insurance while the machinery is in transit

11. Stockton Corporation purchased equipment for $32,000. Stockton also paid $400 for freight and insurance while the equipment was in transit. Sales tax amounted to $240. Insurance, taxes, and maintenance the first year of use cost $1,000. How much should Stockton Corporation capitalize as the cost of the equipment?
    a. $30,000
    b. $30,400
    c. $32,640
    d. $31,640

12. The removal of an old building to make land suitable for its intended use is charged to:
    a. land
    b. land improvements
    c. land improvements expense
    d. renovation and restoration expense

13. Best Company acquired land and buildings for $1,500,000. The land is appraised at $475,000 and the buildings are appraised at $775,000. The debit to the Buildings account will be:
    a. $930,000
    b. $775,000
    c. $712,500
    d. $570,000

14. Which expense below would **not** be considered part of the cost of a plant asset?
    a. the price paid for the plant asset when purchased from the manufacturer
    b. taxes paid on the purchase price of the plant asset
    c. commissions paid to the salesperson that sold the plant asset
    d. repaving a driveway to the building where the plant asset is housed

15. Galaxy Corporation purchased land and a building for $700,000. An appraisal indicates that the land's value is $400,000 and the building's value is $350,000. The amount that Galaxy should debit to the Building account is:
    a. $326,667
    b. $350,000
    c. $373,333
    d. $375,000

Completion

Complete each of the following statements.

1. Two distinguishing characteristics of plant assets are that they are _____ and
   _____.
2. Depreciation is defined as_____.
3. Depreciation is a _____ expense.
4. Most companies use _____ depreciation for tax purposes.
5. The maximum time period over which an intangible asset can be amortized is _____
   years.
6. When two or more assets are purchased in a group, the total cost of the assets is
   allocated to individual assets by the _____ method.
7. To calculate depreciation, you must know the following four items: 1) _____
   2) _____ , 3) _____ , and 4) _____ .
8. Depreciation is an example of the _____ principle.
9. _____ relates to natural resources, while _____ relates to
   intangible assets.
10. _____ is used to depreciate assets for federal tax purposes.
11. Proceeds from the sale of plant assets are listed in the _____ activities
    section of the statement of cash flows.
12. The most widely used depreciation method for financial statements is
    _____.
13. Depreciation expense is listed in the _____ activities section of the
    statement of cash flows.
14. Costs related to plant assets can be classified as either _____ expenditures
    or _____ expenditures.

True/False

For each of the following statements, circle T *for true or* F *for false.*

1.   T F   The expense associated with plant assets is called depreciation.
2.   T F   Historical cost is the price the asset could be sold for.
3.   T F   When an existing building is purchased, its cost excludes the sales and other taxes paid, all expenditures to repair and renovate the building for its intended purpose.
4.   T F   The cost of leasehold improvements should be depreciated over the term of the lease.
5.   T F   Businesses record depreciation based on changes in the market value of their plant assets.
6.   T F   If there is no expected residual value, the full cost of the asset is depreciated.
7.   T F   At the end of its useful life, the asset is said to be fully depreciated.
8.   T F   Most companies use the double-declining-balance depreciation method.
9.   T F   Congress designs tax depreciation to raise tax revenue for the government.
10.   T F   The cost of obtaining a copyright from the government is high.
11.   T F   Most companies use computerized systems to account for fixed assets, which automatically calculate the depreciation expense for each period.
12.   T F   It is ethical for some companies to keep one set of depreciation records for its financial statements and one for reporting to the IRS.
13.   T F   Accelerated depreciation results in lower expenses and lower tax payments early in the asset's life.
14.   T F   Amortization expense for an intangible asset can be written off directly against the asset account rather than held in an accumulated amortization account.
15.   T F   The cost of natural resources is expensed through depletion.

Exercises

1. A company buys Machines 1, 2, and 3 for $90,000. The market values of the machines are $30,000, $36,000, and $54,000, respectively. What cost will be allocated to each machine?

2. Wendy's Weavings purchased equipment for $54,000 on January 4, 2006. Wendy expects the machine to produce 125,000 units over four years and then expects to sell the machine for $14,000. Wendy produced 30,000 units the first year and 45,000 units the second year. Compute the depreciation expense for 2006 and 2007. Round your answer to the nearest dollar.

	2006	**2007**
Straight-line		
Units-of-production		
Double-declining-balance		

3. On January 2, 2006, Latasha Landscape purchased used equipment for $19,000. Latasha expected the equipment to remain in service for 5 years. She depreciated the equipment on a straight-line basis with $2,000 salvage value. On June 30, 2006, Latasha sold the equipment for $2,800. Record depreciation expense for the equipment for the six months ended June 30, 2006, and also record the sale of the equipment.

Date	Accounts and Explanation	PR	Debit	Credit

4. On August 20, 2006, May Lieu, owner of May's Manufacturing, purchased a new drill press for the business. The new equipment carried an invoice price of $9,700 plus a 6% sales tax. In addition, the purchaser was responsible for $460 of freight charges. The sale was subject to 3/15, n/45 discount/credit terms. Upon receipt of the new equipment, May paid $925 to have the press installed and connected. To finance this purchase, May borrowed $11,000 from the bank for 90 days at 10% interest. May paid the invoice within 15 days, earning the 3% discount.

a. Classify each of the following costs as revenue or capital expenditures.

Cost	Classification
a. $9,700 (equipment)	
b. $582 (sales tax)	
c. $460 (freight)	
d. $291 (discount)	
e. $925 (installation)	
f. $275 (interest on loan)	

b. Based on your answer from 1, calculate the fully capitalized cost of the new equipment.

c. Calculate 2006 depreciation using double-declining-balance assuming a six-year life with estimated residual value of $1,000.

5. On October 1, 2006, Star Company purchased Wars Company for $10,400,000 cash. The market value of Wars's assets was $16,200,000, and Wars had liabilities of $9,000,000.

a. Compute the cost of the goodwill purchased by Star Company.

b. Record the purchase by Star Company.

Date	Accounts and Explanation	PR	Debit	Credit

Critical Thinking

Explain the concept of depreciation. Include in your discussion one common misconception regarding depreciation and its impact on the finances of a business.

Demonstration Problems

1.

On January 1, 2005, Marissa Estrada purchased three pieces of equipment. Details of the cost, economic life, residual value, and method of depreciation are shown below:

Equipment	Cost	Useful Life	Residual Value	Depreciation Method
X	$24,000	6 yrs	$3,000	straight-line
Y	16,000	40,000 units	800	units-of-production
Z	18,000	5 yrs	3,000	double-declining-balance

Required:

1. Prepare a schedule computing the depreciation expense for each piece of equipment over its useful life.
2. Prepare the journal entry to record the disposal of Equipment X. Assume that it has been depreciated over its useful life, and that it cannot be sold or exchanged (it is being scrapped).
3. Prepare the journal entry to record the sale of Equipment Y for $1,000. Assume that it has been depreciated over its useful life.

Requirement 1 (Schedule of depreciation)

	X	Y	Z
Asset Cost			
Less Residual Value			
Depreciable Cost			

Equipment X
Schedule of Depreciation Expense
(Straight-line Method)

Year	Depreciable Cost	Depreciable Rate	Depreciation Expense

Equipment Y
Schedule of Depreciation Expense
(Units-of-Production Method)

Year	Depreciable Cost	Units Produced	Depreciation Expense
		12,400	
		10,750	
		11,230	
		6,100	

Equipment Z
Schedule of Depreciation Expense
(Double-Declining-Balance Method)

Year	Book Value X Rate	Depreciation Expense	Book Value

Requirement 2 (Journal entry – Equipment X)

Date	Accounts and Explanation	PR	Debit	Credit

Requirement 3 (Journal entry – Equipment Y)

Date	Accounts and Explanation	PR	Debit	Credit

2.
On June 10, 2005, Clark Catering purchased new kitchen equipment costing $22,500 plus 6% sales tax. The equipment is expected to last eight years and retain an estimated $1,500 residual value. In addition, Clark paid transportation and insurance charges of $410. The equipment arrived on June 21 and required modification of the existing electrical system. An electrician was scheduled the following day and spent two days installing the new equipment. The electrician's charge was $65 per hour for two 8-hour days, or $1,040 total. The equipment was placed in service on June 24, 2005.

On January 5, 2008, repairs costing $4,500 were made which increased the life of the equipment two additional years. On August 18, 2009, some routine repairs were made costing $480.

On April 10, 2010, Clark decided the 80-hour work weeks were taking too heavy a toll on his personal life and closed the business. He sold the equipment for $4,200 cash.

The company closes its books on December 31 and uses the straight-line method.

Required:

Present journal entries to record the following:

1. the purchase of the equipment on June 10, 2005
2. payment of the transportation charges
3. payment of the electrician's charges
4. depreciation for 2005
5. the repair on January 5, 2008
6. depreciation for 2008
7. the repair on August 18, 2009
8. depreciation for 2009
9. depreciation up to date of sale
10. the equipment sale on April 10, 2010

Date	Accounts and Explanation	PR	Debit	Credit

SOLUTIONS

Matching

1	R	5	J	9	N	13	A	17	M
2	G	6	D	10	Q	14	H	18	I
3	L	7	T	11	O	15	S	19	K
4	B	8	P	12	C	16	E	20	F

Multiple Choice

1	A
2	D
3	D
4	A
5	B
6	C
7	C
8	B
9	B
10	B
11	C
12	A
13	A
14	D
15	A

Completion

1. long-lived, tangible (The physical form (tangibility) of plant assets provides their usefulness.)
2. a systematic allocation of an asset's cost to expense (Depreciation is not a method of asset valuation.)
3. noncash (Cash is expended either at the acquisition of a plant asset or over time as the asset is paid for. The debit to Depreciation Expense is balanced by a credit to Accumulated Depreciation, not Cash.)
4. accelerated (MACRS) (Accelerated depreciation methods cause larger depreciation deductions in the first years of an asset's life. The larger deductions result in lower taxable income and lower taxes.)
5. 40
6. relative-sales-value (The need to depreciate each asset separately makes it necessary to allocate the purchase price by some reasonable manner.)
7. cost; estimated useful life; estimated residual value; depreciation method (Order is not important.)
8. matching (Matching means to identify and measure all expenses incurred during the period and to match them against the revenue earned during that period.)
9. Depletion; amortization
10. MACRS (Modified Accelerated Cost Recovery System)
11. investing
12. straight-line
13. operating
14. capital; revenue (Order not important.)

True/False

1. F   R&D costs are generally treated as revenue expenditures and therefore debited to an expense account.
2. F   Accelerated depreciation records larger amounts of depreciation expense when the asset is newer, and lesser amounts as the asset ages. Therefore, book value (cost less accumulated depreciation) will be lower when the asset is newer.
3. F   The amount of total depreciation is not affected by the method used. Instead, the method determines how the depreciable cost is spread.
4. T
5. F   Revenue expenditures are recorded as expenses.
6. F   Depreciable cost equals cost less residual value.
7. F   Accelerated depreciation results in the opposite—decreasing amounts as the assets become older.
8. T
9. T
10. F   Leasehold improvements are either depreciated or amortized. Depletion relates to natural resources.
11. T
12. F   Amortization, not depreciation, is the term used to spread the cost of an intangible asset over its useful life.
13. F   The acquisition of plant assets is an investing activity, not an operating activity.
14. F   The formula is remaining depreciable basis (not book value) divided by remaining useful life.
15. T

Exercises

1. Machine 1 = [$30,000 / ($30,000 + $36,000 + $54,000)] x $90,000 = $22,500
    Machine 2 = [$36,000 / ($30,000 + $36,000 + $54,000)] x $90,000 = $27,000
    Machine 3 = [$54,000 / ($30,000 + $36,000 + $54,000)] x $90,000 = $40,500
    (Proof: $22,500 + $27,000 + $40,500 = $90,000)

2.

	2006	2007
Straight-line	10,000	10,000
Units-of-production	9,600	14,400
Double-declining-balance	27,000	13,500

Straight-line = ($54,000 - $14,000) / 4 years = $10,000

Units-of-production = (54,000 - 14,000) / 125,000 units = $0.32 per unit
2006 = $30,000 x $0.32 = $9,600
2007 = $45,000 x $0.32 = $14,400

Double-declining-balance:
DDB rate =(1/4)x2=.50 2005 = .50 x $54,000 = $27,000
Book value = $54,000 - $27,000 = $27,000
2007 = .50 ^{X} $27,000 = $13,500

3.

Annual depreciation = ($19,000 – $2,000) / 5 = $3,400
Accumulated depreciation 1 /1 /06 = 2 years @ $3,400 per year = $6,800

Date	Accounts and Explanation	PR	Debit	Credit
6-30	Depreciation Expense		1,700	
	Accumulated Depreciation			1,700
	Depreciation for six months			
6-30	Cash		2,800	
	Loss on Sale of Asset (Plug)		7,700	
	Accumulated Depreciation		8,500	
	Equipment			19,000

4.
A.

Cost	Classification
a. $9,700 (equipment)	Capital
b. $582 (sales tax)	Capital
c. $460 (freight)	Capital
d. $291 (discount)	Reduction of Capital
e. $925 (installation)	Capital
f. $275 (interest on loan)	Revenue

B.
$9,700 + 582 + 460 – 291 + 925 = $11,376

C.
Double-declining-balance = Book value x Rate
Book value = $11,376
Rate = 33 1 /3 %
$11,376 ^{X} 33 1/3 % = $3,792
Depreciation from 8/20/04 — 12/31/04 = 4 months
$3,792 ^{X} 4/12 = $1,264

5.

A.

Purchase Price		$10,400,000
Market Value	16,200,000	
Less: Liabilities	9,000,000	
Market Value of Net Assets		7,200,000
Goodwill		3,200,000

B

Date	Accounts and Explanation	PR	Debit	Credit
10-1	Assets		16,200,000	
	Goodwill		3,200,000	
	Liabilities			9,000,000
	Cash			10,400,000

Critical Thinking

Depreciation is the process of allocating a plant asset's cost to expense over the period the asset is used. This process is designed to match the asset's expense against the revenue generated over the asset's life. The primary purpose of depreciation is to help measure income properly. Depreciation is not a process of valuation, and depreciation does not mean that the business sets aside cash to replace assets as they become fully depreciated. Depreciation is a noncash expense. Depreciation does not impact cash flows from operations. It is a tax-deductible expense, thus decreasing income tax payments.

Demonstration Problems

1.

Requirement 1:

	X	Y	Z
Asset Cost	$24,000	$16,000	$18,000
Less: Depreciable Cost	3,000	800	3,000
Depreciable Cost	21,000	15,200	15,000

Equipment X
Schedule of Depreciation Expense
(Straight-Line Method)

Year	Depreciable Cost	Depreciable Rate	Depreciation Expense
2005	$21,000	1/6	$ 3,500
2005	21,000	1/6	3,500
2006	21,000	1/6	3,500
2007	21,000	1/6	3,500
2008	21,000	1/6	3,500
2009	21,000	1/6	3,500
		Total	$21,000

The book value of the equipment after 2009 is $3,000
(cost - accumulated depreciation = $24,000 − $21,000 = $3,000).

Equipment Y
Schedule of Depreciation Expense
(Units-of-Production)

Year	Depreciable Cost	Units Produced	Depreciation Expense
2004	15,200	12,400	4,712
2005	15,200	10,750	4,085
2006	15,200	11,230	4,267
2007	15,200	6,100	2,136
	Total		15,200

Notes: The per-unit cost is $0.38 ($15,200 / 40,000 units = $0.38)
The book value after 2007 is $800 ($16,000 − $15,200 = $800).
The original production estimate for the equipment was 40,000 units. The actual
production over the life of the equipment was 40,480. Assuming the original estimates
(for total production and residual value) are reasonable, the 2006 depreciation should be
based on 5,620 units, the number required to total 40,000 units.

Equipment Z
Schedule of Depreciation Expense
(Double-Declining-Balance)

Year	Book Value X Rate	Depreciation Expense	Book Value
2004	.4 x 18,000	7,200	10,800
2005	.4 x 10,800	4,320	6,480
2006	.4 x 6,480	2,592	3,888
2007	3,888-3,000	888	3,000
2008		0	3,000

The straight-line depreciation rate for an asset with useful life of 5 years is 1/5 per year, or 20%. Double the straight-line rate is 2/5, or 40%. This rate does not change from 2005 through 2008.

Depreciation expense for Equipment Z in the fourth year is not $1,555 ($3,888 x .40) because in the fourth year depreciation expense is the previous year's book value less the residual value ($3,888 - $3,000 = $888). As the asset is fully depreciated at the end of the fourth year, there is no depreciation recorded for the fifth year.

Requirements 2 & 3:

Date	Accounts and Explanation	PR	Debit	Credit
	2			
	Accumulated Depreciation – X		21,000	
	Loss on Disposal of Equipment (plug)		3,000	
	Equipment X			24,000
	3			
	Cash		1,000	
	Accumulated Depreciation – Y		15,200	
	Equipment Y			16,000
	Gain on Sale of Equipment (plug)			200

When fully depreciated assets cannot be sold or exchanged, an entry removing them from the books is necessary upon disposal. The entry credits the asset account and debits its related Accumulated Depreciation account. If the fully depreciated asset has no residual value, no loss on the disposal occurs. In most cases, however, it will be necessary to record a debit to a Loss on Disposal account to write off the book value of a junked asset. There can never be a gain on the junking or scrapping of an asset.

A gain is recorded when an asset is sold for a price greater than its value. A loss is recorded when the sale price is less than book value. In this case, Equipment Y and its related Accumulated Depreciation account are removed from the books in a manner similar to Equipment X. The gain of $200 is calculated by subtracting the book value of the asset sold ($800) from the cash received ($1,000). The Gain on the Sale of Equipment account is a revenue account and is closed to the Income Summary account at the end of the year.

Demonstration Problem 2:

Entry	Accounts and Explanation	PR	Debit	Credit
1	Equipment		23,850	
	Cash			23,850
2	Equipment		410	
	Cash			410
3	Equipment		1,040	
	Cash			1,040
4	Depreciation Expense – Equipment		1,488	
	Accumulated Depreciation			1,488
5	Equipment		4,500	
	Cash			4,500
6	Depreciation Expense – Equipment		2,752	
	Accumulated Depreciation			2,752
7	Repair Expense		480	
	Cash			480
8	Depreciation Expense – Equipment		2,752	
	Accumulated Depreciation			2,752
9	Depreciation Expense – Equipment		688	
	Accumulated Deprecation			688
10	Cash		4,200	
	Accumulated Depreciation		16,605	
	Loss on Sale of Equipment (plug)		8,995	
	Equipment			29,800

Chapter 8

CURRENT & LONG-TERM LIABILITIES

CHAPTER OBJECTIVES

The learning objectives for this chapter are as follows:

1. Account for current liabilities and contingent liabilities
2. Account for bonds-payable transactions
3. Measure interest expense
4. Understand the advantages and disadvantages of borrowing
5. Report liabilities on the balance sheet

CHAPTER OVERVIEW

Liabilities represent future obligations of a firm. These obligations may involve payment of funds, or providing some good or service. Since liabilities represent a priority claim to assets in a bankruptcy, they are monitored closely by financial statement users. Liabilities are classified into two groups: current and long-term. Current liabilities represent obligations due to be extinguished within one year. Long-term liabilities have a time horizon of longer than one year.

CHAPTER REVIEW

Objective 1—Account for current liabilities and contingent liabilities

Types of Current Liabilities (amount-certain):
- Accounts Payable — amounts due for products or services purchased on credit in the normal course of business. Usually bear no interest.
- Short-term Notes Payable — liabilities due to be paid within one year, and usually bear interest.
- Sales Tax Payable — amounts collected from customer for sales tax, these funds are paid to local or state taxing authorities.
- Current Portion of Long-Term Debt — represents only the principal payable within the next year on some noncurrent debt.
- Accrued Expenses (Accrued Liabilities) — includes salary and wages payable, interest payable, and income tax payable
- Payroll Liabilities — includes funds deducted from employees' paychecks. These funds are in turn remitted to the appropriate payee. These may include income taxes payable, FICA/Medicare taxes payable, insurance premiums, etc.
- Unearned Revenue — funds received from customers prior to the providing of goods or services. The funds remain as liabilities until the revenue is actually earned.

Types of Current Liabilities (amount-uncertain):
- Estimated Warranty Payable — warranties represent a firm's promise to repair faulty products sold to customers. This estimate must sometimes be made years in advance.
- Contingent Liabilities — represent potential liabilities, the existence of which must be determined by the occurrence of some future event. This would be recorded only if payment is probable, and the amount may be reasonably estimated. Lawsuits are a common example of this type of liability.

Objective 2—Account for bonds-payable transactions

Bonds Payable represents large groups of long-term notes payable issued to multiple lenders.

Bond Terminology:
- Underwriter — purchases bonds from issuing corporations and resells them to the ultimate lender
- Term Bond — matures at a specific time
- Serial Bond — matures in installments over a period of time
- Secured Bond — backed by a pledge of certain assets of the firm, which would be forfeit to the lender in the case of default
- Debenture Bond — is unsecured
- Face (par) Value — the amount physically written on the bond certificate itself (principal)
- Premium — the amount over the face value that a bond sells for. This results in Interest Expense being less than the amounts actually paid out
- Discount — the amount under the face value that a bond sells for. This results in Interest Expense being more than the amounts actually paid out
- Time Value of Money — $1 invested today is worth more than $1 in the future, because of interest
- Present Value — today's dollar value of some future event or events. Answers the question "what is that future money worth today?"
- Stated (Face) Interest Rate — the rate of interest physically printed on the bond certificate. This is the rate of interest that will physically paid to the bondholders
- Market Interest Rate — the prevailing interest rate demanded by the pool of all potential bondholders

Bond Price Relationships (assuming various interest rates)

Stated Rate	Market Rate	Bonds Issued At	Funds Received Compared to Face Value
9	9	Face	**Same**
9	10	Discount	Received **Less** Cash than Face
9	8	Premium	Received **More** Cash than Face

Objective 3—Measure interest expense

Semiannual Interest Payment = Face Value x Face Rate x (6/12)
Semiannual Interest Expense = Carrying Value x Market Rate x (6/12)
Premium Amortization = Payment – Expense
Discount Amortization = Expense – Payment
Carrying Value = Unamortized Premium + Face Value or Carrying Value = Face Value – Unamortized Discount

Objective 4—Understand the advantages and disadvantages of borrowing

Convertible Bonds — bonds that may be converted at the bondholder's request into the firm's common stock

Comparing Stock to Debt:
- Issuing stock creates no liabilities or interest expense that must be paid. This is less risky for the issuing corporation, and more risky for investors (as compared to buying the firm's bonds).
- Issuing bonds does not dilute stock ownership or control of the corporation. Bonds must be repaid. Bonds are more risky for the issuing corporation, and less risky for bondholders (as compared to buying the firm's stock).

Leases:
- Operating leases are short-term rental agreements, and are cancelable. They give the lessee the right to use the asset, but no continuing rights or ownership to the asset. Operating leases are not considered liabilities. Payments are simply recorded as rent expense.
- Capital leases are long term agreements that are noncancelable. Capital leases are considered liabilities, and have at least one of the following characteristics:
  - Title passes to the lessee at the end of the lease
  - Lease has a bargain purchase option
  - Lease has a term of 75% of the useful life of the asset
  - The present value of the lease payments is 90% or more of the market value of the asset

Pensions — represents funds paid to employees after retirement. They are either disclosed in the notes to the financial statements if a net liability does not exist (overfunded), or as a liability if the fund is underfunded.

Objective 5—Report liabilities on the balance sheet

Current and long-term liabilities are reported separately on a firm's balance sheet. Selling bonds (inflow) and repaying them (outflow) would appear on the firm's statement of cash flows.

TEST YOURSELF

Matching

Match each numbered item with its lettered definition.

_____ 1. bonds payable
_____ 2. term bonds
_____ 3. payroll
_____ 4. earnings per share (EPS)
_____ 5. lease
_____ 6. stated interest rate
_____ 7. debentures
_____ 8. callable bonds
_____ 9. accrued liability
_____ 10. effective interest rate

_____ 11. trading on the equity
_____ 12. market interest rate
_____ 13. convertible bonds (or notes)
_____ 14. premium (on a bond)
_____ 15. times-interest-earned ratio
_____ 16. discount (on a bond)
_____ 17. present value
_____ 18. serial bonds
_____ 19. underwriter
_____ 20. current installment of
         long-term debt

A. ratio of income from operations to interest expense; measures the number of times that operating income can cover interest expense.
B. earning more income on borrowed money than the related interest expense, thereby increasing the earnings for the owners of the business.
C. interest rate that investors demand for loaning their money.
D. interest rate that determines the amount of cash interest the borrower pays and the investor receives each year.
E. bonds that mature in installments over a period of time.
F. unsecured bonds; bonds backed only by the good faith of the borrower.
G. amount a person would invest now to receive a greater amount at a future date.
H. rental agreement in which the tenant (lessee) agrees to make rent payments to the property owner (lessor) in exchange for the use of the asset.
I. excess of a bond's maturity (par value) over its issue price.
J. amount of a company's net income per share of its outstanding common stock.
K. the amount of the principal that is payable within one year.
L. another term for "market interest rate."
M. organization that purchases the bonds from an issuing company and resells them to its clients or sells the bonds for a commission, agreeing to buy all unsold bonds.
N. bonds that the issuer may call (pay off) at a specified price whenever the issuer wants.
O. bonds (or notes) that may be converted into the issuing company's common stock at the investor's option.
P. employee compensation, a major expense of many businesses.
Q. excess of a bond's issue price over its maturity (par) value.
R. groups of notes payable (bonds) issued to multiple lenders called bondholders.
S. an expense incurred but not yet paid in cash.
T. bonds that all mature at the same time for a particular issue.

Multiple Choice

Circle the best answer.

1. Current liabilities are obligations due within:
   a. one year or within the company's normal operating cycle if it is longer than one year
   b. one year or within the company's normal operating cycle if it is shorter than one year
   c. one month or within the company's normal operating cycle if it is longer than one month
   d. one month or within the company's normal operating cycle if it is shorter than one month

2. Failure to record an accrued liability causes a company to:
   a. overstate assets
   b. overstate expenses
   c. overstate liabilities
   d. overstate owners' equity

3. Warranty expense should be recorded in the period:
   a. that the product sold is repaired or replaced
   b. the product is sold
   c. immediately following the period in which the product is sold
   d. that the product is paid for by the customer

4. On December 16, 2005, the G. Baker Corporation purchases $15,000 of equipment by issuing a 30-day, 12% note payable. The amount of accrued interest on December 31, 2005, is:
   a. $75
   b. $150
   c. $750
   d. $800

5. Referring to question 4, the total amount of interest due on the note is:
   a. $75
   b. $150
   c. $800
   d. $1,800

6. Referring to question 4, the entry on the maturity date of the note will include a:
   a. debit to Interest Payable for $75
   b. debit to Interest Expense for $150
   c. credit to Interest Payable for $75
   d. credit to Interest Expense for $150

7. The journal entry to record accrued interest on a short-term note payable must include a:
   a. debit to Interest Payable
   b. debit to Note Payable
   c. debit to Interest Expense
   d. credit to Interest Expense

8. Current liabilities fall into two categories, which are referred to as:
   a. contra liabilities and contingent liabilities
   b. contingent liabilities and noncontingent liabilities
   c. liabilities of a known amount and liabilities whose amount must be estimated
   d. liabilities of a known amount and contingent liabilities

9. Gary's Lakefront Hardware Company includes an 8.50% sales tax in the amount credited to the sales account. If the sales account has a balance of $675,250, the amount of the sales tax payable to the state is:
   a. $54,020
   b. $50,019
   c. $57,396
   d. $52,900

10. Short-term notes payable:
    a. are generally due within three months, with a maximum time period of six months
    b. are shown as a reduction to notes receivable on the balance sheet, with an appropriate footnote disclosure
    c. are shown on the balance sheet with current liabilities
    d. are shown on the balance sheet after bonds payable

11. Jensen Distribution Company's sales for the day totaled $10,552. Jenkins collected an additional 7.50% in sales tax. The entry to record the day's sales includes a:
    a. debit to Sales Tax Expense
    b. debit to Sales Tax Payable
    c. credit to Sales Tax Expense
    d. credit to Sales Tax Payable

12. Jefferson-Davis Company includes the sales tax in the amount recorded in the Sales account. The adjusting entry at the end of the period includes a:
    a. debit to Sales Tax Payable
    b. debit to Sales Tax Expense
    c. credit to Sales
    d. debit to Sales

13. Potential liabilities that depend on future events arising out of past events are called:
    a. long-term liabilities
    b. estimated liabilities
    c. actual liabilities
    d. contingent liabilities

14. A company has a probable contingent gain that can be reasonably estimated. What reporting does the FASB require regarding this contingency?
    a. It should either be recorded on the financial statements or reported in the notes to the financial statements.
    b. It should be ignored until the actual gain materializes.
    c. It should be reported in the notes to the financial statements.
    d. It should be accrued and reported on the financial statements.

15. Secured bonds are also called:
    a. mortgage bonds
    b. callable bonds
    c. debenture bonds
    d. convertible bonds

Completion

Complete each of the following statements.

1. When the market interest rate is _____ than the stated rate. bonds will sell at a premium.
2. When the premium on bonds payable is reduced. the book value of bonds payable _____.
3. Gains or losses on early retirement of debt is _____ and reported separately on the income statement.
4. The liability to make _____ lease payments is not reported on the balance sheet.
5. If a lease transfers ownership of assets at the end of the lease term. the lease is a(n) _____ lease.
6. The _____ method of interest amortization results in the same amount of discount/premium amortization for identical periods of time.
7. Accruing pension and postretirement benefit liabilities is an example of the _____ principle.
8. When the market interest rate is greater than the stated rate. the bonds will sell at a _____.
9. Convertible bonds give the _____ the right to convert the bonds to common stock.
10. When the effective-interest method of amortization is used. the total amount of interest expense over the life of the bonds is _____.
11. Indicate whether each of the following liabilities is a known amount (K) or an estimated amount (E).

A	Accounts Payable	G	Sales Tax Payable
B	Short-term Notes Payable	H	Liability for Vacation Pay
C	Property Taxes Payable	I	Postretirement Benefits
D	Warranty Liability	J	Interest Payable
E	Salaries Expense	K	Pension Premium Payable
F	Income Taxes Payable		

True/False

For each of the following statements, circle T *for true or* F *for false.*

1.   T   F   One of a merchandiser's most common transactions is the credit purchase of inventory.

2.   T   F   At the end of each year, a company reclassifies the amount of its long-term debt that must be paid during the upcoming year.

3.   T   F   A bonus is a percentage of the sales the employee has made.

4.   T   F   The matching principle demands that the company record the warranty expense in the same period that the business records sales revenue.

5.   T   F   There is no need to report a contingent loss that is unlikely to occur.

6.   T   F   Large corporations borrow money by issuing bonds to the public.

7.   T   F   Bonds are always sold at their stated price.

8.   T   F   Callable bonds give the issuer the benefit of being able to pay off the bonds whenever it is most favorable to do so.

9.   T   F   Higher interest rates in the market may convince management to pay off bonds now.

10.   T   F   Conversion of notes payable into stock will decrease the company's debt and increase its equity.

11.   T   F   Earnings per share is probably the most important statistic used to evaluate companies because it is a standard measure of operating performance.

12.   T   F   A capital lease is a long-term and noncancelable financing obligation that is a form of debt.

13.   T   F   When a bond's contract interest rate differs from the market interest rate, the company's interest expense differs from period to period.

14.   T   F   Bonds payable are debts of the issuing company.

15.   T   F   If the plan assets exceed the accumulated benefit obligation, the plan is said to overfunded.

Exercises

1. Siberspace Inc. issued $6,000,000 in 20-year bonds with a stated interest rate of 7 3/4%. The bonds were issued at par on June 1, 2006. Interest is paid December 1 and June 1.

Give the journal entries for:
  A. Issuance of the bonds on June 1, 2006.
  B. Payment of interest on December 1, 2006.
  C. Maturity payment of bonds on June 1, 2026.

Date	Accounts and Explanation	PR	Debit	Credit
	A			
	B			
	C			

2. Record journal entries for the following transactions:
   a. a company borrows $8,000 on October 1 giving a 10%, 1-year note payable
   b. record an adjusting entry on December 31 for the note in (a)

Date	Accounts and Explanation	PR	Debit	Credit
	A			
	B			

3. Minnifield Corporation issued $500,000 in 7-year bonds with a stated interest rate of 8%. The bonds were sold on January 1, 2005, for $477,956 to yield 9%. Interest is paid July 1 and January 1. Minnifield uses the straight-line method to amortize Discount on Bonds Payable. (Assume an October 31 year end.)

Record the journal entries for:

   A. Issuance of bonds on January 1, 2005.
   B. Payment of interest on July 1, 2005.
   C. Accrual of interest and related amortization on October 31, 2005 (year end).
   D. Payment of interest on January 1, 2006.
   E. Maturity payment of bonds on January 1, 2011.

Date	Accounts and Explanation	PR	Debit	Credit
	A			
	B			
	C			
	D			
	E			

4. Young Corporation issued $500,000 in 7-year callable bonds with a stated interest rate of 8%. The bonds were sold on January 1, 2005, for $558,420 to yield 6%. Interest is paid July 1 and January 1. Young uses the effective-interest method to amortize Premium on Bonds Payable. (Assume a December 31 year end.)

Record the journal entries for:

A. Issuance of bonds on January 1, 2005.
B. Payment of interest on July 1, 2005.
C. Accrual of interest and related amortization on December 31, 2005 (year end).
D. Payment of interest on January 1, 2006.
E. Maturity payment of bonds on January 1, 2012.

Date	Accounts and Explanation	PR	Debit	Credit
A				
B				
C				
D				
E				

5. Review the information in Exercise 4 and assume Young Corporation exercised its option to call the bonds on July 1, 2007 at 105. Record the following entries:

    a. the interest payment on July 1, 2007
    b. the cash payment to bondholders on July 1, 2007

Date	Accounts and Explanation	PR	Debit	Credit
	A			
	B			

Critical Thinking

Review the information in Exercises 3 and 4 above and assume, in each case, that each $1,000 bond is convertible, at the option of the holder, into 31.25 shares of the corporation's common stock. Determine when an investor should seriously consider exercising the option to convert the bonds to stock.

Demonstration Problems

1.

The following events occurred in December:

1. On December 1, borrowed $75,000 from the bank, signing a 9-month note at 8% interest.
2. On December 10, the company accepted advance payments from two customers as follows:
   a) A $60,000 payment from Simex for 20 custom-made polishers. As of December 31, six polishers had been produced.
   b) A 10% down payment on a $100,000 contract for a piece of equipment to be delivered by May 1 of the following year. As of December 31, no work had been started on the equipment.
3. During December, a competitor filed a lawsuit against the company alleging violation of anti-trust regulations. If the company loses the suit, it is estimated damages will exceed $1 million.
4. The December payroll totaled $145,000, which will be paid on January 10. Employees accrue vacation benefits at the rate of 2% of monthly payroll. (Ignore payroll deductions and the employer's payroll tax expense.)
5. Sales for the month amounted to 1,200 units at $350 each, subject to a retail sales tax of 6%. Each unit carries a 90-day warranty requiring the company to repair or replace the unit if it becomes defective during the warranty period. The estimated cost to the company to honor the warranty is $55, and past experience has shown that approximately 3% of the units will be returned during the warranty period.

Required:

Record the external transactions and, where appropriate, the required adjusting entry at December 31.

Date	Accounts and Explanation	PR	Debit	Credit

2.

Viera Corporation has outstanding an issue of 10% callable bonds that mature in 2014. The bonds are dated January 1, 2004, and pay interest each July 1 and January 1. Additional bond data:

     a.   Fiscal year end for Viera Corporation: September 30.
     b.   Maturity value of the bonds: $500,000.
     c.   Contract interest rate: 10%.
     d.   Interest is paid 5% semiannually, $25,000 ($500,000 x .05).
     e.   Market interest rate at time of issue: 9% annually, 4.5% semiannually.
     f.   Issue price: 106.

Required:

1.   Complete the interest method amortization table through January 1, 2006. Round pennies to the nearest dollar. See the form below.

2.   Using the amortization table that you have completed, record the following transactions:
     a.   Issuance of the bonds on January 1, 2004.
     b.   Payment of interest and amortization of premium on July 1, 2004.
     c.   Accrued interest and amortization of premium as of September 30, 2004.
     d.   Payment of interest and amortization of premium on January 1, 2005.
     e.   Retirement of the bonds on January 2, 2005. Callable price of bonds was 108.

	A	**B**	**C**	**D**	
Semi-annual Interest Date	Interest Payment (5% of Maturity Value)	Interest Expense (5% of Preceding Bond Carrying Value	Premium Amortization (A-B)	Premium Account Balance (D-C)	Bond Carrying Value ($500,000 + D)
1/1/2004					
7/1/2004					
1/1/2005					
7/1/2005					
1/1/2006					

Date	Accounts and Explanation	PR	Debit	Credit

SOLUTIONS

Matching

1	R	5	H	9	S	13	O	17	G
2	T	6	D	10	L	14	Q	18	E
3	P	7	F	11	B	15	A	19	M
4	J	8	N	12	C	16	I	20	K

Multiple Choice

1	A
2	D
3	B
4	A
5	B
6	A
7	C
8	C
9	D
10	C
11	D
12	D
13	D
14	B
15	A

Completion

1. lower (when market rate > stated rate, then discount; when market rate < stated rate, then premium)
2. decreases (The book value or carrying value amount of a bond is equal to the face amount of the bond plus (minus) the unamortized premium (discount).)
3. extraordinary (Though not meeting the normal "infrequent and unusual" requirement for other extraordinary items, GAAP specifies that such gains and losses are extraordinary items.)
4. operating (Operating leases are normally short term and transfer none of the rights of ownership to the lessee. Accordingly, neither an asset nor a liability is recorded for such leases.)
5. capital (Capital leases require that the lessee record the leased property as an asset and the obligation to make future lease payments as a liability.)
6. straight-line (This method divides the amount of the discount/premium by the number of time periods resulting in the same figure each period.)

7. matching
8. discount (because the lender expects a greater return on the loan than the stated rate provides)
9. lender (not the borrower; convertibility make the bonds more attractive to prospective lenders because of the potential for greater returns)
10. a constant percentage (as compared with the straight-line method where the amount of discount/ premium is constant). The effective rate is required, although the straight-line method can be used if the difference between the two is not material.
11.

K	A	Accounts Payable	K	G	Sales Tax Payable
K	B	Short-term Notes Payable	E or K	H	Liability for Vacation Pay
E or K	C	Property Taxes Payable	E	I	Postretirement Benefits
E	D	Warranty Liability	K	J	Interest Payable
E	E	Salaries Expense	E or K	K	Pension Premium Payable
E or K	F	Income Taxes Payable			

True/False

1	T	
2	T	
3	F	A commission is a percentage of sales. A bonus may also be expressed as a percentage, but is based on an employee's salary.
4	T	
5	T	
6	F	Bonds are sold to financial institutions due to their large denomination.
7	F	The selling price of bonds is derived by and through the market rate of interest, as contrasted to the stated or face interest rate.
8	T	
9	F	Lower interest rates might convince management to retire (pay off) older debt that carries a higher interest rates
10	T	
11	T	
12	T	
13	T	
14	T	
15	T	

Exercises

1.

Date	Accounts and Explanation	PR	Debit	Credit
	A			
	Cash		6,000,000	
	Bonds Payable			6,000,000
	B			
	Interest Expense		232,500	
	Cash			232,500
	$6,000,000 x .0775 x 6/12			
	C			
	Bonds Payable		6,000,000	
	Cash			6,000,000

2.

Date	Accounts and Explanation	PR	Debit	Credit
	A			
	Cash		8,000	
	Notes Payable			8,000
	B			
	Interest Expense		200	
	Interest Payable			200

3.

Date	Accounts and Explanation	PR	Debit	Credit
	A			
	Cash		477,956	
	Discount on Bonds Payable		22,044	
	Bonds Payable			500,000
	B			
	Interest Expense (20,000+1,575)		21,575	
	Cash (500,000 x .08 x 6/12)			20,000
	Discount on Bonds Payable			1,575
	(22,044 / 14 payments)			
	C			
	Interest Expense (13,333 + 1,050)		14,383	
	Interest Payable (500,000 x .08 x 4/12)			13,333
	Discount on Bonds Payable			1,050
	(22,044 / 14 x 2/3)			
	D			
	Interest Expense (20,000 −13,333) + 525		14,383	
	Interest Payable		13,333	
	Cash (500,000 x .08 x 6/12)			20,000
	Discount on Bonds Payable			525
	(22,044 / 14 x 1/3)			
	E			
	Bonds Payable		500,000	
	Cash			500,000

4.

Date	Accounts and Explanation	PR	Debit	Credit
	A			
	Cash		558,420	
	Bonds Payable			500,000
	Premium on Bonds Payable			58,420
	B			
	Interest Expense (558,420 x.06 x 6/12)		16,753	
	Premium on Bonds Payable		3,247	
	Cash (500,000 x .08 x 6/12)			20,000
	C			
	Interest Expense ([558,420-3,247] x.06 x 6/12)		16,655	
	Premium on Bonds Payable		3,345	
	Cash (500,000 x .08 x 6/12)			20,000
	D			
	Interest Payable		20,000	
	Cash			20,000
	E			
	Bonds Payable		500,000	
	Cash			500,000

5.

In order to record the July 1, 2007 interest payment, you need to update the amortization of the premium through July 1, 2007 as follows:

Carrying value of the bonds on 1/1/2006 is $551,828 (as in solution above)
Carrying value of the bonds on 7/1/2006 is: $500,000 + (51,828 – 3,445) = $548,383
Carrying value of the bonds on 1/1/2007 is: $500,000 + (48,383 + 3,549) = $544,834

Date	Accounts and Explanation	PR	Debit	Credit
	A			
	Interest Expense (544,834 x .06 x 6/12)		16,345	
	Premium on Bonds Payable		3,655	
	Cash (500,000 x .08 x 6/12)			20,000
	B			
	Bonds Payable		500,000	
	Premium on Bonds Payable		41,179	
	Cash			525,000
	Extraordinary Gain on Retirement of Bonds			16,179

Critical Thinking

If each $1,000 bond can be converted into 31.25 shares of common stock, then a quick calculation indicates an investor should seriously think about converting when the market price of the stock reaches $32 per share ($1,000 divided by 31.25 shares). However, this assumes the investor paid face value for the bonds. In Exercise 3, investors purchased the bonds at a discount of 95.59% of face value or $955.90 for each $1,000 bond. Therefore, investors in Minnifield's bonds could consider converting at a lower price of approximately $30.59 per share ($955.90 divided by 31.25). In Exercise 4, the investors paid a premium for the bonds because they were purchased at 111.68% of face value ($558,420 divided by $500,000). These investors would not be interested in converting until the price rose to $35.74 ($1,116.80 divided by 31.25 shares).

Demonstration Problems

1.

Date	Accounts and Explanation	PR	Debit	Credit
	1			
12/1	Cash		75,000	
	Notes Payable			75,000
12/31	Interest Expense		500	
	Interest Payable			500
	2a			
12/10	Cash		60,000	
	Unearned Revenues			60,000
12/31	Unearned Revenues		18,000	
	Revenues Earned			18,000
	2b			
12/10	Cash		10,000	
	Unearned Revenues			10,000
12/31	No Entry Needed			
	3			
	No Entry Needed			
	4			
12/31	Salary Expense		145,000	
	Salary Payable			145,000
	Vacation Pay Expense		2,900	
	Estimated Vacation Pay Liability			2,900
	5			
12/31	Accounts Receivable		445,200	
	Sales			420,000
	Sales Tax Payable			25,200
	Warranty Expense		1,980	
	Estimated Warranty Liability			1,980
	1,200 x .03 x $55			

Demonstration Problem #2 Solved and Explained

Requirement 1:

Semi-annual Interest Date	A Interest Payment (5% of Maturity Value)	B Interest Expense (5% of Preceding Bond Carrying Value)	C Premium Amortization (A-B)	D Premium Account Balance (D-C)	Bond Carrying Value ($500,000 + D)
1/1/2004				30,000	530,000
7/1/2004	25,000	23,850	1,150	28,850	528,850
1/1/2005	25,000	23,798	1,202	27,648	527,648
7/1/2005	25,000	23,744	1,256	26,392	526,392
1/1/2006	25,000	23,688	1,312	25,080	525,080

Requirement 2:

Date	Accounts and Explanation	PR	Debit	Credit
	a			
1/1/2004	Cash (500,000 x 1.06)		530,000	
	Premium on Bonds Payable			30,000
	Bonds Payable			500,000
	b			
7/1/2004	Interest Expense (25,000 – 1,105)		23,850	
	Premium on Bonds Payable		1,150	
	Cash			25,000
	C			
9/30/2004	Interest Expense (12,500 – 601)		11,899	
	Premium on Bonds Payable (1,202 x 3/6)		601	
	Interest Payable			12,500
	d			
1/1/2005	Interest Expense (12,500 – 601)		11,899	
	Interest Payable		12,500	
	Premium on Bonds Payable (1,202 x 3/6)		601	
	Cash			25,000
	e			
1/2/2005	Bonds Payable		500,000	
	Premium on Bonds Payable		27,648	
	Extraordinary Loss — Retirement of Bonds		12,352	
	Cash (500,000 x 1.08)			540,000

This entry removes the Bonds Payable and related Premium account from the corporate records, and records the extraordinary loss on retirement. The carrying value of the bonds ($527,648) is less than the cost to call the bonds ($540,000) resulting in the $12,352 loss. Had the price paid to call the bonds been less than the carrying value, the entry would have recorded an extraordinary gain. Extraordinary gains and losses are reported separately on the income statement.

Points to Remember

The interest rate stated on a debt instrument such as a corporate bond will typically differ from the actual market rate of interest when the bond is ultimately issued to the public. This occurs because of the lag in time that frequently occurs between the approval of the bond by the corporation (and regulatory agencies), its actual printings, and, finally, its issuance to the public. Rather than reprint the bond and potentially miss the rapidly changing market interest rate again, bonds are sold at a discount or premium. Occasionally, bonds are sold at face amount.

A bond is sold at a discount when the stated interest rate of the bond is below the current market rate. A premium is paid when the contract rate is higher than interest rates paid by comparable investments.

Premiums and discounts are, in effect, an adjustment to the interest rates. Thus, premiums and discounts should be amortized over the life of the bond.

Study Tip:
1. A good rule to remember is that bonds payable are always recorded at the face amount of the bond. Premiums and discounts are recorded in separate accounts.

2. The actual interest paid to the bondholders at the periodic payment dates (generally, semiannually) will always be the face value of the bond multiplied by the stated interest rate. A discount or premium will not affect these periodic cash payments.

The carrying amount (or book value) of a bond is conceptually similar to the book value of a fixed asset. Premiums are added to the face amount of bonds payable, and discounts are subtracted.

    Bonds Payable
 + Bond Premium or
 –   Bond Discount
 = Carrying Value

Note that bonds sold at a premium will have a carrying amount greater than the face amount owed and discounted bonds will have a smaller value. In both cases, the carrying value will always move toward the face amount of the bond as the discount or premium is amortized. (Because of this, it is possible to quickly double-check your amortization entries—be sure the bond carrying value is moving in the right direction.)

Chapter 9

STOCKHOLDERS' EQUITY

CHAPTER OBJECTIVES

The learning objectives for this chapter are as follows:

1. Explain the advantages and disadvantages of a corporation
2. Measure the effect of issuing stock on a company's financial position
3. Describe how treasury stock transactions affect a company
4. Account for dividends and measure their impact on a company
5. Use different stock values in decision making
6. Evaluate a company's return on assets and return on common equity
7. Report stockholders' equity transactions on the statement of cash flows

CHAPTER OVERVIEW

This chapter analyzes the stockholders' equity section of the balance sheet. Contemporary corporate finance uses a variety of different methods to effectively analyze a firm's ownership structure. Important issues include what type of stock to issue, how much to issue, how much to pay in dividends (if any), and whether or not to repurchase a firm's own shares on the open market.

CHAPTER REVIEW

Objective 1—Explain the advantages and disadvantages of a corporation

Distinguishing Characteristics of a Corporation
- Separate legal entity — a corporation is an artificial entity, distinct and apart from its owners
- Continuous life — a corporation continues operations indefinitely.
- Transferability of ownership — stockholders in publicly traded corporations may sell their shares at will. New owners may invest at will.
- Limited liability — stockholders have no personal liability for the corporation's debts or legal losses. The most a stockholder may lose is his or her investment in the stock.
- Separation of ownership and management — owners hire professional managers to run the corporation.
- Corporate taxation — corporate profits are taxed twice. First, corporate profits are taxed at the firm level as corporate income taxes. Second, profits paid to stockholders as dividends are taxed to the individual owner as dividend income.
- Government regulation — corporations are subject to a great deal of government regulation and oversight, at the local, regional, state, and federal levels.

Stockholders' Rights
- Vote — ability to vote on business matters.
- Dividends — the right to receive a proportionate share of the corporate profits.
- Liquidation — the right to receive a proportionate share of any assets remaining after all creditors are paid.
- Preemption — the right to maintain one's proportionate interest in the firm. If a stockholder owns 5% of a corporation's stock, that stockholder has the first right to purchase an additional 5% of any new stock sales to the public.

Parts of Stockholders' Equity
1. Paid-in Capital — this is also known as contributed capital. This is the amount of the stockholders' direct investment in the corporation. This section is made up of two parts:
   - Stock accounts
   - Additional paid-in capital
2. Retained Earnings — this is the amount of the firm's profits that have been withheld by the corporation. These amounts may be reinvested in the firm, or potentially paid to stockholders in the form of dividends.

Stock Volumes
- Authorized — the maximum number of shares that may be issued by the firm.
- Issued — the number of shares that have ever been distributed by the firm.
- Outstanding — the number of shares that are currently held by owners. The only difference between issued and outstanding shares is Treasury Stock — shares that have been repurchased by the firm. Treasury shares are included in shares issued, and excluded from shares outstanding.

Classes of Stock
- Common or Preferred
  - Common stock is the basic form of capital stock. Common stock has voting rights, and a residual right to profits
  - Preferred stock has superior features compared to common stock. Preferred stockholders have a superior claim to dividends – preferred dividends are paid before any dividends are paid to common holders.
- Par or No-Par
  - Par value is an amount physically written on the face of the stock certificate. It represents a legal floor below which the firm's stock may not trade.
  - No-par stock has no amount written on its face. It therefore has no legal floor restricting its trading value.

Objective 2—Measure the effect of issuing stock on a company's financial position

Sell Common Stock at Par Value Assets are usually Cash, but could be Fixed Assets as well							
Assets	=	Liabilities	+	Stockholders' Equity			
				Preferred Stock	Common Stock	Additional Paid-in Capital	Retained Earnings
+					+		

Sell Common Stock at Amount above Par Value (Addition Paid-in Capital = [Selling Price – Par Value] X # Shares)							
Assets	=	Liabilities	+	Stockholders' Equity			
				Preferred Stock	Common Stock	Additional Paid-in Capital	Retained Earnings
+					+	+	

Sell No-Par Common Stock							
Assets	=	Liabilities	+	Stockholders' Equity			
				Preferred Stock	Common Stock	Additional Paid-in Capital	Retained Earnings
+					+	**never**	

Sell Preferred Stock							
Assets	=	Liabilities	+	Stockholders' Equity			
				Preferred Stock	Common Stock	Additional Paid-in Capital	Retained Earnings
+				+			

Objective 3—Describe how treasury stock transactions affect a company

Treasury stock is a company's own stock that it has issued and later reacquired. Reasons include: trying to raise the stock's market price and/or earnings per share, trying to avoid a takeover by another company, for general corporate needs.

Treasury Stock appears in the Owner's Equity section of the balance sheet as a negative or contra-equity account.

			Buy Treasury Stock				
Assets	=	Liabilities	+	Stockholders' Equity			
			Preferred Stock	Common Stock	Additional Paid-in Capital	Retained Earnings	<Treasury Stock>
-							-

			Resell Treasury Stock for more than the firm paid for it				
Assets	=	Liabilities	+	Stockholders' Equity			
			Preferred Stock	Common Stock	Additional Paid-in Capital	Retained Earnings	<Treasury Stock>
+						+	+

			Resell Treasury Stock for less than the firm paid for it				
Assets	=	Liabilities	+	Stockholders' Equity			
			Preferred Stock	Common Stock	Additional Paid-in Capital	Retained Earnings	<Treasury Stock>
+						-	+

Objective 4—Account for dividends and measure their impact on a company

Dividends are a corporation's return to its stockholders of the benefits of earnings. Dividends can be in cash or in stock.

Preferred stock dividends can be cumulative or non-cumulative. Cumulative dividends accrue or build up until they are paid; unpaid annual dividends are not lost to stockholders. They must be paid in the future. Noncumulative dividends that are not paid in the current period are lost to the stockholders.

			Declaration Date for a Dividend				
Assets	=	Liabilities	+	Stockholders' Equity			
			Preferred Stock	Common Stock	Additional Paid-in Capital	Retained Earnings	<Treasury Stock>
		+				—	

Date of Record for a Dividend: No entry						
Assets	= Liabilities	+	Stockholders' Equity			
			Preferred Stock	Common Stock	Additional Paid-in Capital	Retained Earnings	<Treasury Stock>
n/a						

Date of Payment for a Dividend						
Assets	= Liabilities	+	Stockholders' Equity			
			Preferred Stock	Common Stock	Additional Paid-in Capital	Retained Earnings	<Treasury Stock>
−	−					

Issuing a Stock Dividend						
Assets	= Liabilities	+	Stockholders' Equity			
			Preferred Stock	Common Stock	Additional Paid-in Capital	Retained Earnings	<Treasury Stock>
				+	+	−

Stock splits are an increase in the number of authorized, issued, and outstanding shares of stock, coupled with a proportionate reduction in the stock's par value. For example, a 2-for-1 stock split would double the number of shares outstanding, while cutting their par value in half. No journal entries are necessary for stock splits.

Objective 5—Use different stock values in decision making

Market Value — the price a person can buy or sell a share of stock for

Redemption Value — the price at which a firm may repurchase its own shares of preferred stock.

Liquidation Value — the amount that a company must pay a preferred stockholder in the event that the company liquidates (sells out) and closes its doors.

Book Value — the amount of owner's equity on the company's books for each share of its stock.

Book Value Per Share of Common Stock	=	$\dfrac{\text{Total Stockholders' Equity} - \text{Preferred Equity}}{\text{\# of Shares of Common Stock Outstanding}}$

Objective 6—Evaluate a company's return on assets and return on common equity

Return on Assets (ROA) — measures a company's use of its assets to earn income for the two groups who finance the business (creditors and stockholders)

Rate of Return on Total Assets (ROA)	=	$\dfrac{\text{Net Income} + \text{Interest Expense}}{\text{Average Total Assets}}$

Return on Equity (ROE) — shows the relationship between net income and average common stockholders' equity.

Rate of Return on Common Stockholders' (ROE)	=	$\dfrac{\text{Net Income} + \text{Preferred Dividends}}{\text{Average Common Stockholders' Equity}}$

In both cases, "average" is simply the beginning and ending balances, divided by two.

Objective 7—Report stockholders' equity transactions on the statement of cash flows

Generally speaking, most cash transactions involving stockholders' equity will appear in the Financing Activities section of the statement of cash flows:

Selling stock for cash, preferred or common	Inflow
Purchase of Treasury Stock	Outflow
Resale of Treasury Stock	Inflow
Cash Dividends	Outflow
Stock Dividends, or Stock Splits	Not Reported

TEST YOURSELF

Matching

Match each numbered item with its lettered definition.

_____	1.	deficit	_____ 11.	retained earnings
_____	2.	bylaws	_____ 12.	chairperson
_____	3.	paid-in capital	_____ 13.	return on equity
_____	4.	stated value	_____ 14.	stockholders' equity
_____	5.	treasury stock	_____ 15.	legal capital
_____	6.	president	_____ 16.	book value (of a stock)
_____	7.	return on assets	_____ 17.	stock dividend
_____	8.	dividend	_____ 18.	board of directors
_____	9.	limited liability	_____ 19.	market value (of a stock)
_____	10.	stock split	_____ 20.	double taxation

A. the amount of stockholders' equity that the corporation has earned through profitable operation of the business and has not given back to stockholders.

B. distribution (usually cash) by a corporation to its stockholders.

C. the stockholders' ownership interest in the assets of a corporation.

D. a stockholder can lose no more on an investment in a corporation's stock than the cost of the investment.

E. elected by a corporation's board of directors, usually the most powerful person in the corporation.

F. an increase in the number of authorized, issued, and outstanding shares of stock coupled with a proportionate reduction in the stock's par value.

G. group elected by the stockholders to set policy for a corporation and to appoint its officers.

H. measures a company's success in using its assets to earn income for the persons who finance the business.

I. shows the relationship between net income and average common stockholders' equity.

J. a corporation's own stock that it has issued and later reacquired.

K. price for which a person could buy or sell a share of stock.

L. an arbitrary amount assigned to no-par stock.

M. corporations pay income taxes on corporate income, then the stockholders pay personal income tax on the cash dividends that they receive from corporations.

N. constitution for governing a corporation.

O. amount of owners' equity on the company's books for each share of its stock.

P. the amount of stockholders' equity that stockholders have contributed to the corporation.

Q. chief operating officer in charge of managing the day-to-day operations of a corporation.

R. debit balance in the Retained Earnings account.

S. a proportional distribution by a corporation of its own stock to its stockholders.

T. minimum amount of stockholders' equity that a corporation must maintain for the protection of creditors.

Multiple Choice

Circle the best answer.

1. Which of the following is **not** a characteristic that distinguishes corporations from proprietorships and partnerships?
    a. Corporations are separate legal entities apart from the owners.
    b. Corporate earnings are subject to double taxation.
    c. Corporations have mutual agency.
    d. Corporations have continuous lives regardless of changes in ownership.

2. Corporations are separate taxable entities. The earnings of a corporation are subject to:
    a. federal unemployment taxes
    b. taxation by the SEC
    c. double taxation
    d. the same method of taxation as partnership earnings

3. All of the following are advantages of the corporate form of business **except**:
    a. limited liability of stockholders
    b. continuous life
    c. no mutual agency
    d. corporate taxation

4. The number of stocks currently in the hands of stockholders is the same as the number of stocks:
    a. issued
    b. authorized
    c. outstanding
    d. proposed by the board of directors

5. Which of the following types of business organizations terminates when its ownership structure changes?
    a. partnerships and proprietorships
    b. partnerships and corporations
    c. proprietorships and corporations
    d. only corporations

6. Which of the following is a disadvantage of the corporate form of business organization?
    a. mutual agency
    b. unlimited liability
    c. difficulty in transferring ownership
    d. governmental regulation at both the federal and state levels

7. The par value of common stock is:
    a. always $1.00 in value
    b. an arbitrary amount assigned by the issuing company
    c. the market price of the stock on the date it is first issued
    d. always less than the stock's stated value

8. Paid-in capital is also known as:
    a. contributed capital
    b. retained earnings
    c. total stockholders' equity
    d. common stockholders' equity

9. The ultimate control of the corporation rests with the:
    a. SEC and Congress
    b. chief executive officer
    c. stockholders
    d. employees

10. Paid-in capital is:
    a. the amount of stockholders' equity that the corporation has earned through profitable operations
    b. the amount of stockholders' equity that the stockholders have contributed to the corporation
    c. the amount of stockholders' equity that the stockholders have contributed to the corporation *less* the amount of stockholders' equity that the corporation has given back to the stockholders (dividends)
    d. the amount of stockholders' equity that the stockholders have contributed to the corporation *plus* the amount of stockholders' equity that the corporation has earned through profitable operations

11. All of the following are basic rights of a stockholder **except**:
    a. the right to vote
    b. the right to receive a proportionate share of any assets remaining before the corporation pays its liabilities in the event of liquidation
    c. the right to maintain one's proportionate ownership in the corporation
    d. the right to receive a proportionate part of any dividend

12. If a corporation issues only one class of stock, it must be:
    a. par value
    b. preferred
    c. common
    d. common or preferred

13. The price that the stockholder pays to acquire stock from the corporation is the:
    a. issue price
    b. stated price
    c. par price
    d. authorized price

14. Assets received in exchange for the issuance of stock should be recorded at:
    a. historical cost
    b. historical cost less accumulated depreciation taken to date
    c. fair market value as determined by a good-faith estimate from independent appraisers
    d. none of the above answers

15. In a corporation, the two basic sources of stockholders' equity are:
    a. paid-in capital and operating capital
    b. paid-in capital and retained earnings
    c. donated capital and paid-in capital
    d. donated capital and retained earnings

Completion

Complete each of the following statements.

1. Every corporation issues _____ stock.
2. _____ stock does not receive cash dividends.
3. Preferred stockholders have preference over common stockholders in _____ and _____.
4. Dividends are declared by _____.
5. A corporation may buy treasury stock in order to _____.
6. Stockholders' equity minus preferred equity equals _____.
7. The date of _____ determines who receives the dividend.
8. The date of _____ establishes the liability to pay a dividend.
9. Stock in the hands of stockholders is called _____ stock.
10. Corporations come into existence when a_____ is approved by the _____ government.
11. ROA stands for _____.
12. ROE stands for _____.
13. _____ value is physically written on the face of a stock certificate.
14. _____ value is the current trading price of the stock.
15. _____ stock does not have a par value.

True/False

For each of the following statements, circle T for true or F for false.

1. T F Corporations have continuous lives regardless of changes in the ownership of their stock.
2. T F The purchase of treasury stock increases the company's assets and equity.
3. T F Corporate earnings are subject to double taxation of their income.
4. T F A stock's book value is the price for which a person could buy or sell a share of the stock.
5. T F Return on assets and return on equity are two measures of profitability.
6. T F Ownership of stock entitles stockholders to vote, dividends, liquidation, and preemption.
7. T F The Treasury Stock account has a credit balance.
8. T F Issuing stock for assets other than cash can pose an ethical challenge.
9. T F The Retained Earnings account is a reservoir of cash waiting for the board of directors to pay dividends to the stockholders.
10. T F Successful companies grow by reinvesting back into the business the assets they generate through profitable operations.
11. T F Only the president of the company has the authority to declare a dividend.
12. T F When a company has issued both preferred and common stock, the preferred stockholders receive their dividends first.
13. T F Leverages increases net income when the company's income exceeds its interest expense from borrowing.
14. T F If the preferred stock is cumulative, the corporation is not obligated to pay dividends in arrears.
15. T F Stock dividends increase the Stock account and decrease Retained Earnings.

Exercises

1. Buyitnow.com declared a cash dividend of $1.10 a share on common stock on November 10. The dividend was paid on December 20 to stockholders of record on December 1. Buyitnow.com has 2,250,000 shares of common stock outstanding.

Prepare the journal entries required on November 10, December 1, and December 20.

Date	Accounts and Explanation	PR	Debit	Credit
November 10				
December 1				
December 20				

2. The charter of Spinke-Garman, Inc., authorizes the issuance of 100,000 shares of preferred stock and 5,000,000 shares of common stock. During the first month of operation, Spinke-Garman, Inc., completed the following stock-issuance transactions:

February 1   Issued 600,000 shares of $1 par common stock for cash of $18 per share.

February 10   Issued 20,000 shares of 7%, no-par preferred stock with a stated value of $50 per share. The issue price was $50 per share.

February 28   Received inventory valued at $80,000 and equipment with a market value of $120,000 in exchange for 20,000 shares of $1 par common stock.

Record the necessary journal entries for the above three transactions (omit explanations).

Date	Accounts and Explanation	PR	Debit	Credit
	February 1			
	February 10			
	February 28			

3. Using your answers from Exercise 2 above, prepare the stockholders' equity section of the Spinke-Garman Inc., balance sheet at the end of the first month. Assume Retained Earnings has a balance of $25,000.

Stockholders' Equity	

4. Sanders Corporation has 10,000 shares of $100 par, cumulative, 5% preferred stock outstanding. There were no dividends in arrears at the end of 2002, and no dividends were paid in 2004 or 2005. Sanders also has 20,000 shares of $1 par common stock outstanding.

    A. If Sanders pays a total of $220,000 in dividends in 2006, how much will each class of stockholders receive?

    B. If Sanders pays a total of $140,000 in dividends in 2006, how much will each class of stockholders receive?

5. Indicate the effect of each of the following transactions on Assets, Liabilities, Paid-in Capital, and Retained Earnings. Use + for increase, − for decrease, and 0 for no effect.

		Assets	Liabilities	Paid-in Capital	Retained Earnings
A	Declaration of a Cash Dividend				
B	Payment of a Cash Dividend				
C	Declaration of a Stock Dividend				
D	Issuance of a Stock Dividend				
E	A Stock Split				
F	Cash Purchase of Treasury Stock				
G	Sale of Treasury Stock above Cost				

6. Flex-Tech Corporation had 800,000 shares of $10 par common stock outstanding on March 1. Prepare a journal entry for the following transaction:

3/15   Declared and issued a 5% stock dividend. The market price was $60 per share.

Date	Accounts and Explanation	PR	Debit	Credit

7.   Prepare journal entries for the following transactions:

    2/10   Purchased 800 shares of $5 par treasury stock for $24 per share.
    7/1   Sold 500 shares of treasury stock for $28 per share.
   12/12   Sold 300 shares of treasury stock for $36 per share

Date	Accounts and Explanation	PR	Debit	Credit

Critical Thinking

Review the facts in Exercise 6 with the following changes:

10/10   Declared a 21-for-20 stock split. The market price was $60 per share.
10/30   Issued the shares.

Present the journal entries for the above stock split.

Date	Accounts and Explanation	PR	Debit	Credit

Demonstration Problems

1.

On January 1, 2005, the State of California Corporation Department authorized DVD.com to issue 500,000 shares of 6%, $50 par cumulative preferred stock and 1,000,000 shares of common stock with a no par or stated value. During its start-up phase, the company completed the following selected transactions related to its stockholders' equity:

1/10   Sold 300,000 shares of common stock at $22 per share.
1/11   Issued 10,000 shares of preferred stock for cash of $55 per share.
1/17   Issued 40,000 shares of common stock in exchange for equipment valued at $700,000.
1/24   An old building and small parcel of land were acquired by the corporation for a future office site that would employ 60 people. The site value was $1,000,000; the building was worthless. DVD.com issued 80,000 shares of common stock for the site and building.
1/31   Earned a small profit for January resulting in a $12,000 credit balance in the Retained Earnings account.

Required:

1. Record the transactions in the general journal. No entry is required on 1/31.
2. Post the journal entries into the equity accounts provided.
3. Prepare the stockholders' equity section of DVD.com balance sheet at January 31, 2005.
4. Compute the book value per share of the preferred stock and the common stock. The preferred stock has a liquidation value of $52.50 per share. No dividends are in arrears.

Requirement 1:

Date	Accounts and Explanation	PR	Debit	Credit

Requirement 2:

Assets	=	Liabilities	+	Stockholders' Equity				
				Preferred Stock	Common Stock	Additional Paid-in Capital	Retained Earnings	<Treasury Stock>

Requirement 3:

Stockholders' Equity	

Requirement 4:

Demonstration Problem #2

Dynamic Pensions reported the following stockholders' equity:

Stockholders' Equity:	
Preferred Stock, 8%, $25 par value	$3,750,000
Authorized – 1,000,000 shares	
Issued – 150,000	
Common Stock, $1 par value	800,000
Authorized – 5,000,000	
Issued – 800,000	
Paid-in Capital in Excess of Par – Common stock	6,000,000
Retained Earnings	6,855,180
Less: Treasury Stock at cost (2,000 common shares)	(14,000)
Total Stockholders' Equity	17,391,180

Required: (Work space to complete each of these questions is provided on the following pages.)

1. What was the average issue price per share of the common stock?
2. What was the average issue price per share of the preferred stock?
3. Assume the board of directors declares dividends totaling $1,797,000 to the shareholders. The preferred stock is cumulative and no dividends were declared last year. Calculate the amount per share each class of stock will receive.
4. Journalize the issuance of 10,000 additional shares of common stock at $22.50 per share. Use the same account titles as shown in the problem.
5. How many shares of common stock are outstanding after the 10,000 additional shares have been sold?
6. How many shares of common stock would be outstanding after the corporation split its common stock 2 for 1? What is the new par value?
7. Journalize the declaration of a 10% stock dividend on common stock when the market price of the stock is $1 1.25 per share. Assume the stock dividend is declared after the 2-for-1 split.
8. Journalize the following treasury stock transactions in the order given:
   A. Dynamic Pensions purchases 2,500 shares of treasury stock at $25 per share.
   B. One month later, the corporation sells 1,000 shares of the same treasury stock for $27 per share (credit Paid-in Capital from Treasury Stock Transactions).

Work Space:

1.

2.

3.

4.

Date	Accounts and Explanation	PR	Debit	Credit

5.

6.

7.

Date	Accounts and Explanation	PR	Debit	Credit

8.

Date	Accounts and Explanation	PR	Debit	Credit

SOLUTIONS

Matching

1	R	5	J	9	D	13	I	17	S
2	N	6	Q	10	F	14	C	18	G
3	P	7	H	11	A	15	T	19	K
4	L	8	B	12	E	16	O	20	M

Multiple Choice

1	C
2	C
3	D
4	C
5	A
6	D
7	B
8	A
9	C
10	B
11	B
12	C
13	A
14	C
15	B

Completion

1. common (Corporations may also issue preferred stocks, but that is optional.)
2. Treasury
3. receiving dividends and in event of a liquidation
4. the board of directors
5. avoid a takeover; distribute to employees; buy low and sell high
6. common stockholders' equity
7. record
8. declaration
9. outstanding
10. charter; state
11. return on assets
12. return on equity
13. Par
14. Market
15. No-par

True/False

1.   T
2.   F   Net income is added to interest expense, not income tax expense.
3.   F   Only preferred stock will have a liquidation value—common shareholders simply receive a proportionate share of assets remaining after all creditors have been paid and the preferred shareholders have received their cash (liquidation value plus dividends in arrears).
4.   F   This is a very "tricky" statement. It is true that a 50% stock dividend will result in the same numbers of shares as a 3-for-2 stock split. However, the stock dividend results in additional shares having the same par (or stated) value as the original shares, whereas the stock split results in shares having a lesser par (or stated) value.
5.   F   Small stock dividends are recorded at market value as of the declaration date, the date when the liability is established.
6.   T
7.   F   The payment of a cash dividend results in a decrease in assets and liabilities—stockholders' equity is not affected.
8.   F   A gain (or loss) is never recorded on treasury stock transactions.
9.   F   Treasury stock is reported in the stockholders' equity section, as a reduction.
10.   T
11.   T
12.   F   Outstanding stock refers to the number of shares of stock held by owners. Issued stock refers to the total number of shares the corporation has ever sold. If there is treasury stock, the outstanding shares will equal issued shares less the treasury shares.
13.   T
14.   F   The preemptive right allows a current shareholder to purchase additional shares in proportion to the owner's current amount.
15.   T

Exercises

1.

Date	Accounts and Explanation	PR	Debit	Credit
	November 10			
	Retained Earnings		2,475,000	
	Dividends Payable			2,475,000
	(2,250,000 shares x $1.10)			
	December 1			
	No entry needed			
	December 20			
	Dividends Payable		2,475,000	
	Cash			2,475,000

2.

Date	Accounts and Explanation	PR	Debit	Credit
	February 1			
	Cash		10,800,000	
	Common Stock (600,000 x $1)			600,000
	Paid-in Capital in Excess of Par Value			10,200,000
	[600,000 x ($18-$1)]			
	February 10			
	Cash		1,000,000	
	Preferred Stock (20,000 x $50)			1,000,000
	February 28			
	Merchandise Inventory		80,000	
	Equipment		120,000	
	Common Stock (20,000 X $1)			20,000
	Paid-in Capital in Excess of Par Value			180,000
	($200,000 - $20,000)			

3.

Stockholders' Equity	
Paid-in Capital:	
Preferred Stock, 7%, no-par $50 stated value, 100,000 shares authorized, 20,000 shares issued	$1,000,000
Common Stock, $1 par, 5,000,000 authorized, 620,000 shares issued	620,000
Paid-in Capital in Excess of Par – Common stock	10,380,000
Total Paid-in Capital	12,000,000
Retained Earnings	25,000
Total Stockholders' Equity	12,025,000

4.

A. Preferred: 3 years x 10,000 shares x $100 par x 5% = $150,000 (or $15 per share)
Common: $220,000 – $150,000 = $70,000 (or $3.50 per share)

B. Preferred: 3 years x 10,000 shares x $100 par x 5% = $150,000
Since $140,000 is less than the $150,000 preferred stockholders must receive in dividends before common stockholders receive anything, all $140,000 goes to the preferred stockholders. The common shareholders receive nothing, and the preferred now have $10,000 dividends in arrears.

5.

		Assets	Liabilities	Paid-in Capital	Retained Earnings
A	Declaration of a Cash Dividend	0	+	0	–
B	Payment of a Cash Dividend	–	–	0	0
C	Declaration of a Stock Dividend	0	0	+	–
D	Issuance of a Stock Dividend	0	0	0	0
E	A Stock Split	0	0	0	0
F	Cash Purchase of Treasury Stock	–	0	0*	0*
G	Sale of Treasury Stock above Cost	+	0	+	0

*While a cash purchase of treasury stock does not affect Paid-in Capital or Retained Earnings, it does reduce total Stockholders' Equity

6.

Date	Accounts and Explanation	PR	Debit	Credit
	Retained Earnings (800,000 x .05 x $60)		2,400,000	
	Common Stock (800,000 x .05 x $10)			400,000
	Paid-in Capital in Excess of Par (plug)			2,000,000

7.

Date	Accounts and Explanation	PR	Debit	Credit
2/10	Treasury Stock (800 x $24)		19,200	
	Cash			19,200
7/1	Cash (500 x $28)		14,000	
	Treasury Stock (500 x $24)			12,000
	Paid-in Capital from Treasury Stock Transactions (plug)			2,000
12/12	Cash (500 x $36)		10,800	
	Treasury Stock (300 X $24)			7,200
	Paid-in Capital from Treasury Stock Transactions (plug)			3,600

Critical Thinking

No journal entries are required when a company declares a stock split. The outstanding shares are returned to the company and replaced with new shares. Each new share will have a par value of $9.52 ($10 divided by 21/20). The total paid-in capital remains unchanged, however.

Demonstration Problems

1.
Requirement 1:

Date	Accounts and Explanation	PR	Debit	Credit
1/10	Cash		6,600,000	
	Common Stock (300,000 x $22)			6,600,000
1/11	Cash (10,000 x $55)		550,000	
	Preferred Stock (10,000 x $50)			500,000
	Paid-in Capital in Excess of Par – Preferred (plug)			50,000
1/17	Equipment		700,000	
	Common Stock			700,000
1/24	Land		1,000,000	
	Common Stock			1,000,000

Requirement 2:

Assets	=	Liabilities	+	Stockholders' Equity				
				Preferred Stock	Common Stock	Additional Paid-in Capital	Retained Earnings	<Treasury Stock>
				500,000	6,600,000	50,000	12,000	
					700,000			
					1,000,000			
Bal				500,000	8,300,000	50,000	12,000	

Requirement 3:

Stockholders' Equity	
Preferred Stock, 6%, $50 par, 500,000 shares authorized	$500,000
Paid-in Capital in Excess of Par – Preferred	50,000
Common Stock, 1,000,000 shares authorized	8,300,000
Total Paid-in Capital	8,850,000
Retained Earnings	12,000
Total Stockholders' Equity	8,862,000

Requirement 4:

Preferred:	
Liquidation value (10,000 x $52.50)	$525,000
Cumulative dividends in arrears	0
Stockholders' equity allocated to preferred	525,000
Book value per share ($525,000 / 10,000 shares)	$52.50
Common:	
Total stockholders' equity	$8,862,000
Less: Stockholders' equity allocated to preferred	525,000
Stockholders' equity allocated to common	8,337,000
Book value per share ($8,337,000 / 420,000 shares)	$19.85

Demonstration Problem 2

1. Average issue price of the common stock was $8.50 per share:

Common stock at par ($1 x 800,000 shares)	$800,000
Paid-in capital in excess of par—common	6,000,000
Total paid in for common stock	6,800,000
Number of issued shares	÷ 800,000
Average issue price	$8.50

2. Average issue price of the preferred stock was $25 per share:

Preferred stock at par ($25 x 150,000 shares)	$3,750,000
Paid-in capital in excess of par--preferred	0
Total paid in for preferred stock	3,750,000
Number of issued shares	÷150,000
Average issue price	$ 25.00

3. Preferred: $ 2 per share (8% x $25) x 2 years = $4 per share
          $ 4 per share x 150,000 shares = $600,000

Common: $1,197,000 available ($1,797,000 less $600,000 to preferred)
          $1,197,000 ÷ 798,000 shares = $1.50 per share

Note there are 800,000 shares of common stock issued but only 798,000 outstanding because 2,000 shares are in the treasury. Treasury stock does not receive dividends.

4.

Date	Accounts and Explanation	PR	Debit	Credit
	Cash (10,000 x $22.50)		225,000	
	Common Stock (10,000 x $1)			10,000
	Paid-in Capital in Excess of Par – Common (plug)			215,000

5.   Shares outstanding = 808,000
        810,000 shares issued* less 2,000 shares treasury stock = 808,000
      * 800,000 shares issued, plus 10,000 shares from answer 5 above.

6.   Shares outstanding after 2-for-1 split = 1,616,000:
        808,000 shares outstanding immediately before split x 2/1 = 1,616,000 shares
            outstanding
      The new par value of the common stock is $0.50 ($1.00 ^{X}1/2)

7.

Date	Accounts and Explanation	PR	Debit	Credit
	Retained Earnings (1,616,000 shares x 10% x $11.25		1,818,000	
	Common Stock Dividend Distributable (161,600 x $.50)			80,800
	Paid-in Capital in Excess of Par – Common (161,600 x $10.75)			1,737,200

8.

Date	Accounts and Explanation	PR	Debit	Credit
A	Treasury Stock (2,500 x $25)		62,500	
	Cash			62,500
B	Cash (1,000 x $27)		27,000	
	Treasury Stock (1,000 x $25)			25,000
	Paid-in Capital from Treasury Stock			
	Transactions (plug)			2,000

Chapter 10

LONG-TERM INVESTMENTS & INTERNATIONAL OPERATIONS

CHAPTER OBJECTIVES

The learning objectives for this chapter are as follows:

1. Account for available-for-sale investments
2. Use the equity method for investments
3. Understand consolidated financial statements
4. Account for long-term investments in bonds
5. Account for international operations
6. Report investing transactions on the statement of cash flows

CHAPTER OVERVIEW

Successful management of large firms includes the ability to deal with long-term investments and international operations. Long-term investments are an integral part of many complex organizations. They represent a way for a firm to increase the firm's stockholders' equity through diversifying the asset base beyond its current day-to-day operations. International operations represent a special type of long-term investment, representing the firm's global presence.

CHAPTER REVIEW

Objective 1—Account for available-for-sale investments

Long-term investments are a type of noncurrent assets. This category includes both stocks and bonds that the firm expects to hold longer than one year. Long-term investments are reported on the firm's balance sheet, immediately following Current Assets, but before Fixed Assets (Property, Plant and Equipment).

An investor is an entity that owns part of another firm.
An investee is an entity that is partially owned by another firm.

Long-term investments are accounted for based on the percentage ownership of the parent firm (investing company). Consider the following chart:

% Ownership by the Parent (investing) Company	Investor's Level of Influence Upon Investee Firm	GAAP Accounting Method
Up to 20%	None / Very Little	Available-for-sale
20 – 50%	Significant	Equity
Over 50%	Control	Consolidation

Available-for-sale investments are stock investments other than trading securities. They are classified as current assets if the firm expects to sell them within the next year. All other available-for-sale investments are classified as noncurrent assets.

Available-for-sale investments are accounted for at market value because the company expects to sell the stock at its market price. Cost is only used as the initial amount for recording the investments. Thereafter, these investments are reported on the balance sheet at current market value. An end-of-period adjustment is made to "mark to market" the investment. The investment is "written up" or "written down" to reflect unrealized (holding) gains or losses caused by shifts in market prices. A special asset valuation account, "Allowance to Adjust Investment to Market," is used to reflect these holding gains and losses. The investment's carrying value is the historical cost of the investment, plus a debit balance in the allowance account (gains), or minus a credit balance in the allowance account (losses). Unrealized (holding) gains and losses are a part of comprehensive income. Realized (transaction-based) gains and losses are reported in the "Other" section of the income statement. Dividends received from available-for-sale securities are simply recorded as revenue on the income statement. Review the following entries on the accounting equation:

Purchasing an available-for-sale investment										
Assets	=	Liab	+	Equity Ret Engs	+	Revenues	+	Gains	–	Losses
+ investments – cash										

Receiving an available-for-sale cash dividend										
Assets	=	Liab	+	Equity Ret Engs	+	Revenues	+	Gains	–	Losses
+						+				

Marking an available-for-sale investment to market (gain)										
Assets	=	Liab	+	Equity Ret Engs	+	Revenues	+	Gains	–	Losses
+				+						

Marking an available-for-sale investment to market (loss)											
Assets	=	Liab	+	Equity Ret Engs	+	Revenues	+	Gains	–	Losses
–				**–**						

Selling an available-for-sale investment at a loss											
Assets	=	Liab	+	Equity Ret Engs	+	Revenues	+	Gains	–	Losses
+ Cash – investments										**+**

Selling an available-for-sale investment at a gain											
Assets	=	Liab	+	Equity Ret Engs	+	Revenues	+	Gains	–	Losses
+ Cash – investments								**+**		

Objective 2—Use the equity method for investments

The equity method is used for investments representing ownership between 20 and 50% of the investee's stock. Equity-method investments are not marked to market. Rather, a pro-rata portion of the investee's income, losses, and dividends are reported on the investor's books. The investment is valued as follows:

	Original Historical Cost
+	% Share of Investee's Income
–	% Share of Investee's Losses
+	% Share of Investee's Dividends
=	Amount reported on investor's balance sheet

Purchase of equity-method investment										
Assets	=	Liab	+	Equity Ret Engs	+	Revenues	+	Gains	–	Losses
+ Investment – cash										

Recording pro-rata income share on equity-method investment										
Assets	=	Liab	+	Equity Ret Engs	+	Revenues	+	Gains	–	Losses
+						**+**				

Recording pro-rata dividend on equity-method investment										
Assets	=	Liab	+	Equity Ret Engs	+	Revenues	+	Gains	–	Losses
+ Cash – Investment										

Selling equity-method investment at a loss										
Assets	=	Liab	+	Equity Ret Engs	+	Revenues	+	Gains	–	Losses
+ Cash – investment										**+**

Selling equity-method investment at a gain									
Assets	=	Liab	+	Equity Ret Engs	+	Revenues	+	Gains	– Losses
+ Cash – investment								**+**	

Objective 3—Understand consolidated financial statements

Consolidation accounting is a method of combining the financial statements of multiple companies who share a common set of owners.
Consolidated financial statements are a single set of statements collectively representing the parent company and all majority-owned subsidiaries.

Review the following flow chart:

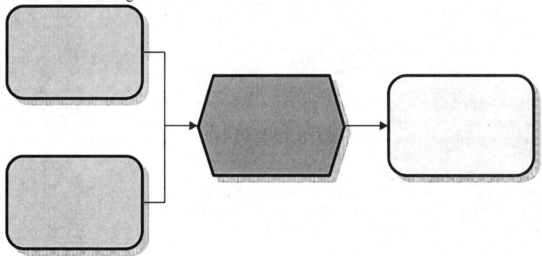

Elimination entries do exactly what their name suggests: eliminate the effects (especially profits and losses) of any intercompany transactions.

Since goodwill arises out of some business combination, it can appear only on consolidated financial statements.

Should a parent own a minority interest in a subsidiary (less than 100%), it includes a pro-rata portion of that subsidiary's income or loss on the consolidated set of financial statements.

Objective 4—Account for long-term investments in bonds

Bond investments are initially recorded at cost. This may reflect a difference from the face value of the bonds. If the bonds are purchased at a discount (less than face value), the carrying value of the bonds is calculated by subtracting the discount from the face value. This difference is gradually written off (amortized) over time. The carrying value will increase over time, and eventually equal the face value.

Conversely, bonds may be purchased at a premium (excess over face value). In this case, the carrying value of the bonds is calculated by adding the premium to the face value of the bonds. As before, the difference is gradually written off (amortized) over time. The carrying value will decrease over time, and eventually equals the face value

Objective 5—Account for international operations

International transactions and subsidiaries must be reported on the parent's consolidated financial statements in US dollars. Accordingly, accountants must use a foreign-currency exchange rate in converting transactions into US dollars.

National currencies' values are constantly shifting. Some currencies become more expensive (strong), and some become less expensive (weak). Factors that influence a currency's exchange rate include:
- The ratio of a country's imports to exports
- The rate of return available in the country's capital markets.

Transactions paid in cash (not on credit, or "on account") record no gains or losses from currency transactions. Only transactions involving time (such as credit or "on account") have the potential of exposing the firm to gains or losses from foreign-currency changes. Settling a transaction with a currency that has become stronger compared to the US dollar will result in a foreign-currency transaction loss. Settling a transaction with a currency that has become weaker to the US dollar will result in a foreign-currency transaction gain. These gains and losses are reflected on the firms income statement in the "Other Revenues and Gains" or "Other Expenses and Losses" section.

A hedge is a legal contract locking in future foreign currency exchange rates. Hedges are extremely complex contracts requiring a great deal of expertise. Managed effectively, these contracts can protect a firm from currency volatility. Managed poorly, these contracts can prove ruinous to a company.

Transactions are not the only items that need to be converted into US dollars. International subsidiaries also need to have their financial statements consolidated into the parent statements. This part of the consolidation process will give rise to foreign currency translation adjustments. No transaction needs to have occurred. This adjustment may result in a gain or a loss. These gains or losses are reported as part of comprehensive income.

Objective 6—Report investing transactions on the statement of cash flows

Cash inflows and outflows arising from long-term investments and international operations are reflected in the Investing Activities section of the Statement of Cash Flows.

TEST YOURSELF

Matching

Match each numbered item with its lettered definition.

_____ 1. subsidiary company	_____ 11. strong currency
_____ 2. minority interest	_____ 12. market value method
_____ 3. hedging	_____ 13. held-to-maturity investments
_____ 4. equity method	_____ 14. majority interest
_____ 5. minority interest	_____ 15. long-term investments
_____ 6. weak currency	_____ 16. available-for-sale investments
_____ 7. marketable securities	_____ 17. internal accounting
_____ 8. foreign-currency exchange rate	_____ 18. short-term investments
_____ 9. parent company	_____ 19. consolidation accounting
_____ 10. consolidated statements	_____ 20. foreign-currency translation adjustment

A. investment that a company plans to hold for one year or less.

B. a currency whose exchange rate is rising relative to other nations' currencies.

C. any investment that the investor expects to hold longer than a year or that is not readily marketable.

D. the measure of one country's currency against another country's currency.

E. accounting for business activities across national boundaries.

F. used to account for all available-for-sale securities which are reported at their current market value.

G. financial statements of the parent company plus those of majority-owned subsidiaries as if the combination were a single legal entity.

H. a currency whose exchange rate is falling relative to that of other nations.

I. ownership of more than 50% of an investee company's voting stock.

J. investment that a company plans to hold for one year or less.

K. an investee company in which a parent company owns more than 50% of the voting stock.

L. the balancing figure that brings the dollar amount of the total liabilities and stockholders' equity of the foreign subsidiary into agreement with the dollar amount of its total assets.

M. a subsidiary company's equity that is held by stockholders other than the parent company.

N. all investments not classified as held-to-maturity or trading securities.

O. a subsidiary company's equity that is held by stockholders other than the parent company.

P. an investor company that owns more than 50% of the voting stock of a subsidiary company.

Q. the method used to account for investments in which the investor has 20-50% of the investee's voting stock and can significantly influence the decisions of the investee.

R. method of combining the financial statements of all the companies that are controlled by the same stockholders.

S. to protect oneself from losing money in one transaction by engaging in a counterbalancing transaction.

T. bonds and notes that an investor intends to hold until maturity.

Multiple Choice

Circle the best answer.

1. Available-for-sale investments in stock are reported on the balance sheet at:
    a. their current market value
    b. their amortized cost
    c. their historical cost or current market value on the balance sheet date
    d. the lower-of-cost-or-market value on the balance sheet date

2. The Allowance to Adjust Investment to Market account may appear in which financial statement?
    a. the balance sheet under the "liabilities" section
    b. the balance sheet under the "assets" section
    c. the balance sheet as part of stockholders' equity
    d. the income statement under the "other income or expenses" section

3. The receipt of a cash dividend arising from an available-for-sale investment held by a company requires a:
    a. credit to Cash
    b. debit to Retained Earnings
    c. credit to Retained Earnings
    d. credit to Dividend Revenue

4. The receipt of a stock dividend arising from an available-for-sale investment held by a company will require a credit to:
    a. Retained Earnings account
    b. Dividend Revenue account
    c. Common Stock account
    d. none of the above answers

5. The gain or loss on the sale of an investment classified as "available-for-sale" is measured by comparing the amount received from the sale of investment with the:
    a. cost of the investment
    b. market value of the investment
    c. amortized cost of the investment
    d. lower-of-cost-or-market value of the investment

6. The Unrealized Gain/Loss on Investment account may appear on which financial statement?
   a. the balance sheet under the "liabilities" section
   b. the balance sheet as part of the stockholders' equity
   c. the balance sheet under the "assets" section as a contra asset
   d. section the income statement under the "other income/expense" section

7. An investment in common stock acquired during 2005 at a cost of $45,000 has a market value on December 31, 2005, of $45,725. The year-end adjusting entry requires a:
   a. credit to Allowance to Adjust Investment to Market for $725
   b. debit to Unrealized Gain on Investment for $725
   c. debit to Long-Term Investment for $725
   d. debit to Allowance to Adjust Investment to Market for $725

8. The receipt of a stock dividend from an available-for-sale investment will require a:
   a. credit to Dividend Revenue
   b. credit to Retained Earnings
   c. debit to Long-Term Investment
   d. recalculation of the cost basis per share of stock owned by the investor

9. The journal entry to record the sale of an available-for-sale investment includes a loss on sale of investment for $500. The income statement will reflect:
   a. nothing, since the entry impacts only asset accounts
   b. other expense of $500
   c. an extraordinary loss of $500
   d. a decrease in net sales of $500

10. The Allowance to Adjust Investment to Market account has a current debit balance of $726. Available-for-sale investments with a cost of $10,000 have a current market value of $11,612. The adjusting entry will require a:
    a. credit to Allowance to Adjust Investment to Market for $886
    b. debit to Allowance to Adjust Investment to Market for $886
    c. credit to Allowance to Adjust Investment to Market for $1,612
    d. debit to Unrealized Loss on Investment for $726

11. The Allowance to Adjust Investment to Market account has a current credit balance of $812. Available-for-sale investments with a cost of $22,000 have a current market value of $22,600. The adjusting entry will require a:
    a. credit to Allowance to Adjust Investment to Market for $1,412
    b. debit to Allowance to Adjust Investment to Market for $1,412
    c. debit to Allowance to Adjust Investment to Market for $600
    d. debit to Allowance to Adjust Investment to Market for $212

12. The adjusting entry for available-for-sale investments contains a credit to Unrealized Gain on Investment for $651. The income statement will reflect:
   a. revenue of $651
   b. an extraordinary gain of $651
   c. the net-of-tax amount as part of "other comprehensive income"
   d. nothing, because unrealized gain is not reported on the income statement

13. Investments accounted for using the equity method are initially recorded at:
   a. fair market value of the investee company multiplied by the percentage of ownership acquired
   b. the total of the investee's equity accounts multiplied by the percentage of ownership acquired
   c. cost
   d. the lower of the cost or fair market value as of the balance sheet date

14. The investor should generally use the equity method of accounting for the investee if the investor owns what percentage of the outstanding stock of the investee?
   a. 0%-15%
   b. 20%-50%
   c. any percentage greater than 50%
   d. any percentage greater than 60%

15. Under the equity method of accounting, the investor will:
   a. reduce the Investment account for investee dividends and increase the Investment account to record investee income
   b. increase the Investment account to record dividends and income of the investee
   c. reduce the Investment account to record dividends and income of the investee
   d. increase the Investment account for investee dividends, and reduce the Investment account to record investee income

Completion

Complete each of the following statements.

1. The price at which stock changes hands is determined by the _____.
2. Two main factors that determine the supply and demand for a particular currency are the country's _____ and _____.
3. Investments in stock are initially recorded at _____.
4. The _____ method is used to account for investments when the investor can significantly influence the actions of the investee.
5. A(n) _____ is ownership of at least 50% of the voting stock of a company.
6. Goodwill is a(n) _____ asset.
7. A change in the currency exchange rates between the date of purchase and the date of payment will result in a(n) _____.
8. Cash used to purchase bonds is reported on the statement of cash flows as a(n) _____ activity.
9. When a parent owns less than 100% of a subsidiary, the other owners are called the _____.
10. Unrealized gains and losses are reported on the _____ in the _____ section.

True/False

For each of the following statements, circle T for true or F for false.

1. T F Unrealized gains and losses result from sales of investments.
2. T F An investment is an asset to the investor.
3. T F Trading investments are classified as current assets.
4. T F As the investee's owners' equity decreases, the Investment account on the investor's books increases.
5. T F Market value is the amount for which you can buy or sell an investment.
6. T F Short-term investments in bonds are the most common.
7. T F Investments accounted for by the equity method are recorded initially at cost.
8. T F A controlling interest is the ownership of more than 50% of the investee's voting stock.
9. T F Accounting for business activities across national boundaries is called national accounting.
10. T F Investee companies are often referred to as affiliates.
11. T F Held-to-maturity investments are reported at their amortized cost.
12. T F Consolidated financial statements reflect the financial statements of only the parent corporation, and no subsidiaries.
13. T F Companies seek to minimize their foreign-currency losses by a strategy called hedging.
14. T F Goodwill may appear on the financial statements of a subsidiary firm.
15. T F Minority interest arises when a parent company purchases less than 100% of the stock of a subsidiary company.

Exercises

1.
Tiger Company purchased 110,000 shares of Woods Corporation on January 1, 2005, for $600,000. Woods Corporation has 1,375,000 shares outstanding. Woods earned income of $300,000 and paid dividends of $100,000 during 2005. Woods Corporation stock was trading at $12.63 on 12/31/04.

    A. What method should be used to account for the investment in Woods?

    B. How much revenue will be recorded by Tiger in 2005 from the investment in Woods?

    C. What is the balance in Tiger's Investment account at the end of 2005?

2.
Billy Company purchased 40% of Bob Corporation on January 1, 2005, for $12,000,000. Bob Corporation earned income of $1,600,000 and paid dividends of $400,000 during 2005.

    A. What method should be used to account for the investment in Bob Corporation?

    B. How much revenue will be recorded by Billy Co. in 2005 from the investment in Bob Corporation?

C.   What is the balance in the Investment account at the end of 2005?

3.

Diablo Company invested in Valley Corporation on January 1, 2005, by purchasing 60% of the total stock of Valley Corporation for $675,000. Valley Corporation had common stock of $400,000 and retained earnings of $725,000.

A.   What amount of Minority Interest will appear on a consolidated balance sheet prepared on January 1, 2005?

B.   If Diablo Company owes Valley Corporation $72,000 on a note payable, prepare the two elimination entries in general journal form.

Date	Accounts and Explanation	PR	Debit	Credit

4.

Contra Company purchased 100% of the common stock of Costa Corporation for $1,315,000. Costa Corporation showed common stock of $280,000 and retained earnings of $510,000. Compute the amount of goodwill resulting from the purchase.

5.

Prepare journal entries for the following available-for-sale stock investment:

6/10   Purchased 6,000 shares of Integrity.com common stock at $35.25, plus a broker's
        commission of $200.
10/2   Received a $.90 per share cash dividend.
11/15   Sold 1,000 shares at $40.25 per share, less a commission of $80.
12/31   Integrity.com stock closed at $42.13.

Date	Accounts and Explanation	PR	Debit	Credit

6.
Prepare journal entries for the following foreign currency transactions.

1/5   Purchased 5,000 cases of dry cider from a British wholesaler for 4.55 pounds
        sterling per case. Today's exchange rate is $1.51 = 1 pound sterling.
1/20 Purchased 2,000 cases of red wine from a cooperative in Coustouge, France. The
        price was 24 euros per case. Today's exchange rate is $1.00 = .975 euros.
2/10 Paid the British wholesaler. Today's exchange rate is $1.43 = 1 pound sterling.
3/20 Paid for the French wine. Today's exchange rate is $1.00 = .96 euros.

Date	Accounts and Explanation	PR	Debit	Credit

Critical Thinking

Review the information in Exercise 5 and change the 10/2 entry to the following:
10/2 Received a 15% stock dividend. The stock was trading at $38 per share.

Prepare journal entries for 6/10, 10/2, 11/15, and 12/31.

Date	Accounts and Explanation	PR	Debit	Credit

Demonstration Problems

1.
Requirement 1:
On 12/31/05, Rouge Corporation paid $375,000 for 90% of the common stock of Blanc Corporation. Blanc owes Rouge $60,000 on a note payable. Complete the following work sheet:

	Rouge Corp.	Blanc Corp.	Eliminations Debit	Credit	12-31 Consolidated Amounts
Assets					
Cash	58,000	26,000			
Notes Receivable from Blanc	60,000				
Investment in Blanc	375,000				
Goodwill					
Plant & Equipment, net	218,000	328,000			
Other Assets	37,000	92,000			
Total	748,000	446,000			
Liabilities & Stockholders' Equity					
Accounts Payable	38,000	41,000			
Notes Payable	170,000	125,000			
Minority Interest					
Common Stock	500,000	110,000			
Retained Earnings	40,000	170,000			
Total	748,000	446,000			

Requirement 2:
Using the following form, present a consolidated balance sheet for Rouge Corporation.

Rouge Corporation
Consolidated Balance Sheet
12/31/05

Demonstration Problem 2.

At 12/31/05, Alpha Corporation had the following long-term investments in its portfolio:

	Cost	Market Value
Available-for-sale securities		
4,000 shares Ajax, Inc	$25.13	$28.00
10,000 shares Dot.com	10.38	18.50
3,800 shares Handy Co.	48.00	37.75
2,500 shares TJCO	63.50	66.25
Held-to-Maturity Bonds		
$100,000, 9% BioLabs, Inc., due 10/1/2010	$100,000	$100,000

Requirement 1

In the space below, present the long-term investments as they would appear on Alpha Corporation's 12/31/05 balance sheet. None of the stock investments are influential. The bonds pay interest semiannually on 4/1 and 10/1.

Requirement 2:
Record the following 2005 events related to Alpha Corporation's long-term investments:

Ajax, Inc.— these shares paid quarterly dividends of $.15/share on 2/10 and 5/10. The shares were sold on 7/2 for $32/share, less a broker's commission of $185.

Dot.com— these shares pay no cash dividends; however, a 10% stock dividend was received on 8/10. The investment remained in the portfolio at the end of the year, at which time its market value was $24 1/4 per share.

Handy Co.— these shares continued to decline in value throughout January, and management decided to sell them on 2/8 for $31/share, less a commission of $205.

TJCO— these shares remained in the portfolio throughout the year. On 9/15 the stock split 3 for 2. At year end, the shares were trading for $55/share.

BioLabs, Inc.— checks for interest were received 4/1 and 10/1. The bonds remained in the portfolio and were trading at face value at year end.

On 6/5/05, Alpha Corporation paid $9.50 a share for 300,000 shares of iTight.com. This ownership represents 30% of the iTight.com outstanding shares and is influential. iTight.com paid 2 cents per share dividends on 8/10 and 11/10 and reported an $850,000 net loss at year end. The stock was trading at $9 on 12/31/05.

On 11/1/05 Alpha Corporation purchased $250,000, 10-year, 6% bonds from Wood, Inc. The bonds pay semiannual interest on 5/1 and 11/1 and were purchased at 97.

Date	Accounts and Explanation	PR	Debit	Credit

Requirement 3:
Record the necessary 12/31/05 adjusting entries

Date	Accounts and Explanation	PR	Debit	Credit

Requirement 4:
Present the long-term investments as they would appear on Alpha Corporations's 12/31/05 balance sheet, taking into consideration the events described in Requirement 2 above.

SOLUTIONS

Matching

1	K	5	O	9	P	13	T	17	E
2	M	6	H	10	R	14	I	18	A
3	S	7	J	11	B	15	C	19	G
4	Q	8	D	12	F	16	N	20	L

Multiple Choice

1	A
2	B
3	D
4	D
5	A
6	B
7	D
8	D
9	B
10	B
11	B
12	C
13	C
14	B
15	A

Completion

1. market (the market allows buyers and sellers with opposing interests to arrive at a price acceptable to both)
2. import/export ratio, rate of return available in its capital markets
3. cost
4. equity
5. controlling interest
6. intangible
7. foreign-currency transaction gain or loss
8. investing
9. minority interest
10. balance sheet; stockholders' equity

True/False

1	F	Unrealized gains and losses are estimates made by using current market values of investments. By definition, a transaction such as a sale has not occurred.
2	T	
3	T	
4	F	Generally speaking, these accounts should reflect changes in parallel. If and investee's owners equity decreases, the investors Investment account should also decrease by a proportional amount.
5	T	
6	F	Bonds are long-term instruments, and are often held to term.
7	T	
8	T	
9	F	Accounting for multi-national activities is called international accounting
10	T	
11	T	
12	F	By definition, consolidated financial statements consolidate, or gather together, the statements of the parent and all subsidiaries.
13	T	
14	F	Goodwill only appears on the financial statements of the parent firm.
15	T	

Exercises

1. A. market value
    B. 8% of $100,000 = $8,000 dividend revenue
    C. $1,389,300 ($600,000 balance in the Investment account plus $789,300 (12.63 x 110,000 shares less $600,000) in the Allowance to Adjust Investment account)

2. A. equity method
    B. $.40 \times \$1,600,000 = \$640,000$
    C. $\$12,000,000 + \$640,000 - (.40 \times \$400,000) = \$12,480,000$

3.

A. .40 x ($400,000 + $725,000) = $450,000

B.

Date	Accounts and Explanation	PR	Debit	Credit
1	Note Payable to Valley		72,000	
	Note Receivable from Diablo			72,000
2	Common Stock (Valley)		400,000	
	Retained Earnings (Valley)		725,000	
	Investment in Valley			675,000
	Minority Interest			450,000

4.

$1,315,000 – ($280,000 + $510,000) = $525,000

5.

Date	Accounts and Explanation	PR	Debit	Credit
6/10	Investment – Integrity.com		211,700	
	Cash			211,700
	(6,000 shares x $35.25) + $200			
	Actual cost/share:			
	211,700 / 6,000 = $35.283			
10/2	Cash		5,400	
	Dividend Revenue			5,400
11/15	Cash		40,170	
	Investment – Integrity.com			35,284
	Gain on Sale of Investment			4,886
	Cost is 1/6 of $211,700			
12/31	Allowance to Adjust Investment to Market		34,234	
	Unrealized Gain on Investment			34,234
	Cost = 176,416 (211,700 – 35,284)			
	Market = 210,650 (5,000 x $42.13)			

6.

Date	Accounts and Explanation	PR	Debit	Credit
1/5	Inventory		34,352.50	
	Accounts Payable			34,352.50
1/20	Inventory		49,230.77	
	Accounts Payable			49,230.77
	(5,000 cases x 4.55 pounds sterling x $1.51)			
2/10	Accounts Payable		34,352.50	
	Foreign-Currency Translation Gain			1,820.00
	Cash			32,532.50
	(5,000 cases x 4.55 pounds sterling x $1.43)			
3/20	Accounts Payable		49,230.77	
	Foreign-Currency Translation Loss		769.23	
	Cash			50,000.00
	(2,000 cases x 24 euros / $0.96)			

Because the dollar strengthened relative to the British pound (on 1/5 it took $1.51 to purchase 1 pound sterling - a month later the same pound would only cost $1.43) a foreign-currency transaction gain was realized when we paid the bill. Conversely, the dollar weakened relative to the euro, so we realized a foreign-currency transaction loss. Foreign-currency transaction gains and losses are reported on the income statement as "Other Revenues and Expenses."

Critical Thinking

Date	Accounts and Explanation	PR	Debit	Credit
6/10	Investment – Integrity.com		211,700	
	Cash			211,700
	(6,000 shares x $35.25) + $200			
10/2	No Entry needed			
	Memorandum Entry Only:			
	We now own 6,900 shares at a cost of $211,700, or ~$30.68 per share			
11/15	Cash		40,170	
	Investment – Integrity.com			30,680
	Gain on Sale of Investment			9,490
	See Note #1			
12/31	Allowance to Adjust Investment to Market		67,555.000	
	Unrealized Gain on Investment			67,555.00
	See Note #2			

Note #1:
Our cost per share was $30.68 (rounded)-see 10/2 details. We sold 1,000 shares at $40.25/share, less the $80 commission. The gain is the difference between our proceeds (1,000 shares x $40.25 less $80) and the cost basis of those shares, $30.68 ^{x} 1,000.

Note #2:
You need to give some thought to this adjustment. Remember our adjusted cost per share is $30.68 and we have 5,900 shares (the original 6,000 plus the 900 share dividend less the 1,000 shares sold on 11/15.) Therefore, our cost basis for those remaining shares is $181,012 (5,900 shares x $30.68/share). On 12/31 the shares were trading at $42.13, so their market value is $248,567.00; the unrealized gain is the difference between $248,567.00 and $181,012 or $67,555.00. Available-for-sale stock securities are reported on the balance sheet at their market value. The amount in the Allowance to Adjust account will be added to the balance in the Investment account, thereby reporting the investment in stock at the market value.

Demonstration Problems

Demonstration Problem #1.
Requirement 1

	Rouge Corp.	Blanc Corp.	Eliminations Debit		Eliminations Credit		12-31 Consolidated Amounts
Assets							
Cash	58,000	26,000					84,000
Notes Receivable from Blanc	60,000			a	60,000		
Investment in Blanc	375,000			b	375,000		
Goodwill			b	123,000			123,000
Plant & Equipment, net	218,000	328,000					546,000
Other Assets	37,000	92,000					129,000
Total	748,000	446,000					882,000
Liabilities & Stockholders' Equity							
Accounts Payable	38,000	41,000					79,000
Notes Payable	170,000	125,000	a	60,000			235,000
Minority Interest					b	28,000	28,000
Common Stock	500,000	110,000	b	110,000			500,000
Retained Earnings	40,000	170,000	b	170,000			40,000
Total	748,000	446,000		463,000		463,000	882,000

Entry (a) eliminated Rouge's $60,000 intercompany note receivable against the note payable owed by Blanc. Note that the consolidated total represents the amount owed to outside creditors ($170,000 owed by Rouge + $125,000 owed by Blanc less $60,000 intercompany debt = $235,000).

Entry (b) eliminates Rouge's $375,000 investment balance against the $280,000 in Blanc's equity. Rouge acquired a 90% interest, so the minority interest is $28,000 (10% x $280,000). Goodwill is the difference between the investment ($375,000) and 90% of Blanc's common stock and retained earnings, or $123,000 ($375,000 - 90% $280,000).

Requirement 2:

Rouge Corporation
Consolidated Balance Sheet
12/31/2005

Assets

Cash	84,000	
Plant and Equipment (net)	546,000	
Goodwill	123,000	
Other Assets	129,000	
Total Assets		882,000

Liabilities & Stockholders' Equity

Liabilities

Accounts Payable	79,000	
Notes Payable	235,000	
Minority Interest	28,000	
Total Liabilities and Minority Interest		342,000

Stockholders' Equity

Common Stock	500,000	
Retained Earnings	40,000	
Total Stockholders' Equity		540,000
Total Liabilities and Stockholders' Equity		882,000

Demonstration Problem #2.
Requirement 1:

Long-term Investments (at market value) $706,075

The cost of the combined long-term investments (both equity and debt) is $645,470, while the 12/31/05 market value of the portfolio is $706,075. Recall that long-term investments are reported on the balance sheet at market value. Prior to the preparation of the balance sheet, an adjusting entry would have been recorded, as follows:

Allowance to Adjust Investment to Market	60,605	
Unrealized Gain on Long-term Investments		60,605

The effect of this adjustment is to increase the investments to their market value. Most companies would report the investments at market value, and then report the cost in a footnote. The unrealized gain would be added into the stockholders' equity section. Alpha would also have adjusted for the accrued interest on the BioLabs bond; however, the amount ($2,250) is NOT included with the long-term investments, but reported separately as interest receivable in the current asset section.

Requirement #2:

Date	Accounts and Explanation	PR	Debit	Credit
	Ajax, Inc.			
2/10	Cash		600	
	Dividend Revenue			600
5/10	Cash		600	
	Dividend Revenue			600
7/2	Cash		127,815	
	Long-term Investment			100,520
	Gain on Sale of Investment			27,295
	Gain = Proceeds – Cost Proceeds = (4,000 shares x $32) - $185 commission Cost = 4,000 shares x $25.13			
	Dot.com			
8/10	No entry needed			
	Memorandum Entry only – 11,000 shares now owned			
	Handy Co.			
2/8	Cash		117,595	
	Loss on Sale of Investment		64,805	
	Long-term Investment			182,400
	Gain = Proceeds – Cost Proceeds = (3,800 shares x $31 - $205 commission Cost = 3,800 shares x $48			
	TJCO			

9/15	No entry needed			
	Memorandum Entry only – 3,750 shares now owned			
	BioLabs			
4/1	Cash		4,500	
	Interest Receivable			2,250
	Interest Revenue			2,250
10/1	Cash		4,500	
	Interest Revenue			4,500
	iTight.com			
6/5	Long-term Investment – iTight.com		2,850,000	
	Cash			2,850,000
8/10	Cash		6,000	
	Long-term Investment – iTight.com			6,000
11/10	Cash		6,000	
	Long-term Investment – iTight.com			6,000
12/31	Unrealized Loss on Long-term Investment		255,000	
	Long-term Investment – iTight.com			255,000
	Note #1			
	Wood, Inc.			
11/1	Long-term Investment		242,500	
	Cash			242,500

Note 1:

Because the investment in iTight.com is influential, the equity method, not the market value method, is used; therefore, dividends received reduce the Investment account balance. Because iTight.com reported a net loss for the year, Alpha's proportional "equity" in the loss is also charged against the Investment account. If iTight.com had reported net income, the Investment account would have been increased.

Requirement 3:

Date	Accounts and Explanation	PR	Debit	Credit
12/31	Allowance to Adjust Investments to Market		149,845	
	Unrealized Gain on Long-term Investments			149,845
	Note #1			
12/31	Interest Receivable		2,250	
	Interest Revenue			2,250
	$100,000 x .09 x 3/12			
12/31	Interest Receivable		2,500	
	Long-term Investment		125	
	Interest Revenue			2,625
	Interest: $250,000 x .06 x 2/12			
	Discount: $7,500 / 10 years x 2/12			

Note 1:

As of the end of 2005, the Allowance to Adjust account has a debit balance of $60,675 (see Requirement 1 Solution). At the end of 2005, the cost and market values of the remaining available-for-sale equity securities are as follows:

	Cost	Market
Dot.com (11.000 shares)	$103.800	$266.750
TJCO (3,750 shares)	158,750	206,250
Totals	$262,550	$473,000

The iTight.com investment is not included in this adjustment. Why? Because the equity method is used, not the market value method.

These totals reflect a difference of $210,450. Given the existing debit balance of $60,605, we need to adjust for $149,845 to increase the Allowance account to the desired $210,500 figure.

Requirement 4:

Long-term Investments (at market)　$815,625
Long-term Investments (at equity)　$2,583,000

The balance in the Long-term Investments (at market) account consists of the following:

Stocks ($262,550 cost + $210,450 allowance)　　　$473,000
Bonds BioLabs　　　　　　　　　　　　　　　　　100,000
Wood, Inc. ($242,500 + $125)　　　　　　　　　　242,625
Total　　　　　　　　　　　　　　　　　　　　　$815,625

The balance in the Long-term Investments (at equity) comes from the iTight.com account, as follows:　$2,850,000 − $6,000 − $6,000 − $255,000 = $2,583,000.

Chapter 11

THE INCOME STATEMENT & THE STATEMENT
OF STOCKHOLDERS' EQUITY

CHAPTER OBJECTIVES

The learning objectives for this chapter are as follows:

1. Analyze a complex income statement
2. Account for a corporation's income tax
3. Analyze a statement of stockholders' equity
4. Understand managers' and auditors' responsibilities for the financial statements

CHAPTER OVERVIEW

The income statement reports the relative success (net income) or failure (net loss) of a business over a period of time. While these two "bottom lines" are the most commonly quoted figures off an income statement, they represent only a fragment of information presented in a typical profit-and-loss statement. It is also important for a financial statement user to be able to follow the movement of profit or loss from the income statement, to the statement of retained earnings, then to the statement of changes in stockholders' equity, finally ending up on the Stockholders' Equity section on the balance sheet.

CHAPTER REVIEW

Objective 1—Analyze a complex income statement

A complex income statement is nothing more than a multiple-step income statement. The complex income statement includes a number of important subtotals that allow users to draw conclusions about the relative quality of earnings. Specifically, did profits arise from day-to-day operations, or did they come from more-or-less one-time transactions unlikely to recur? Profits arising from the former would be considered "higher quality" than those arising from the latter.

Major Income Statement Sections
- Continuing Operations
  - Gross Margin
    - Measures the success or failure of sales only by contrast with cost of goods sold
  - Operating Income (Loss)
    - Measures the success or failure of the firm's day-to-day operations
  - Other Gains/Losses
    - Includes restructuring expenses, and gains/losses from sale of assets

- o Income from Continuing Operations before Income Taxes
  - ▪ Reflects profits/losses from continuing, ongoing operations before income taxes are deducted
- o Income from Continuing Operations
  - ▪ Reflects the net profit/loss from continuing, ongoing operations
- Discontinued Operations
  - o Reported net of income tax benefits, this line reports the losses associated with business lines that have been discontinued and will either be closed or sold off
- Extraordinary Gains and Losses
  - o Must be unusual and infrequent, such as natural disasters
  - o Lawsuits, restructuring costs, and the sale of assets are not extraordinary in nature
- Cumulative Effect of a Change in Accounting Method
  - o Reports the net effects of changing from one accounting method to another, such as changing inventory methods from FIFO to LIFO
- Net Income or Loss
- Earnings per Share
  - o Formula:

Net Income – Preferred Dividends	÷	Average Number of Shares of Common Stock Outstanding

- Comprehensive Income
  - o Includes:
    - ▪ Unrealized gains and losses on available-for-sale investments
    - ▪ Foreign-currency translation adjustments

Objective 2—Account for a corporation's income tax
The current federal corporate income tax rate is approximately 35%. Many states also tax corporate income. The combined federal/state income tax rate is about 40%.

Two accounts are involved in accounting for income taxes:
1. Income Tax Expense – an expense on the income statement
2. Income Tax Payable – a liability on the balance sheet

Income Tax Expense	=	Income before Income Taxes (from the income statement)	X	Income Tax Rate

Income Tax Payable	=	Taxable Income (from the income tax return filed with the IRS)	X	Income Tax Rate

The difference between income tax payable and income tax expense is called deferred taxes. This account may be an asset or a liability.

Objective 3—Analyze a statement of stockholders' equity

Retained earnings includes the current-period net income. Retained earnings may also include prior-period adjustments, which represent corrections of errors that occurred in earlier accounting periods.

Commonly-seen transactions reported in the statement of stockholders' equity:
- Issuing stock (an increase)
- Net Income (an increase)
- Net Loss (a decrease)
- Cash Dividends (a decrease)
- Stock Dividends (no net effect)
- Purchase of Treasury Stock (a decrease)
- Sale of Treasury Stock (an increase)

Commonly seen transactions reported in the statement of stockholders' equity affecting comprehensive income:
- Unrealized Gains and Losses on Investments
- Foreign-currency Translation Adjustments

Objective 4—Understand managers' and auditors' responsibilities for the financial statements

It is management's responsibility to issue financial statements and state their conformance to GAAP.

Independent auditors are hired by the firm to examine the company's financial statements. The auditors then issue one of four types of reports on the financial statements:
- Unqualified — the statements are reliable
- Qualified — the statements are reliable, except for one or more specified items
- Adverse — the statements are unreliable
- Disclaimer — the auditor was unable to reach a professional opinion on the financial statements

TEST YOURSELF

Matching

Match each numbered item with its lettered definition.

_____ 1. disclaimer
_____ 2. investment capitalization rate
_____ 3. taxable income
_____ 4. qualified opinion
_____ 5. extraordinary gains and losses
_____ 6. prior-period adjustment
_____ 7. clean opinion
_____ 8. earnings per share (EPS)
_____ 9. adverse opinion
_____ 10. segment of the business

_____ 11. unqualified opinion
_____ 12. comprehensive income
_____ 13. pretax accounting income
_____ 14. diluted
_____ 15. income tax expense
_____ 16. income tax payable
_____ 17. statement of responsibility
_____ 18. income tax return
_____ 19. deferred taxes
_____ 20. statement of stockholders' equity

A. a company's change in total stockholders' equity from all sources other than from the owners of the business.
B. a correction to beginning balance of Retained Earnings for an error of an earlier period.
C. a liability on the balance sheet.
D. one of various separate divisions of a company.
E. an audit opinion stating that the financial statements are reliable.
F. amount of a company's net income per share of its outstanding common stock.
G. reports the changes in all categories of stockholders' equity during the period.
H. an expense on the income statement.
I. audit opinion stating that the financial statements are reliable, except for one or more items for which the opinion is said to be qualified.
J. is filed with the Internal Revenue Service to measure how much tax to pay the Government.
K. an audit opinion stating that the auditor was unable to reach a professional opinion regarding the quality of the financial statements.
L. when management issues a statement declaring its responsibility for the financial statements and states that they conform to GAAP.
M. usually long-term, but may be an asset or a liability.
N. an audit opinion stating that the financial statements are unreliable.
O. the basis for computing the amount of tax to pay the government.
P. when preferred stock is converted to common stock because more common shares are divided into net income it is reduced.
Q. extraordinary items which are unusual for the company and infrequent.
R. an audit opinion stating that the financial statements are reliable.
S. earnings rate used to estimate the value of an investment in the capital stock of another company.
T. income before tax on the income statement.

Multiple Choice

Circle the best answer.

1. When a company sells a segment of its business, the gain or loss on the disposal of the segment is shown as:
    a. other gains or losses on the income statement
    b. part of the discontinued operations section on the income statement
    c. an extraordinary item appearing on the income statement
    d. an adjustment to the beginning balance of retained earnings

2. The value of a company's stock can be quantitatively estimated by:
    a. dividing the company's investment capitalization rate by retained earnings
    b. dividing the company's current annual income in the future by the investment capitalization rate
    c. dividing the company's retained earnings by the estimated annual income in the future
    d. dividing the company's estimated annual income in the future by the investment capitalization rate

3. A business incurs a loss from a hurricane. It is the first time the business has had a loss from such an event. This loss would probably be classified on an income statement as:
    a. an operating expense
    b. an other expense item
    c. an extraordinary item
    d. an adjustment to the beginning balance of Retained Earnings

4. Changing depreciation methods or inventory methods will be classified on the income statement as:
    a. an extraordinary gain or loss
    b. an other income or other expense item
    c. an adjustment to the beginning balance of Retained Earnings
    d. a cumulative effect of a change in accounting principle

5. The gain on the early retirement of debt is usually classified on the income statement as:
    a. other income
    b. an addition to sales
    c. an extraordinary gain
    d. a reduction in cost of goods sold

6. An analyst with a securities firm calculates the estimated value of a company's stock. Upon further analysis, it is found that the estimated value of the stock exceeds the current market value of the company. Given this, the analyst should make an investment decision to:
   a. hold the company's stock
   b. sell the company's stock
   c. buy the company's stock
   d. The analyst does not have sufficient information to make a prudent investment decision in this situation.

7. Which of the following criteria must be met before an item is considered extraordinary?
   a. The item must be unusual in its nature.
   b. The item must be infrequent in its occurrence.
   c. The item must be both unusual in nature *and* infrequent in occurrence.
   d. The item must either unusual in nature *or* infrequent in its occurrence.

8. Losses due to natural disasters would usually be shown as:
   a. prior-period adjustments
   b. extraordinary items
   c. other gains or losses
   d. a cumulative effect of a change in accounting principle, requiring the restating the beginning balance of Retained Earnings

9. A company incurs a loss due to restructuring. This is the first time the company has gone through restructuring. The loss from this event would be shown as:
   a. an extraordinary item
   b. other gains and losses
   c. prior-period adjustments
   d. a normal business occurrence requiring an adjustment to the beginning balance in Retained Earnings

10. A company that switches from straight-line depreciation to double-declining-balance depreciation during an accounting period must report this change on the financial statements as:
    a. an extraordinary item
    b. income from continuing operations
    c. a prior-period adjustment
    d. a cumulative effect of a change in accounting principle

11. Earnings per share (EPS) is calculated by:
    a. dividing the average number of shares of common stock outstanding throughout the year by net income
    b. dividing net income by the average number of shares of common stock outstanding throughout the year
    c. dividing net income by the number of shares of common stock outstanding at the end of the year
    d. dividing the number of shares of common stock outstanding at the end of the year by net income

12. The dollar amount of a company's net income for each share of outstanding common stock is referred to as:
    a. the price-to-earnings ratio
    b. income as a percentage of equity
    c. earnings per share
    d. cumulative retained earnings ratio

13. Preferred stock dividends must be accounted for in the earnings-per-share calculation. Preferred dividends are:
    a. added to net income in the numerator of the EPS calculation
    b. subtracted from common shares in the denominator of the EPS calculation
    c. added to common shares in the denominator of the EPS calculation
    d. subtracted from net income in the numerator of the EPS calculation

14. EPS is a key measure of a business's success. Which statement below is true regarding EPS and a company's financial statements?
    a. The EPS calculation never takes into consideration preferred stock or preferred stock dividends.
    b. EPS is based on the weighted-average shares of common stock outstanding for an accounting period.
    c. An EPS figure should be calculated and presented for each significant element of net income on the income statement.
    d. EPS based on the actual outstanding number of common shares of stock is called *diluted* EPS.

15. In what situation would a company have to calculate and report *diluted* EPS on the financial statements?
    a. a company that has both convertible preferred and common stock issued and outstanding
    b. a company whose common stock's fair market value has dropped 20% from the prior financial statement reporting period
    c. a company that has both nonconvertible preferred and common stock issued and outstanding
    d. a company that has only common stock issued and outstanding

Completion

Complete each of the following statements.

1. Income tax expense is calculated by multiplying the applicable tax rate times
_____.

2. Income tax payable is calculated by multiplying the applicable tax rate times
_____.

3. The difference between income tax expense and income tax payable is called
_____.

4. Extraordinary gains and losses are both _____ and
_____.

5. To calculate earnings per share, divide _____ by
_____.

6. Number the following income statement categories to show the order in which they should appear. Use * to indicate those categories that should be shown net of tax.

      A. _____ Effect of change in accounting principle
      B. _____ Discontinued operations
      C. _____ Extraordinary items
      D. _____ Continuing operations

7. The P/E is an abbreviation for the _____.
8. The denominator for the P/E ratio is _____.
9. An error affecting net income in a previous accounting period is called a
_____.

10. The four categories of audit reports are
_____,_____,
_____, and _____.

True/False

For each of the following statements, circle T for true or F for false.

1. T F   Fully diluted earnings per share will always be lower than primary earnings per share.
2. T F   Realized gains on the sale of assets are reported as extraordinary items.
3. T F   A company's market value is determined by multiplying the earnings per share times the number of outstanding shares of common stock.
4. T F   To qualify as extraordinary, an item/event must be either unusual or infrequent.
5. T F   To calculate EPS, net income is divided by the number of common shares outstanding at year end.
6. T F   Deferred Tax Liability could be credited or debited when recording a corporation's income tax expense.
7. T F   Prior-period adjustments are reported on the income statement as extraordinary gains or losses.
8. T F   The statement of stockholders' equity will include amounts for net income, dividends, and the sale of investments.
9. T F   Pro forma earnings and forecasted earnings are synonymous terms.
10. T F   Financial information on business segments is found in the notes to the financial statements.
11. T F   The total return on a stock investment can be a positive or negative value.
12. T F   Generally, interim statements are unaudited.
13. T F   Independent auditors are employees of the corporation.
14. T F   A "clean" auditor's opinion is the same as an unqualified opinion.
15. T F   An underfunded pension plan results when the fair market value of the plan's assets are less than the accumulated benefit obligations.

Exercises

1.

For the current year, Mercedes Corporation reported after-tax net income of $420,000. During the year, $63,000 was paid to preferred shareholders and $102,000 was paid to common shareholders. At the beginning of the year, Mercedes had 180,000 shares of common stock outstanding. On 4/1 an additional 60,000 shares were issued. On 10/1, the corporation reacquired 30,000 shares. Calculate earnings per share for the current year. Average common shares outstanding were 217,500.

2.

Trujillo, Inc., reported retained earnings of $1,615,000 as of 12/31/05. During 2006, the company declared and paid $20,000 in preferred dividends and $104,000 in common dividends. Net income for 2006 was $395,000. A prior-period adjustment was recorded, resulting in a charge against retained earnings of $117,000. An extraordinary loss of $186,000 (net of taxes) was also incurred. In the space below, present a retained earnings statement for Trujillo, Inc., for 2006.

Trujillo, Inc. Statement of Retained Earnings 2006		

3.

Quan-Brown Corporation reported pretax income of $235,000 on their income statement and $198,000 taxable income on their tax return. Assume a corporate tax rate of 40%, present the journal entry to record Quan-Brown taxes for the year.

Date	Accounts and Explanation	PR	Debit	Credit

4.

Whitfield Corporation reported the following income statement items for the year:

Extraordinary Loss	($540,000)
Cumulative Effect of Change in Inventory Valuation	110,000
Income from Continuing Operations	410,000
Discontinued Operations:	
Operating Loss	($12,950)
Loss on Sale	($263,000)

Whitfield is subject to a 40% combined income tax rate. Using the form below, show the correct presentation for the above items.

5.
Refer to your solution for Exercise 4. Assuming Whitfield Corporation has 75,000
average shares of common stock outstanding, present the earnings per share information:

Critical Thinking

Examine the information in Exercise 1. Assume the following additional facts: the
company's preferred stock is convertible into 50,000 shares of common stock and
company executives hold options on 100,000 shares of common stock. Calculate fully
diluted earnings per share.

Demonstration Problems

Demonstration Problem #1.

The following amounts were reported for Taylormaid Corporation for the current year.

Administrative Expenses	220,750
Cost of Goods Sold	1,385,000
Cumulative Effect of Change in Depreciation (debit)	-49,200
Discontinued Operations:	
Gain on Sale	22,910
Operating Loss	-205,610
Dividend Revenues	31,000
Gain on Retirement of Bonds	42,000
Gain on Sale of Short-term Investments	87,000
Interest Expense	29,040
Loss from Hurricane	91,000
Loss on Sale of Plant Assets	101,600
Sales Revenue	2,230,000
Selling Expenses	362,500

Taylormaid Corporation is subject to a combined 40% income tax rate.

Requirement 1:
Present a properly classified income statement for Taylormaid Corporation for the current year.

Taylormaid Corporation
Income Statement
Current Year

Requirement 2
Present earnings per share information for Taylormaid Corporation for the current year, assuming an average of 100,000 shares were outstanding throughout the year.

Requirement 3
Assuming Taylormaid Corporation's stock was trading for $8.50 at year end, calculate the P/E ratio based on income from continuing operations and the P/E ratio based on net income.

P/E ratio, based on income from continuing operations.

P/E ratio, based on net income.

Demonstration Problem #2.

At the end of 2005, Baxter International had the following stockholders' equity:

Preferred Stock (6%, $50 par, 1,000,000 shares authorized, 150,000 shares issued	7,500,000
Common Stock ($1 par, 5,000,000 shares authorized, 2,850,000 issued)	2,850,000
Paid-in Capital in Excess of Par	14,250,000
Total Paid-in Capital	24,600,000
Retained Earnings	66,185,000
Less: Treasury Stock (45,000)	-990,000
Cumulative Translation Adjustment	-1,250,000
Total Stockholders' Equity	88,545,000

Requirement 1:

Answer the following questions:

a. What was the average price paid for the preferred shares?

b. What was the average price paid for the common shares?

c. What was the average price paid for the treasury shares?

d. At the end of 2005, the preferred shares were trading at par and the common shares were trading at $31.25. What was the market value of Baxter International?

Requirement 2:

During 2006, the following events occurred:

1. Preferred shareholders received their dividends, as follows:

Declaration Date	Record Date	Payment Date
February 10	March 10	March 30
May 10	June 10	June 30
August 10	September 10	September 30
November 10	December 10	December 30

2. On April 20, a $.90 per share dividend was declared on the common stock to shareholders of record on May 20. The dividend was paid on June 20.

3. On May 29, the corporation paid $36.13 per share for 150,000 shares of common stock.

4. On June 5, the depreciation expense for 2005 was re-calculated. The amount reported for 2005 was overstated by $105,000.

5. Certain key employees hold options to purchase 1,000,000 shares of common stock at varying prices. On August 30, options to purchase 240,000 were exercised at $25 per share.

6. On September 5, the board declared a 10% stock dividend on the common stock to shareholders of record on October 5. On September 5, the shares were trading at $45.25. The additional shares were distributed on November 5.

7.   At the end of 2006, Baxter International reported after-tax profits of $2,615,000.

Journalize the required 2006 entries.

Date	Accounts and Explanation	PR	Debit	Credit

Requirement 3
Using the forms provided, present a retained earnings statement and a statement of stockholders' equity for Baxter International for 2006. At the end of 2006, the amount of the cumulative translation adjustment was ($1,004,500).

Baxter International
Statement of Retained Earnings
For the Year Ended 12/31/06

Baxter International
Statement of Stockholders' Equity
For the Year Ended 12/31/06

	Preferred Stock	Common Stock	Additional Paid-in Capital	Retained Earnings	Treasury Stock	Cumulative Translation Adjustment	Total Stockholders' Equity
Balance, 12/31/04	7,500,000	2,850,000	14,250,000	66,185,000	-990,000	-1,250,000	88,545,000
Cash Dividends							
10% Stock Dividends							
Prior-Period Adjustment							
Purchase of Treasury Stock							
Exercise of Stock Options							
Net Income							
Translation Adjustment							
Balance, 12/31/05							

Requirement 4
At the end of 2006, Baxter's preferred stock was trading at par and the common stock was trading at $51.13. Calculate Baxter's market value as of the end of 2006.

Requirement 5
Calculate the basic earnings per share for 2006. Assume average number of shares outstanding are 2,869,875.

Requirement 6
Calculate the diluted earnings per share for 2006.

Requirement 7
Calculate the price/earnings ratio as of 12/31/06.

SOLUTIONS

Matching

1	K	5	Q	9	N	13	T	17	L
2	S	6	B	10	D	14	P	18	J
3	O	7	R	11	E	15	H	19	M
4	I	8	F	12	A	16	C	20	G

Multiple Choice

1	B
2	D
3	C
4	D
5	C
6	C
7	C
8	B
9	B
10	D
11	B
12	C
13	D
14	C
15	A

Completion

1. pretax accounting income
2. taxable income
3. deferred tax liability
4. unusual and infrequent (order not important)
5. net income less preferred dividends, average number of shares outstanding
6. A. 4
   B. 2
   C. 3
7. D. 1 (income from continuing operations is reported both before and after price/earnings ratio
8. earnings per share
9. prior-period adjustment
10. unqualified, qualified, adverse, disclaimer (order not important)

True/False

1. T
2. F   Gains from the sale of assets are included in the income statement line item "Other Gains/Losses". This line is reported after Operating Income, but part of Income from Continuing Operations.
3. F   A company's market value is determined by multiplying the current market price per share by the number of outstanding shares of common stock
4. F   Extraordinary items must be both unusual and infrequent
5. F   Net income must be reduced by preferred stock dividends before dividing by the number of outstanding common shares.
6. F   Deferred Tax Liability would be credited, but Deferred Tax Asset would be debited.
7. F   Prior-period adjustments are not extraordinary items. They are a separate line item on the income statement, listed after Income from Continuing Operations but before Net Income.
8. F   The Statement of Stockholder's Equity is will include amounts for net income and dividends. Gains and Losses from sales of Investments would be included in net income. Unrealized gains and losses on available-for-sale investments would be listed separately as a part of Comprehensive Income.
9. T
10. T
11. T
12. T
13. F   Independent auditors are not employees of the corporation. They are employed by the CPA firms themselves.
14. T
15. T

Exercises

1.
earnings per share = net income less preferred dividends / average shares of common
                                                            stock outstanding

net income – preferred dividends= $420,000 – $63,000 = $357,000
EPS = $357,000 / 217,500 = $1.64 (rounded)

2.

Trujillo, Inc. Statement of Retained Earnings 2006		
Retained Earnings, 12/31/05 as reported		1,615,000
Less: Prior Period Adjustment		117,000
Retained Earnings, 12/31/05 adjusted		1,498,000
Add: Net Income		395,000
Less: Preferred Dividends	20,000	
Common Dividends	104,000	124,000
Retained Earnings, 12/31/06		1,769,000

3.

Date	Accounts and Explanation	PR	Debit	Credit
	Income Tax Expense		94,000	
	Deferred Tax Liability			14,800
	Income Tax Payable			79,200
	Expense = 235,000 x .4 = 94,000			
	Payable = 198,000 x .4 = 79,200			

4.

Income from continuing operations		410,000
Less: Income Tax Expense (410,000 x .4)		164,000
		246,000
Discontinued Operations:		
Operating Loss (net of tax benefit)	-7,770	
Loss on Sale (net of tax benefit)	-157,800	-165,570
Net income before extraordinary items and cumulative effect of change in inventory valuation		80,430
Extraordinary loss (net of tax benefit)	-324,000	
Cumulative effect of change in inventory valuation (net of tax)	66,000	-258,000
Net Loss		-177,570

5.

Note: most numbers are rounded.

Income from continuing operations (after tax)		3.28
Discontinued Operations:		
Operating Income	-.10	
Loss on Sale	-2.10	-2.20
		1.08
Extraordinary Loss		-4.32
Cumulative effect of change in inventory valuation		.88
Net Income per Share		-2.36

Critical Thinking

Most of the information provided has the effect of diluting primary earnings per share. In other words, if the preferred stock is converted into common stock, the number of outstanding shares will increase, thereby lowering (diluting) the earnings per share. The same is true if the stock options are exercised. To recalculate earnings per share, the denominator changes from 217,500 to 367,500 (217,500 + 50,000 + 100,000). Therefore, EPS (fully diluted) is $357,000 / 367,500 = $.97 (rounded).

Demonstration Problems

Demonstration Problem #1.

Requirement 1:

Taylormaid Corporation
Income Statement
Current Year

Sales revenue		$2,230, 000
Less: Cost of goods sold		1,385,000
Gross margin		845,000
Less: Operating expenses		
Selling expenses	$362,500	
Administrative expenses	220,750	583,250
		261,750
Other revenues (expenses):		
Dividend revenues	31,000	
Gain on sale of short-term investments	87,000	
Interest expense	(29,040)	
Loss on sale of plant assets	(101,600)	(12,640)
Income from continuing operations, before taxes		249,110
Less: Income tax expense ($249,110 x 40%)		99,644
Income from continuing operations		149,466

Discontinued operations:

Operating income (loss), net of tax benefit	(123,366)	
Gain on sale, net of tax	13,746	(109,620)
Income before extraordinary items and cumulative effect of change in depreciation		39,846

Extraordinary items:

Gain on retirement of bonds, net of tax	25,200	
Loss from hurricane, net of tax benefit	(54, 600)	(29,400)
Cumulative effect of change in depreciation, net of tax benefit		(29,520)
Net income (loss)		$ (19,074)

Notes: The items above income from continuing operations could be organized in a single-step format, with income tax expense either included with the other deductions or listed separately.

The items following income from continuing operations are ALWAYS listed net of tax. In addition, the order of the items is discontinued operations, extraordinary items, and, lastly, cumulative effects of changes in accounting principles.

Requirement 2:

Income from continuing operations (after tax)	$1.49
Discontinued operations:	(1.09)
Income before extraordinary items and cumulative effect of change in depreciation	.40
Extraordinary items	(.29)
Cumulative effect of change in depreciation	(.30)
Net income	($.19)

The above amounts are rounded. Note, however, that they reconcile. By far the most important figure above is the EPS from continuing operations. While the corporation did experience a net loss for the year, the items following income from continuing operations should not occur in the future. Therefore, to properly evaluate the company, investors and shareholders will place more emphasis on the continuing operations figure than on the net income amount.

Requirement 3:

P/E, based on income from continuing operations:
$8.50/$1.49=5.7

P/E, based on net income:
This value cannot be calculated because the company experienced an overall net loss.

Demonstration Problem #2

Requirement 1:

a. $7,500,000 / 150,000 shares = $50 per share
b. ($2,850,000 + $14,250,000) / 2,850,000 shares = $6 per share
c. $990,000 / 45,000 shares = $22 per share
d. Preferred market value = 150,000 shares x $50 ea. = $7,500,000
   Common market value = 2,805,000 shares x $31.25 ea. = $87,656,250
   Total market value = $7,500,000 + $87,656,250 = $95,156,250
   * Common shares outstanding equal issued shares less treasury stock

Requirement 2:

Date	Accounts and Explanation	PR	Debit	Credit
2/10	Retained Earnings		112,500	
	Dividends Payable			112,500
	150,000 shares x $.75 / share			
3/30	Dividends Payable		112,500	
	Cash			112,500
5/10	Retained Earnings		112,500	
	Dividends Payable			112,500
6/30	Dividends Payable		112,500	
	Cash			112,500
8/10	Retained Earnings		112,500	
	Dividends Payable			112,500
9/30	Dividends Payable		112,500	
	Cash			112,500
11/10	Retained Earnings		112,500	
	Dividends Payable			112,500
12/30	Dividends Payable		112,500	
	Cash			112,500
4/20	Retained Earnings		2,524,500	
	Dividends Payable			2,524,500
	2,805,000 shares x $.90 / share			

5/29	Treasury Stock		5,419,500	
	Cash			5,419,500
	150,000 shares x $36.13			
6/5	Accumulated Depreciation		105,000	
	Retained Earnings			105,000
6/20	Dividends Payable		2,524,500	
	Cash			2,524,500
8/30	Cash		6,000,000	
	Common Stock			240,000
	Paid-in Capital in Excess of Par- common			5,760,000
9/5	Retained Earnings		13,099,875	
	Common Stock Dividend Distributable			289,500
	Paid-in Capital in Excess of Par – Common			12,810,375
	See Note 1			
11/5	Common Stock Dividends Distributable		289,500	
	Common Stock			289,500

Note 1:

This requires an explanation! The 10% stock dividend is considered a small stock dividend and, therefore, recorded at the market price per share times the number of shares to be distributed. On the date of declaration, there were 2,895,000 shares outstanding, calculated as follows: at the beginning of the year there were 2,805,000 outstanding (2,850,000 authorized less 45,000 in the treasury). On 5/29, an additional 150,000 shares were added to the treasury, and on 8/30 240,000 shares were sold. As of 9/5 there are 2,895,000 outstanding.

$45.25 ^{x} 2,895,0000 \times 10\% = \$13,099,875$

Requirement 3:

Baxter International
Statement of Retained Earnings
For the Year Ended 12/31/06

Retained earnings, 12/31/05		$66,185,000
Add: Prior-period adjustment		105,000
Retained earnings, 12/31/05 adjusted		66,290,000
Net income		2,615,000
		68,905,000
2006 dividends*		
Preferred — cash dividends	$ 450,000	
Common — cash dividends	2,524,500	
Common — stock dividends	13,099,875	16,074,375
Retained earnings, 12/31/06		$52,830,625

* Preferred dividends = 150,000 shares x $50 par x 6% = $450,000

Common dividends:
Cash — In April, there were 2,805,000 shares outstanding (2,850,000 issued less 45,000 shares of treasury stock) x $ .90/share = $2,524,500

Stock — On September 5 there were 2,895,000 shares outstanding (2,805,000 less 150,000 shares purchased on May 29 plus 240,000 shares sold to the key executives on August 30) x 10% x $45.25/share = $13,099,875.

There are now 3,184,500 shares outstanding calculated as follows: 2,895,000 + (10% x 2,895,000) = 2,895,000 + 289,500 = 3,184,500

Small stock dividends are charged against Retained Earnings based on the stock's selling price at the time the dividend is declared.

Baxter International
Statement of Stockholders' Equity
For the Year ended 12/31/06

	Preferred Stock	Common Stock	Additional Paid-in Capital	Retained Earnings	Treasury Stock	Cumulative Translation Adjustment	Total SH Equity
Balance, 12/31/05	7,500,000	2,850,000	14,250,000	66,185,000	-990,000	-1,250,000	88,545,000
Cash Dividends				-2,974,500			-2,974,500
10% Stock Dividends		289,500	12,810,375	-13,099,875			
Prior-Period Adjustment				105,000			105,000
Purchase of Treasury Stock					-5,419,500		-5,419,500
Exercise of Stock Options		240,000	5,760,000				6,000,000
Net Income				2,615,000			2,615,000
Translation Adjustment						245,500	245,500
Balance, 12/31/06	7,500,000	3,379,500	32,820,375	52,830,625	-6,409,500	-1,004,500	89,116,500

Requirement 4

Preferred market value = 150,000 shares x $50 per share = $7,500,000
Common market value = 3,184,500 shares x $51.13 per share = $162,823,485
Total market value = $7,500,000 + $162,823,485 = $170,323,485

Requirement 5

Basic earnings per share= net income less preferred dividends / average shares of
$$\text{common stock outstanding}$$
$$= (\$2,615,000 - \$450,000) / 2,869,875$$
$$= \$.75 \text{ (rounded)}$$

Requirement 6

Basic earnings per share (Requirement 5 above) uses common shares outstanding as the denominator. Diluted earnings per share uses average common shares outstanding PLUS any additional shares that could become outstanding. Remember that 760,000 options could still be exercised (1,000,000 less the 240,000 that were exercised in August). If those additional options are exercised, the total number of outstanding shares increases to 3,629,875 (2,869,875 + 760,000).

Therefore, diluted earnings per share becomes $2,615,000 / 3,629,875 = $.72 (rounded).

Additional items which could "dilute" earnings per share are convertible preferred stock and bonds which have a conversion feature attached to them.

Requirement 7

P/E ratio   = market price per share / earnings per share
               = $51.13 / $.75 (from Requirement 5)
               = 68 (rounded)

Chapter 12

THE STATEMENT OF CASH FLOWS

CHAPTER OBJECTIVES

The learning objectives for this chapter are as follows:

1. Identify the purposes of the statement of cash flows
2. Distinguish among operating, investing, and financing cash flows
3. Prepare a statement of cash flows by the indirect method
4. Prepare a statement of cash flows by the direct method

CHAPTER OVERVIEW

The statement of cash flows is simply an analysis of cash inflows and outflows over a given period of time. Keep this simple: the statement was originally referred to as the "Statement of Where Got and Where Gone." That is what this statement still does: tells the story of where a firm got its money, and where they spent it. This statement is critical since accounting profits do not equal cash flow. It is possible for a profitable firm to be cash-starved. Conversely, it is possible for a marginally profitable firm to have large quantities of cash available.

CHAPTER REVIEW

Objective 1—Identify the purposes of the statement of cash flows

Purposes of the statement of cash flows:
- Predicts future cash flows
- Evaluates management decisions
- Determines ability to pay dividends and interest
- Shows the relationship of net income to cash flows

Cash includes cash equivalents – highly liquid short-term investments that can be converted into cash immediately. These include money market accounts and US government securities.

Objective 2—Distinguish among operating, investing, and financing cash flows

The statement of cash flows has three major sections:
1. Operating – shows cash flows from the day-to-day operations of the firm
2. Investing – shows cash flows from increases and decreases in long-term assets
3. Financing – shows cash flows from changes in long-term liabilities and stockholder's equity (other than income)

Two methods of presenting the Operating Activities section:

1. Indirect method – Starts with net income, reverses out any noncash income statement transactions, and concludes by analyzing changes in current assets and current liabilities. Some users think of this method as a type of balance sheet approach.
2. Direct method – A simple approach that lists cash receipts and cash payments from operations. Some users think of this method as an income statement approach. Though recommended by the FASB, it is not often used in practice.

Investing and Financing Activities sections are unaffected by the selection of indirect/direct method.

Objective 3—Prepare a statement of cash flows by the indirect method

Cash Flow from Operations		Comments
Net Income		*starting figure to convert to cash*
Adjustments to reconcile net income to net cash:		
+ Depreciation/amortization expense		*add back noncash expense*
+ Loss on sale of long-term assets		*add back noncash loss*
– Gain on sale of long-term assets		*take out noncash gain*
+ Increases in current liabilities		*remember the acronym: Add CLICAD*
+ Decreases in current assets		*(Add **C**urrent **L**iability **I**ncreases, **C**urrent **A**sset **D**ecreases)*
– Decreases in current liabilities		*these fail the Add CLICAD acronym, so simply subtract them*
– Increases In current assets		
= Net cash provided (used) by operating activities		*Note: cash and cash equivalents are excluded from this analysis.*
Cash Flow from Financing Activities		*Comments*
+ Cash sales of long-term assets		
– Cash purchases of long-term assets		
+ Collections of notes receivable		

– Issuing notes receivable (making loans)	
= Net cash provided by (used for) financing activities	
Cash Flow from Investing Activities	*Comments*
+ Issuing stock for cash	
+ Sale of treasury stock	
– Purchase of treasury stock	
+ Borrowing	*issuing notes or bonds payable*
– Payment of notes or bonds payable	
– Payment of cash dividends	
= Net cash provided by (used for) financing activities	
= Net increase (decrease) In cash during the year	*represents the sum of the three section subtotals*
+ Cash at end of last year	*appeared on last year's balance sheet*
= Cash at end of the current year	*appears on this year's balance sheet*

Dividends *received* are cash flows from operating activities, but dividends *paid* are cash outflows for financing activities.

Both the direct and the indirect method may have a fourth section: Significant Noncash Investing and Financing Activities. It may seem to be a contradiction to have a noncash section on a statement of cash flows. While not using cash this accounting period, these transactions may affect cash in future periods. An example of this type of event would be purchasing property, plant, and equipment assets by issuing a note payable. This transaction used no cash this period. However, it will use cash in future periods as the note will need to be repaid, probably with interest.

Objective 4—Prepare a statement of cash flows by the direct method

Cash Flow from Operations		Comments
Receipts:		inflows
Collections from customers		
Interest received on notes receivable		
Dividends received on investments in stock		
Total cash receipts		
Payments:		outflows
To suppliers		
To employees		
For interest		
For income tax		
Total cash payments		
= Net cash provided (used) by operating activities		Note: cash and cash equivalents are excluded from this analysis.
Cash Flow from Financing Activities		Comments
+ Cash sales of long-term assets		
– Cash purchases of long-term assets		
+ Collections of notes receivable		
– Issuing notes receivable (making loans)		
= Net cash provided by (used for) financing activities		
Cash Flow from Investing Activities		Comments
+ Issuing stock for cash		
+ Sale of treasury stock		
– Purchase of treasury stock		
+ Borrowing		issuing notes or bonds payable
– Payment of notes or bonds payable		
– Payment of cash dividends		
= Net cash provided by (used for) financing activities		

= Net increase (decrease) In cash during the year	*represents the sum of the three section subtotals*
+ Cash at end of last year	*appeared on last year's balance sheet*
= Cash at end of the current year	*appears on this year's balance sheet*

Both the direct and the indirect method may have a fourth section: Significant Noncash Investing and Financing Activities. It may seem to be a contradiction to have a noncash section on a statement of cash flows. While not using cash this accounting period, these transactions may affect cash in future periods. An example of this type of event would be purchasing property, plant, and equipment assets by issuing a note payable. This transaction used no cash this period. However, it will use cash in future periods as the note will need to be repaid, probably with interest.

Dividends *received* are cash flows from operating activities, but dividends *paid* are cash outflows for financing activities.

Free cash flow is the amount of cash available from operations after paying for planned investments in plant assets:

Free cash flow	=	Net cash provided by operating activities	–	Cash payments earmarked for investments in plant assets

TEST YOURSELF

Matching

Match each numbered item with its lettered definition.

_____ 1. free cash flow
_____ 2. operating activities
_____ 3. indirect method
_____ 4. cash flows
_____ 5. investing activities
_____ 6. statement of cash flows
_____ 7. direct method
_____ 8. cash equivalents

_____ 9. financing activities
_____ 10. noncash activity
_____ 11. depreciation
_____ 12. ending cash balance
_____ 13. gains on asset sale
_____ 14. losses on asset sale
_____ 15. Add CLICAD
_____ 16. Predicting future cash flows

A. activities that increase or decrease the long-term assets available to the business.
B. an activity that consumes no cash in the current period.
C. reports all cash receipts and cash payments from operating activities.
D. noncash expense added back to income in the indirect method.
E. reports cash receipts and cash disbursements classified according to the entity's major activities.
F. activities that obtain from investors and creditors the cash needed to launch and sustain the business.
G. appears on both the balance sheet and the statement of cash flows.
H. the amount of cash available from operations after paying for planned investments in plant, equipment, and other long-term assets.
I. accrual entry subtracted from income on the statement of cash flows.
J. highly liquid short-term investments that can be converted into cash immediately.
K. activities that create revenue or expense in the entity's major line of business.
L. accrual entry added to income on the statement of cash flows.
M. cash receipts and cash payments (disbursements).
N. acronym standing for Add Current Liability Increases and Current Asset Decreases.
O. reconciles from net income to net cash provided by operating activities.
P. one of the major uses of the statement of cash flows.

Multiple Choice

Circle the best answer.

1. A statement of cash flows:
   a. is prepared at the option of management
   b. may be combined with the balance sheet
   c. is a basic financial statement required for publicly held companies
   d. may be combined with the statement of retained earnings at the option of management

2. Cash means more than just cash on hand and cash in the bank. Highly liquid, short-term investments that are easily convertible into cash are called:
   a. common stock
   b. cash equivalents
   c. promissory notes
   d. accounts receivable

3. The statement of cash flows is designed to fulfill all of the following purposes except:
   a. to determine the company's ability to pay dividends to stockholders
   b. to assess the collectibility of accounts receivable
   c. to predict future cash flows
   d. to show the relationship of net income to changes in the company's cash

4. Which of the following transactions would **not** be shown on a statement of cash flows?
   a. purchase of inventory for cash
   b. a stock split
   c. sale of equipment accepting 30% cash and a note receivable for the balance
   d. purchase of land by making a 25% down payment and issuing a note payable for the balance

5. The most important section of a statement of cash flows is the:
   a. operating activities
   b. investing activities
   c. financing activities
   d. all of the sections are equally important

6. Investors analyze the statement of cash flows to determine:
   a. the debt-to-equity ratio
   b. which businesses are expanding and which are shrinking
   c. which companies are reporting unearned revenues
   d. total interest earned during the period

7. All of the following are cash equivalents except:
    a. money market investments
    b. commercial paper
    c. notes receivable
    d. investments in U.S. Government Treasury bills

8. Which of the following activities increase and decrease the long-term assets available to a company?
    a. operating activities
    b. investing activities
    c. financing activities
    d. warehousing activities

9. Cash received from customers would be reported on the statement of cash flows under:
    a. investing activities
    b. operating activities
    c. financing activities
    d. in the schedule of noncash investing and financing activities

10. The issuance of bonds for cash would be reported on a statement of cash flows under the:
    a. operating activities
    b. investing activities
    c. financing activities
    d. no activities because issuing bonds for cash would not be reported on a statement of cash flows

11. After a business is up and running, information about which of the following business activities is most important?
    a. operating activities
    b. investing activities
    c. financing activities
    d. warehousing activities

12. Interest paid on debt would be reported on a statement of cash flows under the:
    a. investing activities
    b. operating activities
    c. financing activities
    d. interest paid on debt would not be reported on a statement of cash flows

13. The receipt of interest on loans would be reported on a statement of cash flows under the:
    a. operating activities
    b. investing activities
    c. financing activities
    d. no activities because interest received on loans would not be reported on a statement of cash flows

14. Which of the following activities creates revenues and expenses in a company's major line of business?
    a. operating activities
    b. investing activities
    c. financing activities
    d. warehousing activities

15. The purchase of available-for-sale securities would be reported on a statement of cash flows under the:
    a. operating activities
    b. investing activities
    c. financing activities
    d. no activities because purchasing available-for-sale securities would not be reported on a statement of cash flows

Completion

Complete each of the following statements.

1. The _____ is the only financial statement that is dated as of the end of the period.
2. The largest cash inflow from operations is _____
3. Both the _____ method and the _____ method of preparing the statements of cash flows are permitted by the FASB.
4. Payments of dividends is a(n) _____ activity on the statement of cash flows.
5. Making loans is a(n) _____ activity on the statement of cash flows.
6. Depreciation is included in the _____ activity section on the statement of cash flows when using the indirect method.
7. The purchase of equipment is a(n) _____ activity on the statement of cash flows.
8. While permitting both methods, FASB recommends the _____ method.
9. The _____ method begins with net income.
10. The difference between the direct and indirect method is found in the _____ section of the statement of cash flows.

True/False

For each of the following statements, circle T *for true or* F *for false.*

1. T F The statement of cash flows is divided into three major sections.

2. T F The statement of cash flows is a supplement to the balance sheet in a company's annual report.

3. T F The statement of cash flows reports the investments the company is making in long-term assets.

4. T F Cash equivalents are highly liquid short-term investments that can be converted into cash quickly.

5. T F Investments in U.S. Government Treasury bills are classified as cash equivalents.

6. T F Businesses invest extra cash in liquid assets rather than let the cash remain idle.

7. T F The main source of cash for a business must come from operating activities if it is to prosper in the future.

8. T F Of the three types of business activities reported on a statement of cash flows— investing, financing, and operating—financing activities are the most important when evaluating a business that is up and running.

9. T F The payment of principal and interest on a loan would be reported in the investing activities section of a statement of cash flows.

10. T F Collections on a loan are reported as a financing activity on the statement of cash flows.

11. T F Of the two formats approved by the FASB for reporting cash flows from operating activities, the FASB clearly prefers the direct method because it reports where cash came from and how it was spent on operating activities.

12. T F Under the indirect method, depreciation expense must be added back to net income under the operating activities.

13. T F Under the direct method, cash receipts from dividend revenue affect both the statement of cash flows and the income statement.

14. T F Only the investing activities section of a statement of cash flows differs between the direct and indirect methods.

15. T F The indirect method of computing cash flows from operating activities begins with net income and reconciles from net income to operating cash flows.

Exercises

1.
Classify each of the following as an operating, investing, or financing activity.

	Classification	Description
a)	_____	payment to employees
b)	_____	lending money
c)	_____	receiving dividends on investments
d)	_____	selling treasury stock
e)	_____	raising funds by selling bonds
f)	_____	receiving cash from customers
g)	_____	paying taxes
h)	_____	purchasing equipment by paying cash
i)	_____	purchasing equipment and signing a note payable
j)	_____	purchasing inventory on account
k)	_____	receiving interest revenue
l)	_____	paying dividends to stockholders
m)	_____	selling short-term investments
n)	_____	selling shares of common stock

2.   Haynes Company had interest expense of $54,000 in 2005. The balance in Interest Payable was $2,100 at the beginning of the year and $3,600 at the end of the year. How much cash was paid for interest during 2005?

3.   Batista Company had cost of goods sold of $600,000, an increase in inventory of $15,000, and an increase in accounts payable of $27,000 in 2005. How much cash was paid to suppliers?

4.   Tran Company had sales of $2,100,000 in 2005. Ninety percent of sales are on credit. During the year, Accounts Receivable increased from $40,000 to $95,000. How much cash was received from customers during 2005?

5.   Saechow Company purchased equipment for $185,000, lent $32,000 to a
      customer, borrowed $42,000, and sold securities that were not cash equivalents
      for $12,000. What was the net cash flow from investing activities?

6.   From the following list of cash receipts and payments, present the cash flows
      from the operating section of the cash flow statement, using the direct method.

Cash receipts from interest revenues	$1,820
Cash paid for taxes	43,110
Cash payments to supplier	328,590
Cash receipts from customers	615,200
Cash paid for dividends	12,700
Cash payments to employees	103,200
Cash receipts from dividend revenues	780
Cash payments for interest	4,965

Critical Thinking

Review the information in Exercises 2 and 4. Calculate the same answer using a different approach.

Demonstration Problems

Demonstration Problem #1

The income statement, schedule of current account changes, and additional data for Village Books follows:

Village Books

Income Statement

For the Year Ended December 31, 2005

Revenues:		
Net sales revenue	$3,512,500	
Dividend revenue	67,500	$3,580,000
Expenses:		
Cost of goods sold	2,702,500	
Salary expense	322,500	
Other operating expense	77,500	
Depreciation expense	137,500	
Interest expense	162,500	
Amortization expense-patents	12,500	3,415,000
Net income		$165,000

Additional data:

a. Collections exceeded sales by $17,500.
b. Dividend revenue equaled cash amounts received, $67,500.
c. Payments to suppliers were $45,000 less than cost of goods sold. Payments for other operating expense and interest expense were the same as 'Other operating expense' and 'Interest expense'.
d. Payments to employees were less than salary expense by $10,000.
e. Acquisition of plant assets totaled $325,000. Of this amount, $50,000 was paid in cash and the balance was financed by signing a note payable.
f. Proceeds from the sale of land were $212,500.
g. Proceeds from the issuance of common stock were $125,000.
h. Full payment was made on a long-term note payable, $100,000.

i. Dividends were paid in the amount of $40,000.
j. A small parcel of land located in an industrial park was purchased for $185,000.
k. Current asset and liability activity changes were as follows:

	December 31	
	2005	2004
Cash and cash equivalents	580,00	230,000
Accounts receivable	590,00	607,500
Inventory	945,00	960,000
Prepaid expense	30,000	30,000
Accounts payable	535,00	505,000
Salary payable	27,500	17,500
Income tax payable	8,000	8,000

Required:
1. Using the direct method, prepare the December 31, 2005, statement of cash flows and accompanying schedule of noncash investing and financing activities for Village Books.
2. Calculate the corporation's free cash flow

Requirement 1:

Village Books
Statement of cash flows
For the Year Ended December 31, 2005

Requirement 2:

Demonstration Problem #2
Using the information in Demonstration Problem #1, prepare a statement of cash flows and accompanying schedule of noncash investing and financing activities using the indirect method.

Village Books
Statement of cash flows
For the Year Ended December 31, 2005

SOLUTIONS

Matching

1	H	5	A	9	F	13	J
2	K	6	E	10	B	14	L
3	O	7	C	11	D	15	N
4	M	8	J	12	G	16	P

Multiple Choice

1	C
2	B
3	B
4	B
5	A
6	B
7	C
8	B
9	B
10	C
11	A
12	B
13	A
14	A
15	B

Completion

1. balance sheet (The income statement, statement of retained earnings, and statement of cash flows all cover a period of time. Only the balance sheet is as of a particular date.)
2. collections of cash from customers
3. direct, indirect (order not important)
4. financing
5. investing
6. operating (Recall from our previous discussion that depreciation is a noncash expense.)
7. investing
8. direct
9. indirect
10. operating activities

True/False

1	T	
2	F	The statement of cash flows is one of the four primary financial statements. It complements, not supplements the balance sheet
3	T	
4	T	
5	T	
6	T	
7	T	
8	F	The term "up and running" refers to the day-to-day operations of the firm. Generally, and in this case, the Operating Activities section is considered the most important section of the statement of cash flows
9	T	
10	F	Collection of a loan would a cash inflow reported in Investing Activities section of the statement of cash flows
11	T	
12	T	
13	T	
14	F	Only the Operating Activities section differs in presentation between the direct and indirect methods of preparing the statement of cash flows.
15	T	

Exercises

1.
a. operating
b. investing
c. operating
d. financing
e. financing
f. operating
g. operating
h. investing
i. none (this is a noncash activity)
j. operating
k. operating
l. financing
m. investing
n. financing

2. Note that this exercise and the next ones may be solved using what you learned in earlier chapters.

	Interest Payable (beginning)	$2,100
+	Interest Expense	54,000
=	Subtotal	56,100
−	Cash payments	?
=	Interest Payable (ending)	$3,600

$2,100 + $54,000 - x = $3,600
x = $52,500

3.

	Cost of Goods Sold	$600,000
+	Increase in Inventory	15,000
=	Subtotal	615,000
-	Increase in Accounts Payable	27,000
=	Cash paid to suppliers	$588,000

4. Cash received from credit sales:

	Accounts Receivable (beginning)	$40,000
+	Credit sales (90% × 2,100,000)	1,890,000
=	Subtotal	1,930,000
−	Cash collected from customers	?
=	Accounts Receivable (ending)	$95,000

Cash received from credit sales ($1,930,000 - $95,000)	$1,835,000
Cash collected from cash sales (10% x 2,100,000)	210,000
= Total cash collected from customers	$2,045,000

5.

Purchase of equipment	$(185,000)
Loan made to customer	(32,000)
Sale of securities	12,000
Net cash flow from investing activities	$(205,000)

Borrowing $42,000 is not an investing activity. It is a financing activity.

6.

Cash flows from operating activities		
Cash receipts from customers	615,200	
Cash receipts from dividends	780	
Cash receipts from interest	1,820	
Cash payments to suppliers	-328,590	
Cash payments to employees	-103,200	
Cash paid for taxes	-43,110	
Cash payments for interest	-4,965	
Net cash inflow from operating activities		137,935

The cash paid for dividends is not an operating activity. Dividends paid to shareholders relate to stockholders' equity on the balance sheet and are, therefore, a financing activity.

Critical Thinking

Exercise 2

Interest Expense	$54,000
* Less increase in Interest Payable	1,500
Payments for interest	$52,500

*The increase in the related liability is deducted because it represents an expense which has not been paid. Similarly, a decrease in the related liability would be added. Remember we are concerned with <u>cash payments.</u>

Exercise 4

Sales	$2,100,000
** Less increase in Accounts Receivable	55,000
Cash received from customers	$2,045,000

**The increase in Accounts Receivable is deducted because it represents credit sales which have not been collected. Similarly a decrease in Accounts Receivable would be added because it represents additional credit sales collected. Remember we are concerned with cash receipts.

Demonstration Problems

Demonstration Problem #1.
Requirement 1 (direct method)

Village Books
Statement of cash flows
For the Year Ended December 31, 2005

Cash Flows from operating activities				
Receipts:				
Collections from customers	3,530,000	A		
Dividends received from investments in stock	67,500	B		
Total cash receipts			3,597,500	
Payments:				
To suppliers	2,735,000	C		
To employees	312,500	D		
For interest	162,500	C		
Total cash payments			3,210,000	
Net cash flows from operating activities			387,500	
Cash flows from investing activities:				
Acquisition of plant assets	-50,000	E		
Proceeds from sale of land	215,500	F		
Acquisition of industrial park land	-185,000	J		
Net cash outflow from investing activities			-22,500	
Cash flows from financing activities:				
Proceeds from common stock issuance	125,000	G		
Payment of long-term note payable	-100,000	H		
Payment of dividends	-40,000	I		
Net cash outflow from financing activities			-15,000	
Net increase in cash			350,000	
Cash balance at beginning of year			230,000	
Cash balance at end of year			580,000	

Noncash investing & financing activities				
Acquisition of plant assets by issuing notes payable			275,000	E

Computations and Explanations

(A) The largest cash inflow from operations will almost always be the collection of cash from customers. Cash sales obviously will bring in cash immediately. Since sales on account increase Accounts Receivable (not Cash), companies need to know the actual collections from customers. Item (a) of the additional data indicates that collections from customers were more than sales by $17,500. Thus, collections must have been $3,530,000 ($3,512,500 sales plus $17,500).

(B) Dividends do not accrue with the passage of time, but rather are recorded when received. Item (b) of the additional data states that $67,500 was received, the identical amount shown in the income statement. Thus, no adjustment is necessary. Note that dividends received result in a cash inflow reported as an operating activity. Although the origin of the dividend was from an investment activity, in accordance with the FASB, dividends received were accounted for as part of operating activities because they have a direct impact on net income.

(C) Payments to suppliers is a broad category which includes all cash payments for inventory and all operating expenses except disbursements for:

1. employee compensation expense
2. interest expense
3. income tax expense

A review of Item (c) indicates that payments to suppliers were $2,735,000 ($2,657,500 + $77,500) as follows:

Cost of goods sold	$2,702,500
Less: Additional amounts owed to suppliers	45,000
Payments for inventory	$2,657,500
Payments for other operating expenses	$77,500

Payments to suppliers include all payments (except those listed above as exceptions) to those who supply the business with its inventory and essential services. Note that interest payment equals interest expense, an item that is separately disclosed in the statement of cash flows.

(D) Payments to employees include all forms of employee compensation. The income statement reports the expense (including accrued amounts), whereas the statement of cash flows reports only the payments. Item (d) indicates that actual payments were $312,500, which is $10,000 less than the $322,500 reported in the income statement as salary expense.

(E) The purchase of $325,000 in plant assets used $50,000 in cash. The balance was financed with a $275,000 promissory note. Because the note is not an outflow of cash, it is separately disclosed as a noncash investing activity at the bottom of the statement of cash flows.

The $185,000 industrial park land (Item j) used $185,000 cash and is shown as a cash outflow or "use." A firm's investment in income-producing assets often signals to investors the direction that the firm is taking.

(F) The receipt of $212,500 from the land sale (Item f) is essentially the opposite of the acquisition of a plant asset, and should be reported as a cash inflow from an investment transaction.

(G) Investors and other financial statement users want to know how an entity obtains its financing. The financing activities section of the cash-flow statement for Village Books discloses the effect of the sale of common stock (inflow of $125,000, Item g), payment of a long-term note (outflow of $100,000, Item h), and payment of cash dividends (outflow of $40,000, Item i).

Requirement 2:

$365,000

Free cash flow is the difference between cash flows from operating activities and cash flows from investing activities. A review of the cash-flow statement shows cash inflows from operating activities of $387,500 and net cash outflows from investing activities of $22,500. Therefore, free cash flows are $387,500 - $22,500 = $365,000.

Demonstration Problem #2:

Village Books
Statement of cash flows
For the Year Ended December 31, 2005

Cash Flows from operating activities				
Net income			165,000	
Add (subtract) items that affect net income and cash flow differently:				
Depreciation	137,500			
Amortization	12,500			
Decrease in Accounts Receivable	17,500			
Decrease in Inventory	15,000			
Increase in Accounts Payable	30,000			
Increase in Salary Payable	10,000			
Net cash flows from operating activities			387,500	
Cash flows from investing activities:				
Acquisition of plant assets	-50,000	E		
Proceeds from sale of land	215,500	F		
Acquisition of industrial park land	-185,000	J		
Net cash outflow from investing activities			-22,500	
Cash flows from financing activities:				
Proceeds from common stock issuance	125,000	G		
Payment of long-term note payable	-100,000	H		
Payment of dividends	-40,000	I		
Net cash outflow from financing activities			-15,000	
Net Increase in cash			350,000	
Cash balance at beginning of year			230,000	
Cash balance at end of year			580,000	
Noncash investing & financing activities				
Acquisition of plant assets by issuing notes payable			275,000	E

As emphasized many times in the chapter, the difference between the direct method and the indirect method appears only in the presentation of the cash flows from operating activities section of the statement. The indirect method begins with net income, then 'adjusts' the net income figure in order to convert it to a cash-based value. Regardless of method, the presentation of cash flows from investing activities and financing activities are the same. FASB permits either method, but recommends the direct method because it is thought to be more "user friendly."

Chapter 13

FINANCIAL STATEMENT ANALYSIS

CHAPTER OBJECTIVES

The learning objectives for this chapter are as follows:

1. Perform a horizontal analysis of comparative financial statements
2. Perform a vertical analysis of financial statements
3. Prepare and use common-size financial statements
4. Use the statement of cash flows for decisions
5. Compute the standard financial ratios
6. Use ratios in decision making
7. Measure the economic value added by operations

CHAPTER OVERVIEW

The previous twelve chapters of this textbook have given you an excellent foundation in the understanding of accounting information and financial statements. Unfortunately, that is not enough to be a successful user of financial statements. A user must be able to compare the financial statements to something.

Consider the unicycle photograph on the cover of your textbook. Is the unicycle large or small? Is the unicycle 2 inches tall, 20 inches tall, or 2 feet tall? There is no way to tell, unless you are given a point of reference to compare it to.

FINANCIAL ACCOUNTING

sixth edition

HARRISON   HORNGREN

The same is true for financial statements. Unless you can compare them to last period's results, the results of a competitor, or some industry average, it is nearly impossible to draw definite conclusions from the financial statements regarding the relative health (or risks) of the firm.

CHAPTER REVIEW

Objective 1—Perform a horizontal analysis of comparative financial statements

Horizontal analysis is exactly what it sounds like: a side-to-side evaluation of a set of multi-period financial statements. The focus is on change from one period to another. The change could be measured in dollars or in a percentage. Measuring changes in terms of percentages is a very important tool for financial statement users. Using percentages standardizes two or more financial statements of different sizes. Instead of reporting income simply in dollars, they can also be reported in percentage changes. In that way, a trend may be observed, as well as the magnitude of the trend. Simply put, a one million dollar increase may be difficult to conceptualize, but most users could understand the same one million dollar increase translated into a 10% increase. Percentages are often easier and simpler to use.

Simpler horizontal analysis compares two years: this year and last year.

| Change measured in dollars | = | Newer Year amount | − | Older Year amount |

$$\text{Change measured in percentages} = \frac{\text{Change measured in dollars}}{\text{Older Year amount}}$$

Another way to remember this formula:

$$\text{Change measured in percentages} = \frac{\text{Newer Year amount} - \text{Older Year amount}}{\text{Older Year amount}}$$

A more complex form of horizontal analysis (called trend analysis) compares two years: any year and the base year. The base year of study is usually the oldest year, and is used to compare each year in the analysis, regardless of how far away the year of study is from the current year.

| Trend Change measured in dollars | = | Any Year amount | − | Base Year amount |

$$\text{Trend Change measured in percentages} = \frac{\text{Trend Change measured in dollars}}{\text{Base Year amount}}$$

Objective 2—Perform a vertical analysis of financial statements

Vertical analysis is, as it's name suggests, an up-down analysis. Financial statements are converted from dollars to percentages, using either total revenues (for income statements) or total assets (for balance sheets) as the base figure.

Vertical analysis formula for income statements:

Vertical Analysis %	=	$\dfrac{\text{Each Income Statement Line Item}}{\text{Total Revenue}}$

Vertical analysis formula for balance sheets:

Vertical Analysis %	=	$\dfrac{\text{Each Balance Sheet Line Item}}{\text{Total Assets}}$

Objective 3—Prepare and use common-size financial statements

Common-size financial statements are a complete set of ordinary financial statements presented in terms of percentages instead of dollars. They may use either the horizontal or vertical approach.

Benchmarking is the comparison of a company to a standard set by others, with a view toward improvement. The standard may be of a competitor, a set of competitors, or some industry average.

Objective 4—Use the statement of cash flows for decisions

Careful evaluation of the statement of cash flows is important in the overall study of a set of financial statements. Remember, the statement of cash flows is the only financial statement that does not contain accounting estimates. A transaction is, or is not, cash. In other words, the statement of cash flows is the most objective component of a set of financial statements, because the level of management influence is limited.

Favorable cash-flow indicators:
- Operations are the major provider of cash (a surplus, if you will).
- Investing activities include more purchases than sales of long-term assets. Purchases of long-term assets provide a strong signal that management believes the outlook of the firm is favorable.
- Financing activities are not dominated by borrowing. Debt must be repaid, with interest. Equity does not.

Objective 5—Compute the standard financial ratios and Objective 6—Use ratios in decision making

Measuring ability to pay current liabilities:

Ratio	Formula	Description	Interpretation
Current	Current Assets ÷ Current Liabilities	Measures the ability to pay bills on time as they become due	Rule of thumb: 2:1. Lower is risky. Higher is inefficient
Acid-test (quick)	(Cash + Short-term Receivables + Net A/R) ÷ Current Liabilities	Measures the ability to pay all bills immediately if necessary	Depending on level of acceptable risk, somewhere between .7:1 and 1:1 is ideal. Lower is risky. Higher is inefficient

Measuring ability to sell inventory and collect receivables:

Ratio	Formula	Description	Interpretation
Inventory Turnover	Cost of Goods Sold ÷ Average Inventory	Indicates the number of times a firm "sells out" of inventory	Higher is better
Accounts Receivable Turnover	Net Credit Sales ÷ Average Net Accounts Receivable	Indicates the number of times a year customers "completely pay off" all of their accounts	Higher is better
Days' Sales in Receivables	Average Net Accounts Receivable ÷ One Day's Credit Sales	Indicates how long it takes the average customer to pay off their account	Lower is better

Measuring ability to pay long-term debt:

Ratio	Formula	Description	Interpretation
Debt Ratio	Total Assets ÷ Total Liabilities	Indicates the percentage of assets financed with debt	Higher is riskier
Times-Interest Earned Ratio	Income from Operations ÷ Interest Expense	Measures how "easily" a firm can afford to cover its interest expense	Lower is riskier

Measuring profitability:

Ratio	Formula	Description	Interpretation
Rate of return on net sales	Net Income ÷ Net Sales	Shows how much ("in cents") of each sales dollar is profit	Higher is better
Rate of return on total assets	(Net Income + Interest Expense) ÷ Average Total Assets	Measures how much profit is earned for every dollar invested in assets	Higher is better
Rate of return on common stockholders' equity	(Net Income – Preferred Dividends) ÷ Average Common Stockholders' Equity	Measures how much profit is earned for every dollar invested by the common shareholder	Higher is better
Earnings per share of common stock	(Net Income – Preferred Dividends) ÷ Average Number of Shares of Common Stock Outstanding	Measures how much profit is earned on each share of common stock	Higher is better

Analyzing stock as an investment:

Ratio	Formula	Description	Interpretation
Price/Earnings Ratio	Market Price per Share of Common Stock ÷ Earnings per share	Measures how relatively "expensive" a share of stock is	Higher is more expensive
Dividend Yield	Dividend per Share of Common (or Preferred) stock ÷ Market price per share of common (or preferred) Stock	Measures how much will be returned to the stockholder in the form of dividends (can be viewed as $ dividend per $1 invested	Higher means more dividends
Book Value per share of common stock	(Total Stockholders' Equity – Preferred Equity) ÷ Average Number of Shares of Common Stock Outstanding	Reports the value per share of stock from the perspective of the firm's own accounting record	Higher is better

Objective 7—Measure the economic value added by operations

Economic Value Added (EVA®) is a different way of evaluating the financial results of a firm. EVA® combines accounting and finance to measure whether operations have increased stockholder wealth.

EVA®	=	Net Income	+	Interest Expense	−	Capital Charge

Capital Charge	=	Notes Payable + Current Maturities of Long-term Debt + Long-term Debt + Stockholders' Equity	X	Cost of Capital

The capital charge may be viewed as invested capital from all sources (debt and equity) times the cost of capital (expressed as an interest rate).

Interpretation of the EVA® is simple: a positive EVA® is favorable; a negative EVA® is unfavorable.

An efficient capital market is one in which market prices fully reflect all information to the public.

TEST YOURSELF

Matching

Match each numbered item with its lettered definition.

_____ 1. benchmarking
_____ 2. vertical analysis
_____ 3. price/earnings ratio
_____ 4. inventory turnover
_____ 5. dividend yield
_____ 6. capital charge
_____ 7. working capital
_____ 8. horizontal analysis
_____ 9. book value per share
_____ 10.earnings per share

_____ 11. common-size statement
_____ 12. trend percentages
_____ 13. efficient capital market
_____ 14. rate of return on net sales
_____ 15. cost of capital
_____ 16. accounts receivable turnover
_____ 17. economic value added (EVA)
_____ 18. quick ratio
_____ 19. debt ratio
_____ 20. current ratio

A. are a form of horizontal analysis which indicate the direction a business is taking.

B. measures a business's ability to meet its short-term obligations with its current assets.

C. ratio of the sum of cash plus short-term investments plus net current receivables to total current liabilities; tells whether the entity can pay all its current liabilities if they come due immediately.

D. study of percentage changes in comparative financial statements.

E. ratio of net income to net sales; measure of profitability.

F. financial statement that reports only percentages (no dollar amounts).

G. measures a company's ability to collect cash from credit customers.

H. amount that stockholders and lenders charge a company for the use of their money.

I. used to evaluate a company's operating performance by combining the concepts of accounting income and corporate finance to measure whether the company's operations have increased stockholder wealth.

J. analysis of a financial statement that reveals the relationship of each statement item to a specified base, which is the 100% figure.

K. ratio of dividends per share of stock to the stock's market price per share; tells the percentage of a stock's market value that the company returns to stockholders as dividends.

L. weighted average of the returns demanded by the company's stockholders and lenders.

M. ratio of cost of goods sold to average inventory; indicates how rapidly inventory is sold.

N. capital market in which market prices fully reflect all information available to the public.

O. the practice of comparing a company to a standard set by other companies, with a view toward improvement.

P. ratio of the market price of a share of common stock to the company's earnings per share.

Q. a measure of evaluating a firm's ability to pay a firm's bills as they become due

R. indicates the percentage of assets financed with debt

S. gives the amount of net income earned for each share of common stock outstanding

T. indicates the recorded accounting amount for each share of common stock outstanding

Multiple Choice

Circle the best answer.

1. Horizontal analysis involves the study of:
   a. percentage changes in comparative financial statements
   b. percentage and/or dollar amount changes in various financial statement amounts from year to year
   c. the change in key financial statement ratios over a certain time frame or horizon
   d. the changes in individual financial statement amounts as a percentage of some related total

2. The percentage change in any individual item shown on comparative financial statements is calculated by dividing the dollar amount of the change from the base period to the current period by:
   a. 100
   b. the amount shown for the current period
   c. the average of the amounts shown for the base and the current periods
   d. the base-period amount

3. The analysis of percentage changes in comparative statements is known as:
   a. economic value added analysis
   b. benchmarking analysis
   c. horizontal analysis
   d. vertical analysis

4. The form of analysis that looks at trend percentages over a representative period is known as:
   a. trend analysis, which is considered a form of horizontal analysis
   b. trend analysis, which is considered a form of vertical analysis
   c. ratio analysis
   d. economic value added analysis

5. A company reported $75,000 of income for 2004, $80,000 for 2005, and $90,000 for 2006. The percentage change in net income from 2005 to 2006 was:
   a. 9.1%
   b. 11.1%
   c. 12.5%
   d. 16.7%

6. Referring to question 5, the percentage change in net income from 2004 to 2005 was:
   a. 6.7%
   b. 6.25%
   c. 5.9%
   d. 10.7%

7. Assuming the Accounts Receivable balance at the end of 2004 is $80,000, and it has decreased by 15% per year since the end of 2003, the balance at the end of 2003 (rounded to the nearest whole dollar) was:
   a. $110,727
   b. $99,188
   c. $94,188
   d. $53,333

8. Assuming the Accounts Payable balance at the end of 2005 is $45,000, and it has increased by 10% per year since the end of 2003, the balance at the end of 2003 (rounded to the nearest whole dollar) was:
   a. $36,450
   b. $37,190
   c. $40,909
   d. $40,500

9. Assuming the balance in Retained Earnings at the end of 2004 is $180,000, and it has increased by 15% since the end of 2001, the balance at the end of 2003 (rounded to the nearest whole dollar) was:
   a. $156,522
   b. $153,000
   c. $159,584
   d. $136,106

10. Assuming the Inventory balance at the end of 2005 is $25,000, and it has decreased by 5% since the end of 2004, the balance at the end of 2004 (rounded to the nearest whole dollar) was:
    a. $23,750
    b. $26,250
    c. $26,316
    d. $27,701

11. Given the following data for total sales:
    2003 $50,000
    2004 $55,000
    2005 $56,000
    2006 $53,000
    A table showing trend percentages for 2003-2006, respectively, using 2003 as the base year, would show:
    a. 100%, 110%, and 95%
    b. 100%, 110%, 112%, and 106%
    c. 100%, 10%, 2%, and (5%)
    d. 94%, 1.04%, 1.06%, and 100%

12. Which of the following would be most likely to reveal that cost of goods sold is 125% of the amount shown for a base year?
    a. trend analysis
    b. ratio analysis
    c. vertical analysis
    d. horizontal analysis

13. When calculating trend percentages, all percentages shown are relative to:
    a. the current year
    b. the base year
    c. the immediately preceding year
    d. the average index calculated for all the years shown

14. Which of the following would be most likely to reveal that cost of goods sold increased by $75,000 from 2004 to 2005?
    a. horizontal analysis
    b. trend analysis
    c. vertical analysis
    d. ratio analysis

15. When performing vertical analysis of an income statement, which of the following is usually used as the base?
    a. gross sales
    b. net sales
    c. net income
    d. gross profit

Completion

Complete each of the following statements.

1. The study of percentage changes in comparative financial statements is called
    _____ analysis.
2. Vertical analysis percentages on the income statement are computed by dividing all
    amounts by _____.
3. Vertical analysis percentages on the balance sheet are computed by dividing all
    amounts by_____.
4. Working capital is _____.
5. _____ and _____ are the two
    most common measures of firm size.
6. Leverage _____ the risk to common stockholders.
7. The _____ ratio indicates the market price of one dollar of
    earnings.
8. The rate of return on total assets equals _____.
9. The most widely quoted of all financial statistics is _____.
10. The _____ is the recorded accounting value of
    each share of common stock outstanding.

True/False

For each of the following statements, circle T *for true or* F *for false.*

1.   T F The study of percentage changes from year to year is called horizontal
             analysis.
2.   T F Most companies never use ratios in their reports because they are virtually
             useless.
3.   T F The decision-making tools based on working-capital data are the current
             ratio and the acid-test ratio.
4.   T F Generally, a higher current ratio indicates a stronger financial position.
5.   T F A business strives for the highest rate of turnover.
6.   T F Two indicators of the ability to pay total liabilities are the debt ratio and
             the times-interest-earned ratio.
7.   T F Earnings per share is the most widely quoted of all financial statistics.
8.   T F Investors sell stock to earn a return on their investment.
9.   T F Many experts believe book value is not useful for investment analysis
             because it bears no relationship to market value and provides little
             information beyond what's reported on the balance sheet.
10.   T F A positive EVA amount suggests an increase in stockholder wealth.
11.   T F Managers cannot fool the market with accounting gimmicks.
12.   T F The most important financial ratios measure a company's ability to pay
             current liabilities.
13.   T F Horizontal analysis of a financial statement reveals the relationship of
             each statement item to a specified base.
14.   T F Common-size statements ease the comparison of different companies and
             may signal the need for corrective action.

15.   T   F   Trend percentages are a form of vertical analysis.

Exercises

1.   Net income was $300,000 in Year 1, $500,000 in Year 2, and $400,000 in Year 3. What were the percentage changes in net income?

2.   Singh Industries had the following information for 2005:

Cost of goods sold	$600,000
Beginning inventory	40,000
Ending inventory	80,000
Net credit sales	1,125,000
Beginning accounts receivable	85,000
Ending accounts receivable	75,000

A. What is inventory turnover?

B. What is the accounts receivable turnover?

C. What is the days' sales in average receivables?

3. The following information is given for Pradesh Corporation for 2005:

Net Sales	$825,000	$825,000
Net Income	60,000	60,000
Average Common Stockholders' Equity	3,150,000	3,150,000
Average Total Assets	4,225,000	4,225,000
Interest Expense	75,000	75,000
Preferred Dividends	20,000	20,000
Common Dividends	55,000	55,000
Shares of Common Stock Outstanding	240,000	240,000 shares

A. What is the rate of return on net sales?

B. What is the rate of return on total assets?

C. What is the rate of return on common stockholders' equity?

4.

The following information is given for Trax.com:

Assets:	
Cash	30,000
Marketable Securities	59,000
Accounts Receivable	107,000
Inventory	70,500
Equipment	120,000
Total Assets	476,500
Liabilities and Stockholders' Equity	
Accounts Payable	52,500
Salary Payable	8,500
Long-term Bonds Payable	82,500
Common Stock	100,000
Retained Earnings	233,000
Total Liabilities and Stockholders' Equity	476,500

A. What is the current ratio?

B. What is the acid-test (quick) ratio?

C. What is the debt ratio?

5. Fashion Connection, Inc., has a price/earnings ratio of 12, dividends of $.90 per share, and earnings per share of $1.28.

A. What is the market price per share?

B. What is the dividend yield?

Critical Thinking

The operating cycle is the length of time between the purchase of merchandise and its conversion to cash following the sale and receipt of payment. Using the information in Exercise 2 above, calculate the operating cycle for Singh Industries.

Demonstration Problems

Demonstration Problem #1.

Zell Industries, headquartered in Richmond, California, manufactures products for the home. Figures from their 2005 annual report (slightly modified for ease of presentation) follow:

Zell Industries
Statement of Consolidated Earnings
For Year Ended December 31, 2005

	(In thousands)
Net sales	$1,073,022
Cost and expenses	
Cost of products sold	687,103
Selling, delivery, and administration	241,711
Depreciation	15,607
Discount on sales of receivables	3,963
Interest expense	17,546
Other (income) expense, net	1,827
Total costs and expenses	967,757
Earnings before income taxes	105,265
Income taxes	42,106
Net earnings	63,159
Average shares outstanding	42,600

Zell Industries
Consolidated Balance Sheet
December 31, 2005

	(In thousands)	
	2005	2004
Assets		
Current assets:		
Cash and short-term investments	8,326	5,225
Accounts receivable, less allowance	125,126	121,763
Inventories	146,002	156,245
Deferred income taxes	20,155	34,038
Prepaid expenses	4,662	3,561
Total current assets	304,271	320,832
Property, plant, and equipment-net	319,677	290,960
Brands, trademarks, patents and other intangibles-net	204,422	202,323
Other assets	32,510	25,831
Total	$860,880	$839,946

Liabilities and Stockholders' Equity
Current liabilities:

Accounts payable	$ 61,168	$ 70,106
Accrued liabilities	110,522	144,863
Income taxes payable	3,474	27,279
Short-term debt	4,013	5,128
Current maturity of long-term debt	116	912
Total current liabilities	179,293	248,288
Long-term debt	199,355	166,279
Other obligations	17,107	18,677
Deferred income taxes	66,300	54,524
Stockholders' equity		
Common stock — authorized, 50,000,000 shares,		
$.01 par value; issued: 43,140,586 shares	431	431
Additional paid-in capital	126,432	121,124
Retained earnings	333,846	278,649
Treasury shares, at cost: 2005, 1,490,000 shares;		
2004, 1,210,700 shares	(52,563)	(40,433)
Cumulative translation adjustments	(9,321)	(7,593)
Total stockholders' equity	398,825	352,178
Total liabilities and stockholders' equity	$860,880	$839,946

Required:

Assume annual dividends of $.80 and a market price of $11.13 per share. Compute the following for 2005:

A)   working capital

B)   current ratio

C)   acid-test (quick) ratio

D)   inventory turnover

E)   accounts receivable turnover

F) days' sales in receivables

G) debt ratio

H) times-interest-earned ratio

I) rate of return on sales

J) rate of return on total assets

K) rate of return on common stockholders' equity

L) earnings per share

M) price/earnings ratio

N) dividend yield

O) book value per share of common stock

Demonstration Problem #2:
Vega Corporation's balance sheets and income statements are presented below:

Vega Corporation
Balance Sheet
Years 2005 and 2004

	2005	2004
Assets		
Current assets:		
Cash	$ 13,300	$ 20,350
Short-term investments	8,200	8,000
Receivables, net	26,000	24,000
Inventories	45,000	40,000
Prepaid expenses	2,500	4,650
Total current assets	95,000	97,000
Property, plant, and equipment—net	185,680	196,500
Land	40,000	35,000
Intangibles and other assets	2,400	2,400
Total assets	$323,080	$330,900
Liabilities and Stockholders' Equity		
Current liabilities:		
Notes payable	$ 10,000	$ 10,500
Current installments of long-term debt	3,550	3,445
Accounts payable-trade	14,447	18,500
Accrued liabilities	3,670	1,605
Total current liabilities	31,667	34,050
Long-term debt, less current installments	95,500	93,330
Capital lease obligations, less current portion	1,100	2,150
Deferred income and deferred income taxes	4,813	4,370
Total common stockholders' equity	190,000	197,000
Total liabilities and stockholders' equity	$323,080	$330,900

Vega Corporation

Income Statements

Years 2005 and 2004

	2005	2004
Net sales	$416,500	$406,316
Cost and expenses:		
Cost of goods sold	322,593	315,812
Operating expenses	41,219	43,200
	363,812	359,012
Income from operations	52,688	47,304
Interest expense	3,251	3,150
Earnings before income taxes	49,437	44,154
Income taxes	7,437	6,554
Net income	$ 42,000	$ 37,600

Required:

1. Prepare a horizontal analysis for 2005 of the balance sheet, using the 2004 amounts as the base.

Vega Corporation				
Balance Sheet				
Years 2005 and 2004				
	2005	2004	Amount Increase (Decrease)	% Change
Assets				
Current assets:				
Cash	$ 13,300	$ 20,350		
Short-term investments	8,200	8,000		
Receivables, net	26,000	24,000		
Inventories	45,000	40,000		
Prepaid expenses	2,500	4,650		
Total current assets	95,000	97,000		
Property, plant, and equipment-net	185,680	196,500		
Land	40,000	35,000		
Intangibles and other assets	2,400	2,400		
Total assets	$323,080	$330,900		

Liabilities and stockholders' equity				
Current liabilities:				
Notes payable	$ 10,000	$ 10,500		
Current installments of long-term debt	3,550	3,445		
Accounts payable-trade	14,447	18,500		
Accrued liabilities	3,670	1,605		
Total current liabilities	31,667	34,050		
Long-term debt, less current installments	95,500	93,330		
Capital lease obligations, less current portion	1,100	2,150		
Deferred income and deferred income taxes	4,813	4,370		
Total common stockholders' equity	190,000	197,000		
Total liabilities and stockholders' equity	$323,080	$330,900		

2. Convert the 2005 and 2004 income statements to common-size statements, using net sales as the base figures.

Vega				
Income Statements				
Years 2005 and 2004				
	2005		2004	
	Amount	%	Amount	%
Net sales	$416,500		$406,316	
Cost and expenses:				
Cost of goods sold	322,593		315,812	
Operating expenses	41,219		43,200	
Total costs and expenses	363,812		359,012	
Income from operations	52,688		47,304	
Interest expense	3,251		3,150	
Earnings before income taxes	49,437		44,154	
Income taxes	7,437		6,554	
Net income	$ 42,000		$ 37,600	

Solutions

Matching

1	O	5	K	9	T	13	N	17	I
2	J	6	H	10	S	14	E	18	C
3	P	7	B	11	F	15	L	19	R
4	M	8	D	12	A	16	G	20	Q

Multiple Choice

1	A
2	D
3	C
4	A
5	C
6	A
7	A
8	B
9	A
10	C
11	B
12	A
13	B
14	A
15	B

Completion

1. horizontal
2. net sales
3. total assets (or total liabilities plus stockholders' equity)
4. current assets minus current liabilities
5. Net sales, total assets
6. increases (Leverage is the practice of increasing the debt financing of an entity with respect to owner financing. Leverage is a two-edged sword, increasing profits (and returns to stockholders') during good times but compounding losses during bad times.)
7. price/earnings
8. (net income plus interest expense) / average total assets
9. earnings per share
10. book value per share of common stock

True/False

1	T	
2	F	Ratios are very important in the use of financial statements, and are often included as supplements in annual reports
3	T	
4	T	
5	T	
6	F	These ratios measure the firm's ability to pay long-term debt, not total liabilities
7	T	
8	F	Investors sell stock to convert their investment into cash. Returns on an investment take the form of Earnings per Share, or Dividends
9	T	
10	T	
11	F	Under the Efficient Capital Market theory, market prices reflect all information available to the public. Since the public market sets market prices and has all information, they would not be fooled by accounting gimmicks
12	T	
13	T	
14	T	
15	F	Trend percentages are a form of horizontal analysis

Exercises

1. Year 2 = $200,000 / $300,000 = 66.7%
   Year 3 = ($100,000) / $500,000 = (20%)

2. A. Cost of goods / Average inventory = [$600,000 / ($40,000 + $80,000) / 2] = 10
   B. Net credit sales / Average accounts receivable
      [$1,125,000 / ($85,000 + $75,000) / 2] =14.06
   C. Average accounts receivable / One day's sales =
      [($85,000 + $75,000) / 2] / ($1,125,000 / 365) = 26 days (rounded)

3. A. Net income / Net sales = $60,000 / $825,000 = .073 = 7.3%
   B. (Net income + Interest expense) / Average total assets =
      ($60,000 + $75,000) / $4,225,000 = .032 = 3.2%
   C. (Net income – Preferred dividends) / Average common stockholders' equity =
      ($60,000 – $20,000) / $3,150,000 = .013 = 1.3%

3. A. Current assets / Current liabilities =
      ($30,000 + $59,000 + $107,000 + $70,500) / ($52,500 + $8,500) = 4.4 (rounded)
   B. (Cash + Short-term investments + Net current receivables) / Current liabilities =
      ($30,000 + $59,000 + $107,000) / ($52,500 + $8,500) = 3.2
   C. Total liabilities / Total assets =
      ($52,500 + $8,500 + $82,500) / $476,500 = .301 = 30.1%

5.   A. Market price per share of common stock / Earnings per share =
       P / $1.28 = 12; P = $15.36.
     B. Dividends per share of common stock / Market price per share of common stock =
       $.90/$15.36=.059=5.9%

Critical Thinking

The operating cycle for Singh Industries is 61.5 days. Instruction (C) in the exercise asked you to calculate the days' sales in average receivables. The correct figure was 26 days. Another way of characterizing this result is to say that it takes approximately 26 days to collect an average account receivable. Instruction (A) asked you to calculate inventory turnover. The correct amount was 10—in other words, inventory "turns" approximately 10 times each year. Divide this result into 365 to convert it to days, or 36.5 days. In other words, on average it takes 36.5 days for an item to sell and 26 days on average to collect a receivable. Therefore, the operating cycle is 62.5 days.

Demonstration Problems

Demonstration Problem #1

A) working capital = current assets – current liabilities = $304,271 – $179,293 = $124,978

B) current ratio = current assets / current liabilities = $304,271 / $179,293 = 1.7 (rounded)

C) acid-test (quick) = quick assets / current liabilities
                      = ($8,326 + $125,126) / $179,293 = 0.74 (rounded)

   This means Zell has 74 cents of quick assets (cash and short-term investment plus net accounts receivable) for every dollar of current liability.

D) inventory turnover = cost of goods sold / average inventory
       $687,103 / [($156,245 + $146,002) / 2] = 4.55 times

   Zell "turns" its inventory 4.55 times each year. Another way of stating this ratio is to convert it to days by dividing the "turn" into 365. For Zell, the turnover averages 80 days (365 / 4.55).

E) accounts receivable turnover = net credit sales / average accounts receivable
       $1,073,022 / [($121,763 + $125,126) / 2] = 8.69 times

F) days' sales in receivables = average net accounts receivable / one day's sales
$123,444 / ($1,073,022 / 365) = 42 days

The numerator for this ratio was the denominator for the previous ratio.

G) debt ratio = total liabilities / total assets $462,055 / $860,880 0.537 or
53.7%

This means that 53.7% of the Zell assets were financed with debt. Notice the numerator (total liabilities) was not presented on the balance sheet but had to be calculated by adding together total current liabilities, long-term debt, other obligations, and deferred income taxes.

H) times-interest-earned = income from operations / interest expense
= $122,811 / $17,546 7 times

Note we used earnings before income taxes plus interest expense as the numerator because interest expense had already been deducted from the earnings before income taxes amount.

I) rate of return on sales = net income / net sales
= $63,159 / 1,073,022 = .0059

J) rate of return on total   (net income + interest expense) / average total
= ($63,159 + $17,546) / [($839,946 + $860,880) / 2]
= 0.095 or 9.5%

This ratio measures the return on assets generated by this year's operations.

K) rate of return on common stockholders' equity = (net income – preferred dividends) /
average common stockholders'
equity
($63,159 – 0) / [($352,178 + $398,825) / 2] = 0.169 or 16.9%

Zell does not have preferred stock outstanding, so the numerator is the same as net earnings.

L) earnings per share = (net income – preferred dividends) / average number of
common shares outstanding
= $63,159 / 42,600= $1.48 (rounded)

This should be calculated for each "net earnings" amount. Companies are required to include these per share amounts on the income statement, not in the footnotes.

M) price/earnings ratio = market price per share of common stock / earnings per share
$11.13 / $1.48 = 7.5 (rounded)

N) dividend yield = dividend per share of common stock / market price of common stock
$.80 / $11.13= 0.0719 or 7.19%

O) book value per share of common stock = (total stockholders' equity – preferred equity) / number of shares of common stock outstanding
= 398,825 / 41,650,586
= $9.57 per share

The dollars are presented "in thousands," so you must add three zeroes to the total stockholders' equity amount. To determine the number of shares outstanding, deduct the treasury shares (1,490,000) from the issued shares (43,140,586). As emphasized in your text, these ratios would have more meaning if you did them over consecutive years. In addition, to properly evaluate a company you would also want to compare the ratios with those of competitors and with the industry as a whole.

Demonstration Problem #2.

Vega Corporation				
Balance Sheet				
Years 2005 and 2004				
	2005	2004	Amount Increase (Decrease)	% Change
Assets				
Current assets:				
Cash	$ 13,300	$ 20,350	$(7,050)	(34.6)
Short-term investments	8,200	8,000	200	2.5
Receivables, net	26,000	24,000	2,000	8.3
Inventories	45,000	40,000	5,000	12.5
Prepaid expenses	2,500	4,650	(2,150)	(46.2)
Total current assets	95,000	97,000	(2,000)	(2.1)
Property, plant, and equipment—net	185,680	196,500	(10,820)	(5.5)
Land	40,000	35,000	5,000	(14.3)
Intangibles and other assets	2,400	2,400	0	0
	$323,080	$330,900	$(7,820)	(2.4)
Liabilities and stockholders' equity				
Current liabilities:				
Notes payable	$10,000	$10,500	$ (500)	(4.8)
Current installments of long-term debt	3,550	3,445	105	(3.0)
Accounts payable-trade	14,447	18,500	(4,053)	(21.9)
Accrued liabilities	3,670	1,605	2,065	128.7
Total current liabilities		34,050	(2,383)	(7.0)
Long-term debt, less current installments	95,500		2,170	2.3
Capital lease obligations, less current	1,100	2,150	(1,050)	(48.9)
Deferred income and deferred income taxes	4,813	4,370	443	10.1
Total common stockholders' equity	190,000	197,000	(7,000)	(3.6)
	$323,080	$330,900	$(7,820)	(2.4)

Vega Corporation				
Income Statements				
Years 2005 and 2004				
	2005		2004	
	Amount	%	Amount	%
Net sales	$416,500	100.0	$406,316	100.0
Cost and expenses:				
Cost of goods sold	322,593	77.5	315,812	77.7
Operating expenses	41,219	9.9	43,200	10.6
	363,812		359,012	
Income from operations	52,688	12.7	47,304	11.6
Interest expense	3,251	0.8	3,150	.8
Earnings before income taxes	49,437	11.9	44,154	10.8
Income taxes	7,437	1.8	6,554	1.6
Net income	$ 42,000	10.1	$ 37,600	9.3

Points to remember:

1. When presenting horizontal analysis, each year's change is divided by the base-year amount (in this case 2004) and converted to a percentage. While the change in any single item in any single year may not be significant, applying horizontal analysis over a number of years may highlight significant changes.

2. Common-size statements for a single year are only meaningful when the results are compared to other companies or industry data. However, common-size statements covering two or more years permit analysis of the particular company being examined. In this case, we see that 2005 results improved over 2004 due to lower cost of goods sold and lower operating expenses.

3. Financial ratios are mathematical formulas that quantify the relationship between two or more items reported in the financial statements. Ratios are used to assess and compare a firm's liquidity, profitability, rate of return, and ability to meet debt obligations.